A MESSAGE TO THE CHILDREN

A guide to writing your autobiography

by

JIM WILLIAMS

Also by Jim Williams

American Values
Irina's Story
The Sadness of Angels
The Demented Lady Detectives' Club
The English Lady Murderers' Society
Tango in Madeira
The Argentinian Virgin
The Strange Death of a Romantic
Recherché
Scherzo
Anti-Soviet Activities
Farewell to Russia
The Hitler Diaries
How to be a Charlatan and Make Millions

Print edition 2018

Licensed by Marble City Publishing

Copyright © 2007 Jim Williams

ISBN-10 1-908943-92-0

ISBN-13 978-1-908943-92-7

Praise for Jim Williams' books

Farewell to Russia

"There are going to be very few novels of any kind that are as well written. Totally authentic. Totally readable. Far too good to miss." *Ted Allbeury*

The Hitler Diaries

"...steadily builds up an impressive atmosphere of menace." *Times Literary Supplement*

"...well written and full of suspense." *Glasgow Herald*

Last Judgement

"...the author journalists read for their next scoop." *Sunday Telegraph*

Scherzo

"Sparkling and utterly charming. Devilishly clever plot and deceitful finale." *Frances Fyfield – Mail on Sunday*

Recherché

"A skilful exercise, bizarre and dangerous in a lineage that includes Fowles' *The Magus.*" *Guardian*

The Strange Death of a Romantic

"This is an extraordinarily witty and assured novel." *T J Binyon – Evening Standard*

"...seriously good...technically brilliant...constantly suggestive... dreamy but sinister glamour." *Times Literary Supplement*

Contents

TO BEGIN

For years I suggested to people that they should write their autobiography. Not for publication, you understand, but for the family: especially for the grandchildren. I even had a few practical suggestions as to how they might set about it.

Of course I did nothing about writing my own autobiography.

I'm like that. Bone-idle and more than happy to give people advice that I don't follow myself.

Then, a few years ago, in a sloppy lazy fashion I began to put pen to paper and wrote some bits and pieces with no particular plan in mind except that they weren't for general publication. Nothing might have come of them, except it occurred to me that my advice on writing – always assuming there was something to it – might be of wider interest. And so, as I wrote my essays, I began to write accompanying notes so that other people could follow the process and pick up hints as to how they might go about it themselves.

This book comprises the pieces I have written about my life, together with the notes explaining my choices and techniques and how you may adapt them to your purposes. The result isn't an autobiography in the conventional sense. In fact I think it's better because it captures more of the texture and feel of life, though that's something you must decide for yourself.

I want to emphasize that writing your autobiography is exciting and the emotions you feel and describe will be genuine, because in Life, unlike Art, the characters *really* experience joy. They *really* suffer. They *really* die.

Writing your autobiography is *dangerous*. The Good

1

Guys don't necessarily win. The Hero may not make it to the end.

I hope that when you've read this book, you'll want to try your hand.

So shall we begin?

A DREAM OF RED TULIPS

Little Jimmy is five years old and lying in bed at home in Warwick Street, Oldham and the year is 1952. Dorothy Mee has told him the King has died, and next year he'll see the Coronation and get a souvenir mug and a case of chicken pox. His mother, Nellie, is fretting about the state of the roof and owes Machin the builder (whose daughter has a "lazy eye" and a good one covered with a pink patch over the lens of her spectacles) seventy-five pounds. It's the largest bill Nellie will ever have to pay and she remembers the exact amount fifty years later.

Most of this is bye the bye. What's important is that Jimmy has been to school and enjoyed himself at his artwork. He's come home excited and now he's lying in bed and a picture forms in his mind.

It's of three red tulips. They have green stalks and green leaves and grow in a brown pot. The background is a vivid yellow. Years later Jimmy discovers Van Gogh's *Chrysanthemums* and can see that Vincent has something of the idea. But they're a pallid affair compared with Jimmy's tulips. Nothing can capture the vivid scarlet of the blooms, the deep emerald green, the vibrant yellow, the radiance of the whole. No other image can generate the same excitement because none will be so fresh as the one he has at the age of five.

Jimmy draws with sticks of hard wax crayon that come in a cheaply printed carton. Nellie buys them together with colouring books on Oldham Tommyfield market. She often takes Jimmy there. The bus fare is a penny each way, but they sometimes walk. The market also sells surplus school exercise books made for the Gold Coast colony. On the back of the cover they have extraordinary tables of

3

weights and measures, full of troy ounces and rods, poles and perches.

At school Jimmy is also allowed to play with Plasticine. He loves the red and the white, but the colours are gradually absorbed into a muddy green. Yet on one occasion he comes by them in their pristine form and makes a figure with a red jacket and white breeches, which he says is Dick Turpin, the highwayman. Somewhere he's seen a picture of a redcoat soldier.

Who can say why history interests him? He learns to read a collection of Arthurian legends and Norse myths and will always know that Loki killed Balder with a piece of mistletoe. He swaps his most valuable soldiers with Alan Hutchinson, his best friend, so he can have one figure in a Napoleonic uniform. Nellie is furious and reverses the exchange. She has no feeling for history at all, even though she does remember the amount of Machin's bill when it's become a part of history.

The morning after his wonderful dream, Jimmy arms himself with wax crayons and sets about realising it on paper. There it is: red tulips, green stalks and leaves, brown pot, yellow background.

'That's nice, Jimmy,' says his teacher, and it is nice. She gives him a gold star and writes "very good" in red ink.

And yet...

The truth is that the dream of red tulips can't survive its translation into this world. The problem isn't a technical weakness in the drawing or the colouring, but in the very fact that the image has been taken from the realm of wonders. Jimmy will no more forget the palpable disappointment at the failure to realise his vision than he will forget the dream itself

But he remains grateful that he had the dream.

NOTES ON "A DREAM OF RED TULIPS"

I'm in a bar in Abu Dhabi with Fabulous Fred Day, and Billy Brooks is telling stories about Ben Ley, who died of a heart attack while swimming. Ben was famous for mangling his words. Billy is from Liverpool and has a deep voice of gravel and spent cigarettes.

'So,' says Billy, 'Ben is telling me about this wedding – he's at this wedding – it's a posh wedding, this wedding he's at. He says, says Ben, "The bridegroom was wearing this fancy suit and a carafe." That's what he says: "a *carafe*", you know? A *carafe*? So I says, "What do you mean, he's wearing a *carafe*?" I mean what's he doing wearing a bloody jug of wine, eh? "Round his neck," says Ben. "He's wearing this carafe tied round his neck."'

This book is about autobiography: how I wrote mine, which you're reading, plus a few ideas about how you might write yours. I've begun these notes with a tale about Ben Ley because it illustrates the natural way in which people tell stories. Read it again and notice how sparse the details are. We don't know when or where the wedding took place, or when or where Ben told his story to Billy. For that matter you don't know – because I didn't bother to say – when it was that Billy repeated the story to me. The fact that we were in Abu Dhabi is immaterial: I might have said Dubai or Derby for all the difference it would make. That little detail is just a trick of storytelling. By locating the incident in real space, I persuade you it really happened – as indeed it did.

Billy Brooks is a funny man and can tell a dozen tales about his mate Ben fit to make you weep. Fabulous Fred Day is another and in the course of this book I'll tell you a few more things about him. If you were to ask most people to tell you in their own fashion about someone they know, they'd probably recite a series of anecdotes about the time when X did this or said that, and the order would follow the significance of the stories. It would reflect their humour, their pathos, the light they throw on the human condition, their impact on the lives of other people, and so forth. However it's very unlikely they'd follow a strict chronology and it would probably be very difficult to assign a date or a place to most of them. And the reason is simple. For the most part Life doesn't have a plot. It's just stuff that happens. The point of the Ben Ley story is his habit of chewing up the language. No other detail matters. The point of my story of red tulips is the remembrance of a childhood vision. I don't recall how it stands in relation to all the other things I did at school (such as being called before the headmistress for peeing in the playground), because that relationship has no significance.

The basis of my approach to writing autobiography is to follow this natural trend of story-telling, setting down incidents that seem to me to be important but without any effort to string them together into a plot. Where I do put the various anecdotes and recollections together, the reason is that I sense a pattern: an outline of a picture of who I am and where I've come from; and here and there a touch of colour.

This is the method I recommend to you and which this book sets out to explain.

NELLIE

'I didn't know my own name 'til I were eleven,' says Nellie.

I partly understand her. Her maiden name is sometimes Nellie Webb and sometimes Nellie Wright. Webb – she says – was her 'real' father, but Wright, her stepfather, was the one she loved. Except, she tells me on another occasion, her 'real' father was a man called Roper, the nephew of the manager of the Sun Mill who went down with his ship in 1916. Which leaves the mysterious Webb where exactly? In life, he fell off a ladder and died, and so exits this story having scarcely come into it except to lend an unwanted name.

'My mother were called Marrow,' Nellie volunteers. She doesn't know the spelling. A whiff of uncertainty clings to it. 'Her mum and dad kept a lodging house for prison officers in Knutsford. I think she had other children before she met Webb, but ' – she adds – ' I don't know who they were or what they were called.' Or, indeed, if they ever existed.

My grandmother was evidently a sporting type, what with a family in Knutsford, the affair with Roper, the interlude with Webb and finally a marriage to Wright, who fathered my Uncles Fred and Joe. She took snuff and drank beer.

'She was a fat, dirty, smelly old woman,' my brother Denis says.

'She were a alcoholic,' says Nellie. 'It were Wright who first learned her to drink. But she didn't like pubs and used to take beer home in jugs.'

Grandma Wright experienced a late conversion.

'One day she said "I've given up drinking",' Nellie

7

explains. But, if so, it did her no good. Nellie shakes her head: "She died a fortnight later.'

I was four years old.

The problematic matter of names extended to Nellie's children. I'm called 'Jim' not 'James'. My sister is 'Anne'. One brother is 'Denis' (single 'n'). The other is 'Jack' not 'John'. None of us has a second name.

I can't explain this meanness. I joke about it. 'It was wartime rationing. You couldn't get the coupons. Either I got a second name or my sister got a winter vest.' However, I suspect one of the more subtle effects of poverty is that it extends into the imagination. I'm not sure my parents thought their children were *entitled* to bear a second name.

My grandmother cleaned houses.

'You couldn't meet a nicer woman when she weren't in drink,' Nellie remembers. As for her stepfather: 'I loved him to death. He were lovely.' Fred Wright was gassed in the Great War and invalided.

Nellie spent her childhood among poverty, disability and alcoholism. And love. She never felt her parents didn't love her. But the poverty was hard. 'At Christmas all we used to get was an orange,' she tells me.

I can't decide if Nellie is bright or not. She may be. The problem is that her horizons are deformed by poverty and, bright or not, she's a silly woman. I can say this without shame because, unfortunately, I happen to be a silly man.

Whatever the case, Nellie won a place at grammar school. It was the greatest disappointment of her life. She shakes her head at the memory. 'I were right pleased and ran home to tell my mum. And she went to see my teacher. When she came back she told me I couldn't go.'

I've heard this story a hundred times and know how Nellie punctuates it. After a pause she says, 'There were a uniform and she couldn't afford to buy it.'

Nellie lost her education for the sake of a suit of clothes. Instead she left school at fourteen and worked in cotton mills around and about Oldham until sometime in the nineteen forties she met my father, Hughie Williams, The Last Cowboy in Wrexham.

The experience of an alcoholic mother gives Nellie a lifelong prejudice against drink. She rails against modern girls. '*I* used to go drinking only three times a week,' she sniffs, 'not like they do nowadays.'

I'm missing something. If three times a week is moderation, the boozing of contemporary women must be awesome.

As a result of her modest visits to the pub, Nellie met Hughie, who had three kids and a wife 'no better than she should be'. Hughie's wife had 'fancy men' and was in the habit of selling the furniture while Hughie was at work and spending the proceeds on immoral purposes. Years later I meet her at my brother Denis's house when she's in her late forties. She seems a pleasant though rather brassy woman. Her current 'fancy man' is a florid type with the air of a publican and they have a nice daughter who looks strikingly like my brother Jack. In some vague way she's therefore a relative but I don't recall her name, assuming I ever knew it.

'And then I fell for you,' Nellie says.

The expression 'falling for' a baby is conventional but captures the accidental nature of pregnancy in Nellie's youth (though she's twenty-nine when she 'falls'). It also has echoes of 'fallen women'. I can feel the lives of Nellie and Hughie teetering on the edge of chaos and disaster. Nellie is unmarried and 'fallen'. Hughie is a country boy cut off from home, hard drinking, quick-tempered and out of his depth. Denis and Jack are shuttled among relatives. Anne is put in a children's home. Hughie, Nellie and Little Jimmy take a mouse-infested room in Greenacres Road and try to build a life from scratch.

My parents ought to fail. I can't really understand why they don't except that there's something fundamentally sound about them. Nellie is thrifty. Both are hard-working.

Neither is vicious. They have good hearts and generous natures and I never doubt they love me. Still, I don't like my father's fiery temper and at the age of five think the man who sells shirts at Bradleys Gentleman's Outfitters, Mumps, is nicer than my dad. (For information, Bradleys' trademark is a Cheshire cat and the father of my friends John and David Parry works there.)

Nellie scrimps and saves and borrows fifty pounds from her brother Joe, and, when Little Jimmy is two, she and Hughie buy a house in Warwick Street for four hundred and fifty pounds. It has a dilapidated roof which, mortgage apart, is the source of a seventy-five pound bill to Machin the builder that will haunt her memory as the biggest debt of her life. Yet it proves a blessing. Her financial management impresses Hughie and he raises her 'wage' so she can pay off the debt and never afterwards reduces it. It marks a growing confidence between them that will outlive their blazing rows.

Despite poverty, money has no grip on Nellie beyond a practical thriftiness. Her lack of interest in material things is sublime. Fifteen years after she buys the house in Warwick Street, she sells it to my exotic Italian Auntie Anna (who married Uncle Bobby the communist) for scarcely more than she paid, and gives her free credit as well. The market price of the house doesn't interest Nellie. She never liked the place and won't take more than her own notion of what it's worth. Similarly in old age she refuses the pension credit to which she's entitled and gets annoyed when I press it on her. It isn't a matter of pride.

'I won't have it,' she says. 'I don't *need* it.'

And she's right. She doesn't need it. She's given away anything superfluous and lives very simply in a house that smells of mothballs, the last that she and Hughie lived in together. She subscribes to the National Lottery but only with an eye to giving any prize to charity.

'I won't give to you,' she says pointedly. She won't

give it to my children either. She explains: 'I don't hold with having a lot of money. It doesn't do you any good.'

She saves out of her small pension then gives the savings away to charity or in small presents. 'I do what I can,' she says and shrugs. Her notions of money reflect the prices of thirty years ago and trivial sums seem large to her, but only as amounts to wonder at. Since she buys nothing, they have no real meaning.

All her measures are set by the smallness of her life. It colours even her notions of luxurious living, which are bizarre.

'She bought a tea towel,' she says of someone or other. 'You know – the sort you can hang on the wall.'

Of someone else: 'They have a bit of money behind them. They live in a bungalow.'

Nellie is uncertain how far her own experiences reflect the general world. Sometimes she assumes a false universality.

'You can always buy sugar cheap at Dixons,' she says to my Aunt Doll from Shrewsbury.

Dixons was the grocer at the corner of Warwick Street. In the days before supermarkets, it was one of a chain of half a dozen in the Oldham area. For Nellie, however, there are Dixons' stores from Derby to Delhi.

In old age she tends to the other direction and expresses surprise if she encounters in Stockport something she knows of in Oldham. This can take bizarre forms.

'Ee, there's a chemist!' she says in wonder (she refers to Boots the Chemist as 'Bootsies'). Or it may be shoe shop. Or, sometimes, she asks what kind of shop she's looking at, and, when I tell her it sells mobile phones, she shakes her head, marvelling that such places exist.

She has an addiction to laxatives and a store of folk wisdom.

'Don't go out with your hair wet!' she tells me.

She repeats her good advice every time we meet. Spells always work better if they're repeated.

11

'You shouldn't drive your car when it's dark, Jimmy.' She fixes me with a witch's glare. 'Now remember: *you drive carefully.*'

I'm fifty-odd years old and have been driving for more than thirty years. Still, you never know: those words '*you drive carefully*' may work their magic.

Oldham, in Nellie's opinion, is a place of fantastic danger, especially as she grows older. Pensioners are habitually murdered in their beds and nary a one ever gets home with her pension.

'It's bad round here,' she says, then contradicts herself, 'I wouldn't want to move. I've a lot of good neighbours.'

Apparently it's far more dangerous for me. If I drive to Oldham at night, I'll be dragged out of my car, beaten up and left for dead *with my hair wet.*

Nellie's sense of danger comes from the natural timidity of the old but also from her reading of the local paper. She's can't put a context to the stories of mayhem she devours every day. She assumes the extraordinary reflects the habitual, and has no idea of how things may be elsewhere than in her hometown.

'You drive home carefully,' she says.

'Mum, I'm only going ten miles to Stockport. Next week I'll be in Bombay.'

Her eyes glaze over. 'Hmm... But you drive home careful.' She pokes my chest. '*And don't stop for no one. It's bad round here.*'

Nellie's world has no history except the personal. Broader history isn't real. She's vaguely aware of it, but the facts mentioned in the romances she reads are confined within the covers, simply parts of the plot. The reign of Charles the Second and the Regency Period are just settings. Nellie can't tell you how far apart from each other they are or which came first. No analogies can be drawn between past and present because the past has no structure. Its incidents

12

are specific and contain no lessons.

Who is 'the Old King'? No one except Nellie ever uses the term to me, though she says it as if it's a title known to everyone.

'That were in the time of the Old King,' she says in order to place some incident. If I'm explaining something to her, she'll ask: 'Were that in the time of the Old King?'

Logic suggests there's a 'New King', but Nellie never refers to him or indicates she's aware of any kings other than 'the Old King.'

Who is he, then? George the Fifth, I think, who died in 1936 when Nellie was eighteen. I tell her, but to no purpose. It means nothing. She gives no sign of having heard of a King George, whether the Fifth or otherwise. Indeed she can't carry the name from one occasion to another so I have to tell her again. It isn't that she's forgetful. It's just that the subject is of no interest.

For years Nellie worked in the cotton mills. The National Trust has a preserved cotton mill at Styal, a museum to the industry, covering all aspects, not just the spinning and weaving of cloth. Shirley and I took Nellie round it. This was a few years ago when she was in her seventies.

'Eee, look at that!' she says.

In one of the long spinning rooms she sees a machine and her eyes light up with familiar memory.

'I used to work on one o' them.'

What was it for?

She doesn't know.

Where does it fit in the process of cotton manufacture?

She doesn't know. All she could do was operate it.

Much of her life is spent in this way, without any context except the immediate. It doesn't bother her, no more than money does.

It's good to 'have a bit of money behind you'.

But only for reasons of security.

Security, not wealth, is the most important value in Nellie's scheme of life. It's understandable. Wealth is abstract: she's never been rich and doesn't know any rich people. But insecurity she knows first-hand from the poverty of her childhood and her 'fallen' condition with Little Jimmy to care for when she was uncertain of her hold on Hughie.

Nellie's desire for security expresses itself as 'settling down'. To be settled down means to achieve a sort of inertness that will go on for ever. It consists of a job, a spouse and a house, none of which will ever change. At times it seems like something that occurs after life in the conventional sense has been lived: a form of un-dead existence in which nothing very much happens except for occasional redecorating or the purchase of a new washing machine: vampirism at a domestic level.

One of the things that women do for men is to settle them down. As Nellie says of my sister-in-law: 'Margie were the best thing that ever happened to Denis. *She settled him down.*' And of my father, 'Once he'd *settled down* he were a smashing chap.'

Nellie believes all endeavours should be directed to 'settling down' at the earliest possible opportunity. She liked my girlfriend, Kathy Redfern, and would have been perfectly happy if I'd got engaged at the age of seventeen. I'd have 'got over' the uncertainty surrounding sex and girls. She'd have liked me to be a teacher. It is a nice steady job for life.

Nellie's moralising has an effect. Taken as a whole, I've lived quietly and not been especially concerned about money or high position. I have loyal friends, a fine family and a good and loving marriage. I've taken my disappointments easily: not expecting very much and accepting the outcome as the proper reward for getting above myself. I don't put forward 'settling down' as a general recommendation to others, but it's suited me and made me happy.

But, to return to where I came in...

'I didn't know my own name 'til I were eleven,' says Nellie.

'No?'

'No. You see, I thowt I were called "Nellie". Everyone called me "Nellie". My Mam and Dad called me "Nellie".' (I assume that "Dad" was Fred Wright, but there are at least two other candidates.)

'I see,' I say. But I don't. My father called her "Nellie" until the day he died. No one has ever called her anything else. So her real name is...?

'*Helen!*' she says with a smile. 'I were eleven years old when I learned I were called "Helen".'

Helen – yes, of course, though she was still known as Nellie.

Today we're in a residential home in Royton – Nellie, Shirley and I. Opposite us sit a young social worker, who speaks with a strong Oldham accent, and a fat trainee, who beams pleasantly and says nothing. They remind me of the stock duo of my teenage years: the pretty one and the fat friend, who seem to haunt every church hall dance I ever go to. What will this one think if she realises I've only half an ear to the conversation while the other half is listening to Johnny Dean and the Graduates rip off Beatles' numbers in Hill Stores Co-op ballroom?

We're here to decide if, after a trial period, Mum is willing to stay on in the home. Is she happy with the place? With the food? With the staff? Today she's in a cheerful mood and answers lucidly – so lucidly you may think she's perfectly capable of managing her own affairs.

'Yes, it's very nice,' she says. 'The staff are nice. The food's good. I've made some friends.' She searches out Shirley and beams at her as if seeing the joke. 'Where am I again?' she asks.

'In a residential home,' says Shirley.

'That's right,' says Nellie without pausing. 'In Royton?

15

Carol put me here.'

Carol is a wonderful, selfless friend to my mother. Carol didn't put Nellie in a home. I did.

The interview continues and Nellie is blithe throughout. Several times she asks where she is. It's characteristic that many of her memories aren't altogether lost but exist in an intermediate state where they no longer come spontaneously to mind but can be prompted by the right cue. Once she's told she's in a home, she recalls immediately that it's in Royton and that Carol put her there.

But no matter how many times she is reminded, she can't hold the notion that I was the one responsible.

'I don't have a memory,' our old friend Monty once said. 'I have a forgettery.'

Nellie has a 'forgettery'. 'My memory's something shocking,' she says, and sighs and shrugs. 'Where am I again?'

The young social worker is satisfied. Her client is clearly incapable of managing on her own and has settled well in her current placement. She smiles.

'So you'll stay here then, will you, Nellie'

Mum doesn't answer, but she grins mischievously.

'Excuse *me,*' she says pleasantly but with characteristic emphasis. 'My name *isn't* Nellie.'

'No?'

'No,' says Mum. She is triumphant. 'It's *Helen*!'

And so it is. The staff of the home have never met Nellie and know only Helen. At the age of eighty-six she has defined her own name and forced its acceptance on the world.

NOTES ON "NELLIE"

Most people can't write a book. The problem isn't that they write badly – they may or may not do – but good and bad writing determine only whether a book is enjoyable, not whether it's written at all. Most people can't write even a bad book. What defeats them is psychology.

A novel of ordinary length typically takes a year or two's work, and demands a major commitment in a life busy with other things. Importantly the act of writing means sitting down, facing and overcoming the obstacles to putting pen to paper not once but maybe hundreds of times. All writers are familiar with the displacement activities they engage in so as to avoid that moment of truth. In fact one joke has it that an experienced author, on being asked by a novice how to write, said, 'First clean your fridge.' A single failure to meet the challenge of the blank page may doom the whole enterprise. Repeated failure will almost certainly do so.

The fundamental problem with writing novels is that the task is lengthy and, what's worse, a waste of time if the book never gets finished. So it isn't an accident that few people write novels (even if it's too many for the comfort of publishers and critics). In contrast, however, most of us have probably turned out a verse or two in our time because verse is generally short and so easier to complete. And the same is true of essays such as we wrote at school.

That last comment is a clue. An exercise in writing is more likely to succeed if it's short and results in a satisfactory completed product. Or, to put it another way, writing your autobiography will be easier to the extent you can organise it so that it's more like writing verse or an essay than like writing a novel.

But isn't life – the subject of an autobiography – in truth a novel? It's tempting to think so if we look at it in chronological terms, as a story that just happens to be real. The plot of a novel – of a conventional novel at any rate – moves from event A to event B over a span of time; and life – though at a slower pace and less artistically organised – moves in a similar linear fashion from birth to death. So it isn't surprising that biography frequently resembles a novel in using this chronological structure, which is also the ordinary form for historical narrative.

However there are important differences. In particular, novels usually have a plot, which determines the beginning and ending and sets the pace of the story. Indeed it's the failure to resolve the plot that makes a novel unsatisfactory and largely valueless if it's left unfinished. We want to know how everything turned out: and, if we aren't told, we feel cheated.

Now, I can't speak for your life, but mine doesn't have a plot: rather, as I've already said, it feels like a pile of stuff that just happened; and today (a Monday in May when Shirley and I have just returned from holiday to find our local burglar is treating the garage as a DIY supermarket and our old cat, Oscar, has vomited on the rug) doesn't represent an artistic climax to anything. Unless I suddenly become a genius, no account by me of my life is going to lead in a dramatically satisfactory way to the events of today – which isn't to say that these events have no meaning or interest. But I have to figure out some other way of dealing with them.

To generalise like a barbarian:
(a) novels are organised chronologically and have a plot – and those that aren't are often tedious;
(b) poetry and essays are organised around motifs and perceptions – and when structured like a novel, are as likely as not dull.

And if this isn't so for every case, it's still true enough for the purpose of illustration.

In my notes to *A Dream of Red Tulips*, I introduced the notion of stories such as Ben Ley and the 'carafe' as self-contained chunks of narrative, tied only loosely to any larger structure such as a plot, and more or less indifferent to exact historical details such as dates and place. This kind of story is commonly called an anecdote, and by some experts a '*pericope*'. You can identify a *pericope* by the fact that the link of cause and effect between what goes before and comes afterwards is negligible. Think about it. Did you predict that the story of my childhood dream would be followed by a sketch of my mother drawn mainly from her old age? There's a connection, but it isn't causal in the rigid sense.

My point about these first two essays is that they're each complete in themselves; and they're intended to be because I don't know how many I'm going to write and I want to be in a position to break off at any time, yet feel the business has been worthwhile. In other words this task is as long or as short as I feel like making it, and at any point it's in some sense finished and satisfactory.

This approach to writing autobiography by means of a series of essays is my basic proposal for overcoming the psychological difficulties that a long piece of writing poses for most of us. It's a technique I've recommended to others on intuitive grounds, and now I'm going to see whether it works for me. I don't suggest this approach is original: only that it should work; and the fact that others have used it is good evidence.

If you care to, you may want to break off here and read Montaigne's *Essays* or Alan Bennett's *Writing Home*. Montaigne is interesting because, on the face of them, his *Essays* cover a wide range of subjects having no apparent connection with his life. Yet he makes it clear to the reader that they're largely an exercise in self-exploration. It really doesn't matter in which order you read the *Essays*, and you'll get something out of them if you read only a couple. Montaigne uses the themes of his writings (cannibalism

19

for example) as a focus for his personal insights. It's in this way that they resemble poetry.

If you look again at *Nellie*, you'll see the essay is framed by the story of how she discovered her 'real' name. It forms the structure on which I've hung the other details, all of which tend towards uncovering my mother's identity rather than her history (though there's a fair amount of the latter).

Dramatically, the incident functions rather as a plot might do in a novel. There's an element of suspense: the outcome is left uncertain – the reader doesn't know what Nellie's real name is or how she finds out, and so is compelled to go on until the mystery is resolved. If you decide to read the other essays, you'll find this technique repeated, and you should ask yourself if it's effective and whether you can make it work for you. I find it helps me to shape my material: the use of a framing incident sets limits the way that a conventional beginning and end do.

Nellie's 'real' name is the motif of this second essay as the red tulips were the motif of the first. Either might have formed a subject for a short poem, which is why I think poetry rather than novels or history offers useful insights into how to write autobiographical essays. However, you shouldn't think this use of motifs is artificial, even though it's clearly in part an artistic device. Behind my present use of these incidents lie real memories. I still remember my dream of red tulips more than fifty years ago. I still recall my shock when Nellie told me she didn't know her name until she was eleven.

An intriguing question is *why* do I remember these particular details of my life? And the answer lies within the essays.

One of the benefits of autobiography is that it helps us understand why we remember what we remember.

SHINY JIM AND ADOLF HITLER

My grandfather and Adolf Hitler were members of the Wrexham St. John's Ambulance Brigade.

There are three photographs of James Edward Williams. The first is a portrait. He wears the uniform of the Royal Welch Fusiliers and sports a large moustache of the kind common before the Great War: in fact he looks like Lord Kitchener. The second was taken in the early thirties. By then he was confined to a wheelchair by a mining accident. In the same picture are his second wife, Lucy and a little girl who, I learn much later, is Millie. The third photograph is of my grandfather and Hitler.

Millie's experience was to give me a key to a man who in most respects is mysterious, though, I admit, I've made few enquiries into his history. Even his dates are uncertain. He died in about 1934 and I suspect he was born a few years either side of 1890: probably earlier rather than later. I'm told he was raised in an orphanage in South Wales.

Two facts come through convincingly. He was adored by his children and admired by everyone else. It was his neighbours in Ruabon who gave him the name 'Shiny Jim' from his spotless turnout. My father first told me so and then Millie confirmed it. She had returned to Ruabon in search of her roots fifty years or more after my grandfather died. Yet enquiring among the old people she found someone who'd known 'Shiny Jim' and volunteered the name.

Foremost he was a soldier. He was a regular and subsequently a territorial and he fought on the Western Front. My father said he was mentioned twice in dispatches and won the Military Medal. I've no reason to disbelieve this. In the twenties he was a miner and he was disabled in one of the great pit disasters, which I presume led to his early death.

He married twice and had six children, one of whom, Stanley, drowned in his teens. I knew all the others. His first wife – my grandmother – died of breast cancer at the age of thirty-two. His second wife, Lucy, always had a bad reputation in the family as a difficult woman, but Millie's story gave me reason to re-evaluate her role. My Auntie Blodwen (alias 'Billie') also softened towards Lucy in old age and expressed sympathy for her.

Millie wasn't a relative at all. She was a foundling: a child out of melodrama or a Catherine Cookson novel. No one ever mentioned her to me and it came as a surprise when she turned up in the early nineties in a polite letter that told me her story, which was this.

Sometime in the late twenties (1927 is the nearest I can get), a woman was going from door to door around the village of Ruabon carrying a baby of three weeks and offering it to anyone who came to the doorstep. My grandfather had five children of his own, but was afraid the woman was about to drown the child if no one took it in. And so he did. He took it without further enquiry and without any paperwork (as a result Millie never knew her own name or her birthday) and raised her for seven years. Millie confessed to me that she adored Shiny Jim: that he was the most wonderful father to her.

I think the reason I knew nothing of Millie was that she was so much younger than the other children and, in a sense, she stayed only briefly. Also, none of them ever spoke much about their own childhood to me. As for Millie, after Shiny Jim's death her real mother turned up again and Lucy had to return her because there'd never been a formal adoption. Millie was spirited away to South Wales; then placed in a Catholic children's home, which she hated. As I say, this is a story from a Catherine Cookson novel.

To return to Lucy. She was a nurse. She was a difficult

woman. She had children of her own and inherited five from Shiny Jim and one from God knows whom. Millie had a point when she said things weren't easy for her – but, she said, Lucy loved my grandfather very much.

Those children who still remained at home left after Shiny Jim's death. It was at about this time, I suspect, that Hughie, who'd be seventeen years old, quit the Wrexham area for Oldham, where he had relatives. Lucy (a hazy figure like the wicked stepmother from a fairy story) vanished from the picture. Yet, Millie told me that she – the mother who was no mother – followed the foundling child down to South Wales and, though she had no rights in the matter, did what she could for Millie as she went through her agony with the Catholic nuns. So, it seems, Lucy loved Millie as much as any mother could. Certainly Millie had no doubts about it. The two stayed in close contact until Lucy died in the mid-sixties. In a confessional letter to me, my Aunt Billie admitted that Shiny Jim's children were hard on Lucy. For all her faults (and Millie suggested she was a martinet), one can't help feeling that there was a great deal to be said for her.

Among the memorabilia I inherited from Billie is the photograph of Shiny Jim and Adolf Hitler. The Führer is clear enough. He sits in the front row in an all black SS uniform among those in the gear of the St. John's Ambulance Brigade. The doubt lies in the identification of Shiny Jim: someone has had to mark him out among all the other men.

Yet, despite the photograph, this story is nonsense. Isn't it?

Maybe. Still there's a persistent urban myth that Hitler worked in the twenties as a painter and decorator in Liverpool. And, if that's true, why shouldn't he have been a member of the Wrexham St. John's Ambulance Brigade?

Now he's part of a family myth of uncertain origin. Did I invent it in the early nineties after I received the box of bits from Billie, or was the photograph merely confirmatory evidence of an earlier story? The latter, I think, but I can't be sure. And even if the story dates from before I acquired the photograph, it may still have its roots in the same source seen at an earlier date by someone else in the family. My memory tells me that Billie mentioned it.

In the end I know more about Adolf Hitler than I do about Shiny Jim. In many ways it's appropriate that, in the photograph, it's Hitler's face that emerges clearly and my grandfather's that struggles to be distinctive against the general mass of similar men. I don't suppose I'll ever learn enough about Shiny Jim to create a true portrait, though, from what I have learned, he seems to have been a good and admirable man, which ought to be enough.

This short essay is not about who my grandfather was, but about what he meant.

NOTES ON "SHINY JIM AND ADOLF HITLER"

If by now you're thinking of trying your hand at writing your own essays, you may be wondering what to take as your first subject. You have a choice because the essay form allows you to take topics in any order you like. In contrast a simple chronology naturally draws you to dealing with events in the order they arise. I suspect though that even now you may find the prospect of actual writing to be rather more than you can face.

The shape of this latest essay was determined by three photographs, which are all I have by way of memorabilia relating to my grandfather. You probably have something similar: a box of old photographs kept somewhere-or-other and recording half-forgotten events. As a limbering up exercise you should turn them out and see what can be made of them.

My suggestion is this: begin your first effort by taking photographs as your subject matter. Family shots – wedding pictures – holiday snaps: each one is worth a paragraph at least. When was the photograph taken? Where is it set? What was the weather like? Who are the people and how do you feel about them? Were you happy or sad on that day?

Photographs are pregnant with memories of things that can't be filmed: scents and sounds, music, laughter, taste, the intangible quality of relationships with others – though these may be slyly hinted at by the cut of clothes or the glance of an eye. Beginning with the most basic information, you can go on to expand in the way that I've done in this essay. So the photograph of Shiny Jim and Adolf Hitler led me to mention my Auntie Billie who gave it to me; and the one of my grandfather in a wheelchair

25

made me write about Lucy and Millie.

The character of your essay will be decided by the way you arrange your photographs. For example, if you put together a number of pictures taken on several holidays the effect will be different than if you take the same number but from a single holiday, because, in the first case, you'll be naturally drawn into making comparisons, but in the second you'll probably discuss the experience of the particular holiday in more depth. To take another example, photographs of several weddings may lead to a discussion of fashions and marriage ceremonies and how they've changed over time; but, in contrast, pictures of a single wedding make one think of the couple: was the marriage a success or a failure? With that in mind, you may want to try several layouts before deciding on one that suits you.

An autobiography driven by photographs will tend to be something of a scrapbook, especially if you exhibit the pictures (later on you'll find some of mine). But that's fine. You're doing it for your enjoyment and that of your family (or their edification, puzzlement or whatever), and there are no rules except what works.

My general point is that photographs without explanation are dumb. Why don't you make a start with just a few of yours and get them to speak to you again? Then turn to fully-fledged essays when you've built up your confidence – or maybe the mixture of text and images will appeal to you and you'll stay with it.

In most families memories and clear traditions go back only as far as grandparents. It's unusual to have known your great-grandparents and anything in the way of stories, documents or mementoes from their time will be sparse. Yet your grandparents are the great-grandparents of your children. And for your children's children they'll scarcely exist at all and everything you know about them will most likely be lost. One reason for including Shiny Jim within the scope of this book is that otherwise even the little that's known will fade from the recollection of my family. Most people don't consider this, and so history is lost by neglect rather than intention.

Among the motives for writing an autobiography (when you wonder why you're bothering) it's worth bearing in mind that the readership for your book may be your grandchildren and even later generations: those who've never known you; who'll hear no voice unless you make yours sound. If they aren't interested − well, that's their problem. But don't underestimate your importance to others. The effort people put into tracing their ancestors − often to arrive at nothing more than a name − suggests your descendants will be very much interested in what you have to say and how the world looked to you. And if your style is ham-fisted, they'll forgive you.

It should be obvious that even an amateur genealogist could discover more about Shiny Jim than I have so far: for example his exact dates of birth and death and something of his military record; and it may be I'll put in the effort one day. However, while the addition of a few hard facts may add to the conviction of my grandfather's reality, I doubt they're going to flesh out the portrait of him. Essentially that relies upon the memory of individuals who knew him, not the paper records held in government offices.

I've got nothing against genealogical research, but it seems to me that it's a bit like trainspotting. Gathering engine-numbers will never make you a train driver. Genealogy has a place, but only a limited one, and shouldn't be allowed to become a displacement activity that distracts you from setting down and making sense of the information and memories that are already to hand.

When it comes down to it, we're not in pursuit of facts. We're looking for meaning.

In this essay I've confessed the limitations of my picture of Shiny Jim and simply set down what I have.

Read the final sentence again. My grandfather's 'real' history and character are probably lost beyond recovery, leaving only a general picture of a good and brave man. All I can hope to convey is what he means for me.

The uncertain information underlying this essay brings me to a general issue, which is the nature of the 'truth' you're searching for and trying to describe when you set about writing your autobiography (I'm using 'you' deliberately, in the hope you've decided to join me). I'm not asking a philosophical question, but a practical one. The answer will determine such matters as what information you need before you're confident to proceed; whether you feel able to set down conversations in direct speech, when the exact words are forgotten; how far you're willing to speculate or commit to an interpretation of your material.

For my part – as should be clear from this essay – I'm more concerned to explore the meaning of events than to get the particulars correct in every respect. If you think again about what I've written earlier, you'll recognise that this is a point of view consistent with the notion of autobiography as a poetic rather than an historical exercise. But, in the remote event that someone else wants to treat my life like a railway timetable, they're welcome to. My approach isn't binding on you or, indeed, anybody.

The tale of Shiny Jim and Adolf Hitler is a legend in my family. You may have myths and legends of your own. Why not add them to your topic list for the purpose of your essays?

THE LAST COWBOY IN WREXHAM

Hughie Williams was an Indian fighter. He and his drinking pal, my Uncle Denis, killed the last one in Wrexham, in the summer of 1954, one morning shortly before breakfast, while Little Jimmy was still in bed.

Hughie and Uncle Denis were boyhood friends and worked in the coalmines until my Dad left for Oldham in the mid-thirties. Hughie had a good tenor voice, but Denis was the real thing, a member of the Rhos Male Voice Choir, which sang all over the world like the Army of the Lord proclaiming the Last Judgment.

When I was very small, Denis and his wife Blanche came to stay for a week or two, which was the cause of a bitter argument between my parents and a grudge on the part of Nellie, which nags at her fifty years later. It's understandable only against the background of our poverty and Nellie's desperate insecurity.

Hughie followed the old practice of controlling the finances and paid Nellie a 'wage' or 'housekeeping', on which she had to manage. There was no discussion: in fact Nellie didn't know how much Hughie earned, and when she discovered he kept most of his money for himself, there was a blazing row. When Denis and his family arrived, Nellie had to put them up and feed them out of her meagre resources while Hughie and Denis went boozing in the evenings, and at the end (so Nellie tells me) Blanche didn't even make an offer of a contribution.

I believe the substance of the story is true, but Denis and Blanche probably expected to reciprocate in the way of a return visit, which never happened. Hughie occasionally went to Wales for a short break, and on one occasion I went with him. But Nellie never did. I doubt she saw Blanche again, and Denis re-appeared only once. It was at Hughie's funeral in 1989 and he was a jolly old man with a high complexion, who looked as though he might well have shot a few Indians in his time.

At heart Hughie was a countryman, never happier than when he was growing tomatoes or chrysanthemums in a greenhouse he rented from our neighbours in Werneth, or a few flowers in our small patch of garden. He was brought up in a pit village, where fields were never more than a hundred yards away.

After Shiny Jim's death the family broke up to escape the tyranny of Lucy. Hughie had an aunt who lived in Oldham and he trekked there some time in the mid-thirties. He was seventeen years old or thereabouts and his native language was Welsh. Though the comparison may seem strange, his situation wasn't dissimilar from that of the young Pakistani peasants who made the journey to Oldham thirty years later. They too were inexperienced country boys, unfamiliar with English and visiting a big town for the first time. They bought the house at Werneth where Little Jimmy once lived and for the same reason that Hughie bought it. It was cheap.

My father's name was Hugh Thomas Williams, but everyone called him Hughie. He was a well-made bantam cock of a man, all five feet five of him, and good-looking in a fierce Celtic way with dark curly hair. He was also honest and hardworking and had no difficulty finding a job in one of the coal mines that still existed in the Oldham area and closed only during my childhood.

He fell in with two brothers called Howard, who had a sister, Edna – the one Nellie hated. He married her and had three children: Denis, Jack and Anne.

According to Nellie, Edna was a slut who went out with other men. According to Denis, Hughie wasn't above hitting her, which I'm prepared to believe. He was a hard man in his youth and handy with his fists, but definitely

30

not a bully. Even now it's difficult to make sense of the tangle of relationships and emotions. Certainly Hughie stayed on friendly terms with the Howard brothers after the break with Edna and was admitted to the Howard house to pay for the keep of Jack, who boarded with 'grandma' Howard – I know because Little Jimmy went with him and thought nothing of this spare grandmother or the brother who didn't live at home. Nellie, too, always spoke well of the Howard men and said she and Hughie used to have a friendly drink with them even after all that had happened.

What did happen was disastrous – or, at least, had the potential for disaster. Hughie was reduced to sleeping in the street or the shelter of gents' toilets. It was his sister, my Auntie Dilys, who rescued him and cleaned him up.

Nellie was always bitter about Edna. It's hardly surprising. She was unmarried and uncertain about her title to Hughie, pregnant with Little Jimmy and burdened with three children by a woman she hated.

At the age of eighty-six she confesses the truth.

'I didn't love them. It were *duty* that made me take them on.'

She feels guilty about this and wants forgiveness.

'You have to understand. We had no money and I didn't know the first thing about bringing up children. And then I fell for you.'

Again the language of 'fallen women'. Nellie needs to be told she's a good person – which, indeed, she is.

When not hunting Indians, Hughie hunts for mice. The house at Werneth is overrun by them; they scamper over Little Jimmy's bed at night. Hughie chases them round the skirtings with a coal shovel, lays traps for them and finally wins his campaign. We have a cat to help out and one night, when he's drunk, Hughie and Denis have to fish it from the outside toilet, where it's been staring at its reflection in the long drop and lost its balance. It has

31

kittens and Hughie drowns them in a bucket of water while Little Jimmy and his sister are watching the Saturday matinee at the Gem cinema.

Hughie often smells of beer because he has a drink with his mates when they finish their shifts.

'I need to get the dust out of my throat, woman!' he says when Nellie complains. And perhaps he does.

His spit is black and his body is tattooed with a skein of fine scars blacked by coal.

He's spectacularly drunk only a couple of times. Because he's a 'hard man', he's learned the trick of doing it. Denis says, 'Dad was able to gamble and drink with the very best. He told me once that, when he had drunk enough, he would make himself sick, just to keep up with the boys, and continue drinking.'

Once Denis has to retrieve him from the coal cellar when he's taken a wrong turning. And once, when Jimmy is five or six, he and Nellie come home to find Hughie asleep under the sitting room rug, which is tucked up to his chin. It's Christmas and Jimmy has been singing *Sospan Bach* in a pub at Bardsley to the delight of miners and their wives. Nellie and Hughie have quarrelled and Hughie has sloped off on a pub-crawl.

His interests are rugby league, football and boxing. My Uncle Fred and he also put an occasional bob on a horse, especially when on holiday, but he isn't a gambler beyond the odd flutter and the pools. He often goes of a Saturday to watch a match, but I go with him only once, to the rugby ground at Watersheddings, where it's foggy and the match is abandoned.

All in all I'm a disappointment to him in this respect because I've no interest in sport.

'Here's a casey for you, Titch,' he says, giving me a present of a leather football. He gives me a pair of boxing gloves and wants to spar. Sometimes we roughhouse on the floor. It's to no effect. I want a teddy bear and books.

Hughie reads one book a year, usually a cowboy story.

He loves cowboys, especially John Wayne and Joel McCree. It takes one to know one. He never lets his disappointment in me show. He's far too tolerant and good-natured and he's concerned for my future though only dimly aware of the possibilities.

'You can stay on at school until you're sixteen,' he says. Anne goes to work in a handbag factory at fifteen, but for Jimmy he's prepared to make the sacrifice. 'You study your sums, Titch, and when you grow up you can become a draughtsman.'

I think the coal mine frightens him at times. At news of an accident he's glued to the radio or the newspaper. 'Hush, sirrah!' he snaps at any interruption. Once he breaks an arm and, for all his courage, he's terrified of hospitals: 'being in dock,' he calls it.

As a result he says, 'I don't want no son of mine going down the dirty stinking pit!' He's vehement; but, all the same, Denis does a stint in the colliery until he pulls himself out by his own efforts. Whatever Hughie wants, he doesn't know how to make it happen. Except to stay at school until sixteen and learn sums.

Like Nellie, my father has no sense of history, but he has a vague radicalism inherited from his Welsh Non-conformist roots.

He's the only man I know who disliked Churchill. Several times he expresses the opinion that, 'The miners'll never forgive Churchill for Tonypandy.'

Someone must have told him about this, because the incident itself was before his day. He resents Churchill out of solidarity with miners long dead.

Yet 'Tonypandy'? What is it?

He doesn't know.

A name.

A dimly recalled crime against miners.

A mystery like the 'Old King' who reigned over England when Nellie was a girl and who might have been

George the Fifth or Old King Cole for all she knows.

After the disastrous visit by Denis and Blanche, Nellie holds a fifty-year grudge and has nothing more to do with them. Hughie keeps contact with his old pal and now and again over the years he returns to Wrexham for a few days. And once only he takes Little Jimmy, who is six.

It's the first time Jimmy has travelled by train. We go from London Road Station in Manchester and the train has a black engine and deep maroon carriages. A few years later, with my friends, John and David Parry, I spend hours hanging around the marshalling yard at Newton Heath, climbing onto the footplates of derelict steam engines such as *The Derbyshire Yeomanry*. The engine that took us to Wales is known as a 'mickey' to *aficionados*, but I've no idea why.

Denis and Blanche live at Johnstown in a pebble-dashed house painted white. Behind it is a scrubby field. That night I go to bed exhausted with a Fox's Glacier Mint in my mouth. In the morning it's still there.

We take a walk after breakfast: me, Hughie and Uncle Denis, across the field behind the house. I find a crow's feather lying in the grass. There are no birds in Werneth other than house sparrows and I've never seen feathers before except the brightly dyed ones in the Indian headdresses sold on the toy stall in Oldham covered market.

'Look! Look!' I say and I show the feather to Hughie. 'What is it? Where's it come from?'

He examines it and grins at Denis. He says, 'It's from a Red Indian, see? Your Uncle Denis and me, we shot him this morning.'

'Did you?' I am open-mouthed. '*Did you?*'

'We used to be cowboys, me and your Uncle Denis, see?'

He gives me back the feather, pats me on the head, and he and Denis carry on talking about having a pint at lunch time and placing a small bet on a horse. But all I can think of is that my dad is a cowboy.

Wow!

Nineteen eighty-nine. It's the last summer of Hughie's life. The previous year, Shirley and I bought a house in Stockport, about a mile from Bramall Park. It has a large garden that makes Hughie's eyes open wide with pleasure. So much room for tomatoes, dahlias and chrysanthemums! I know he loves it and I so much want him to enjoy visiting us and pottering about at odd gardening jobs.

But in fact he's dying of cancer, though he doesn't yet know it, and all I have to remember this day by is a photograph of him and Nellie and my children sitting on the lawn in the sunshine.

We decide to go for a walk to Bramall Park. I find myself strolling alongside my father, who's in a cheerful mood but wistful. He doesn't normally talk about the past – not, I think, because it's a difficult subject but because he has an unreflecting nature and a lot of it simply makes no sense to him: it has no shape from which he can construct a story; only disconnected pieces. Today he talks about his days as a coal miner.

'I was fourteen,' he says. 'They gave me the ponies to look after, see?'

The ponies lived underground and hauled tubs of coal.

'I loved them ponies,' he says and smiles.

One by one Hughie tells me about the ponies he knew sixty years before. He remembers them all: each of their names and the character and idiosyncrasies of every one; and his voice is full of affection.

I suppose a cowboy never forgets his horse.

NOTES ON "THE LAST COWBOY IN WREXHAM"

The essays on Nellie and Hughie supply a foundation for this autobiography. They explain the background to my childhood and suggest the origin of my character and attitudes. For this reason I've placed them early in the collection.

I didn't find it difficult to write about my parents. I had a well-loved and happy childhood, and thinking about them causes me no anxiety. When my Dad died in 1989, I was sad because I loved him; but the process of grieving was an easy one. I think of him often, but the memories simply cause me to smile.

Not everyone is so fortunate. Not even within my family. My brother Jack was always semi-detached and he dropped out of sight in his early twenties. In her teens my sister Anne had considerable difficulties with Nellie. Nellie was frightened that Anne would grow to resemble her mother, Edna, and hounded her until in the end she left home. As for Denis, he had clear recollections of his birth mother, being nine years old when I was born, and although he was willing to accommodate Nellie he was never prepared to deny Edna. He joined the R.A.F. to avoid the problems of home life.

Over time, Anne and Nellie have patched their differences. Anne has my Dad's warm and easy-going nature and is incapable of holding a grudge; and Nellie, to her credit, admits she treated Anne harshly and recognises her many excellent qualities. Denis is a well-balanced man with a good heart. Taken as a whole he's behaved decently and generously towards Nellie, sometimes under considerable provocation, and I admire him for it.

I mention these matters because I'm aware that writing

an autobiography may be painful if it means addressing the relationship with your parents. Still, I'm reluctant to offer advice about dealing with emotional difficulties: partly because it isn't the subject of my book but more because I don't claim any special wisdom or expertise and anything I have to say is probably trite. However, I do have something to say on the more limited topic of getting on with your own book.

If the subject of parents is too distressing I recommend, in the first instance, that you simply avoid it. Put it off until a later date. If you try to cope with it at the same time as developing your abilities as an essayist, the combination of two difficult tasks will probably defeat you. It makes more sense to tackle problems singly. Build up your confidence as a writer by covering the easier topics (later you'll see some suggestions as to what these are); then, when you're at ease with words, turn to the more emotionally fraught subjects if you can. The essay approach doesn't demand that you write up your material in any particular order. These essays haven't been written in the order you are reading them.

That said, I do advise you to write essays about your parents at some time: certainly if you get to the point when you've covered the major part of your life. Partly this is in the interest of comprehensiveness; but more because what you have written will seem lacking in texture and truth if you deny a major influence on your life (if only by silence). Also – and here I am straying into the realm of advice and I repeat my earlier caution – the act of writing about your parents may be cathartic and help resolve the difficulties that have so far held you back.

Writing about both Nellie and Hughie, I've tried to understand the world as it appeared to them. I've taken Nellie's perspective, deformed as it was by poverty and insecurity, and Hughie's as an ignorant economic migrant come from the country. What strikes me still is how ill-equipped my parents were to meet the challenges they faced and how valiantly they struggled – successfully by and large. After the disaster with Edna when he was reduced to sleeping in the streets and public toilets, Dad did succeed in holding the family more or less together; and Nellie, for all that she had to bring up two strange children she didn't love (I exclude Jack who was with the Howards), managed well enough so that they never completely rejected her and most of the time hold her in affection. My parents' life was a small one, but I think their achievements were great because they began with so little, and I saw my Dad visibly becoming a nicer and better man as the years passed.

Nellie fought many ding-dong battles with him but she says: 'We became happier and happier. I do miss Daddy.'

Much grief is caused by things not said (as well as wrong things said and not retracted), matters unacknowledged, conflicts unresolved, anger suppressed – or so I suppose.

Death closes the opportunity for dialogue but, in the form of our essays, we can reopen it by entering imaginatively into our parent's world. Perhaps more importantly, in writing an autobiography we have the opportunity to speak to our children in a calm and measured way and so put over a point of view, which the ordinary circumstances of life prevent us from expressing: perhaps because we're too busy or embarrassed or tongue-tied. None of this is guaranteed to cure grief or grievance, but I suspect it'll help. However I know no more of the subject than anyone else.

At this point it's worth examining the structure of an essay. What makes it interesting? What holds it together in the absence of a conventional chronology and plot? Below I've analysed *The Last Cowboy in Wrexham* schematically. The elements of the essay are set out, with an arrow to indicate a flow or link between one event and the next (or a break if there is none). The approximate date of events is given so you can see that they're not sequential; and the nature of the link is explained. The purpose is to show how the essay holds together through the links. On the other hand, you may find the following diagram a bit technical and confusing – in which case, I suggest you skip it.

I didn't compose *The Last Cowboy in Wrexham* with this structure consciously in mind. In practice I write with a general sense of narrative rhythm: the links naturally suggesting themselves. However you may find that a planned structure of short linked passages, each no more than a few paragraphs, will help you.

Story Unit   *Link*

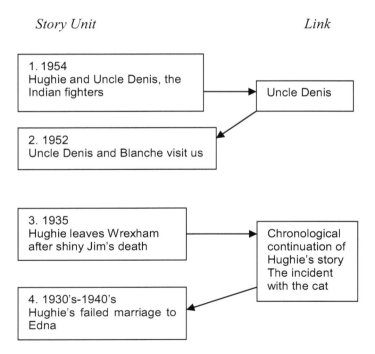

Story Unit   *Link*

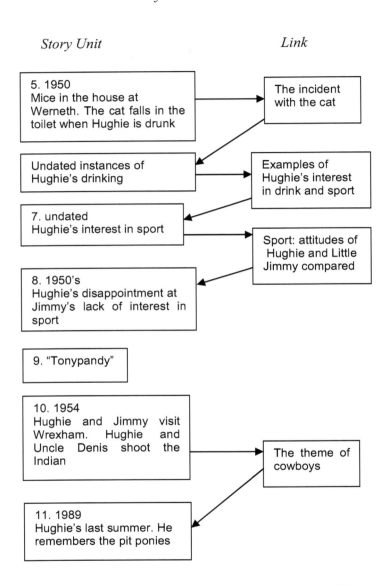

As you can see, the essay comprises eleven units. There are six sequential links and four breaks (after units 2, 4, 8

and 9) where there's no obvious connection between consecutive units. Where there is a link, it's in the nature of a common theme or reference. But even where there's a break, in two cases there are connections to other, non-sequential units. So units 5 and 10, which both follow breaks, are connected to each other and to unit 1 by the subject of cowboys and Indians. These three units, at beginning middle and end, contain the main theme of the essay and provide its frame so that the conclusion in a sense flows from the opening. The only true break is between units 2 and 3 and it isn't especially radical since both units in a larger sense are about Hughie, who is the subject of the whole essay. Unit 9, the 'Tonypandy' story is an aside.

Now compare the chronology of the units: it goes 1954, 1952, 1935, 1940s, two undated units, 1950's, 1954, a third undated unit, and finally 1989. The general trend is forward, which provides a degree of continuity, but it's by no means rigidly sequential and there are few obvious cause and effect relationships between the units. Chronology is essentially secondary to the thematic structure.

Although I've said you ought to consider a formal plan for your essay, once you've established your general theme, you should trust to your instincts to develop it. Only if you get stuck or find the result too disconnected should you focus consciously on developing the links between units. It's also possible to compromise: to devise a plan with four or five units, comprising your main subject, which will be expanded as inspiration takes you.

One of the tricks of writing is to know how to use a small amount of planning as a general compass without being too prescriptive. Experience will help you make this judgment.

Any plan should be short, each unit described in a brief sentence, much as I've done here.

THE LAST VICTORIAN

My childhood was spent in a Victorian world of slums: of mill chimneys, cobbled streets, gas lamps and yellow smogs. This wasn't true for all my contemporaries in nineteen fifties Oldham. The Coppice, for example, was the home of teachers, foremen and small tradesmen (rows of well-built Edwardian houses with 'high class grocers' on every corner); the Garden Suburb was a contribution to the inter-war spread of suburbia; the surrounding belt of council estates a monument to municipal socialism. In a world where motor cars were still uncommon, a child's range was limited and I lived within the compass of a few streets ending at the mysteriously named 'Jammy Lane', half a mile from my house but a place so remote that I had only unclear notions of how to get there. I was nineteen before I first entered a semi-detached middle class house (Fanny Kuler's as it happens), and I thought it impossibly luxurious.

Little Jimmy's parents, Nellie and Hughie, aren't married. They live in a verminous rented room off Greenacres Road. My brother Denis describes it like this: 'Dickensian... true squalor... indescribable... a small wallpaper peeling room within which one person would have had difficulty surviving... everything had to be carried up five flights of stairs... constant drunken fighting.'

Little Jimmy's first memory, however, is of a small terraced house, 5 Warwick Street, Werneth. He is two years old and will forever hold a picture of standing at the rail of his cot, calling to his parents, who are in bed in the same room.

In 1949 the universal ambition to be a homeowner doesn't exist. Council properties are so infinitely better than the swathes of slum terraces that it's clearly preferable to be a tenant of the local authority. However, Nellie and Hughie don't qualify because of their immoral status and have to make do with second best. They buy their first house for £450 only because there's no alternative if they're to escape rented rooms. Even so, there's no avoiding the vermin. The house swarms with mice.

The house is in a terrace of three plus a corner grocery called Dixons. They share a yard with two common toilets at the bottom, opposite our back door. The toilets are made from a length of salt-glazed pipe that falls to a mysterious drop. They're called 'tipplers' and empty erratically, using wastewater from the houses. As I sit silently contemplating the huge grey spiders that run free across the distempered brick walls, the mechanism of the tippler suddenly operates with a violent *galoosh!* I wipe my bum on *The News of the World* which is cut up in squares and hangs from a nail. Throughout childhood my backside is black with newsprint except after my weekly bath.

One day the cat falls down the tippler toilet and Hughie and my brother Denis have to fish it out

Outside toilets are found everywhere and they figure largely in my world, whose geography is less of streets than of alleyways and back yards. Their roofs are easy to climb on and they form turrets from which I can keep lookout and bombard enemies during the military campaigns against other gangs waged by me and my friends the Parrys.

David Parry throws a lighted firecracker into the toilet when his father is in it. He emerges cursing and holding up his pants in mid-shit. Dropping bangers down the pipe and hearing them blow the turds to pieces is most satisfying.

An effect of the toilet being outside is that bedrooms smell of pee – a quality they share with the palace of

Versailles: the cause being the same in both cases, namely the numerous chamber pots. When Hughie has been drinking, the pot is filled near to overflowing and we carry it through the house with extreme care. But, as a change from pee, the place sometimes smells powerfully of the bleach used to clean the 'chamber pots', though that term is too posh for us. We call them 'jerries' and the bleach is called 'Lanry'. Finally there's a stink of mothballs, which Nellie uses liberally.

The Warwick Street house is heated by coal. Hughie gets an ample supply as a miner. It's kept under the stairs by the back door and after a delivery there's a film of dust everywhere. We have electricity, but there are still gas brackets on the walls. The water supply for the entire house is a single brass cold-water tap in the kitchen-living room. It's in a corner by a copper boiler and there's no sink, only a block of unglazed sandstone with a hollow scooped out of it.

Nellie's first home improvement is to have the 'slopstone' removed and replaced by a plain white industrial sink that stands unceremoniously on two columns of bricks – the single brass tap remains. Her second improvement is to remove the cast iron range and replace it with a small tiled fireplace. When a tile falls off the fireplace, my Uncle Joe Wright cements it back with condensed milk. In a similar spirit of improvisation, Hughie and Uncle Fred hang wallpaper up the staircase using flour paste. The tile falls off. So does the paper.

There's no bathroom. On a nail in the yard hangs a galvanized bath, which we bring in as necessary and fill from the copper and pans heated on the gas stove. We bathe once a week and share the water (except that Hughie showers at work). Bath night is Sunday, and afterwards the tub is dragged to the back door and poured into the yard to drain away.

The joy of the house is three decent sized bedrooms. I share a bed briefly with my brother Denis until he leaves to join the RAF when I'm seven or eight. My sister Anne also has her own room. My brother Jack doesn't live with us. He stays with Grandma Howard and I see him now and again when my father pays for his keep. Children take their own families to be the model of all families, and nothing in this arrangement strikes Little Jimmy as odd.

In my world cars are rarities. I know of only three. Joe Holden has one, a small Austin in which he makes deliveries. He's a grocer and owns a shop in which biscuits, ham, coffee, tea, cheese and butter are all served loose. The shop possesses a bacon slicer and magnificent mahogany display counters, and is a rich and unforgettable mix of savours. The second car is a green Jaguar and belongs to the chemist. He sells eggnog, Sanatogen Tonic Wine and 'British sherry', and I call on him every two or three weeks to fill a brown medicine bottle with Hughie's chest mixture. Finally, Roy Sutton's dad owns a huge black American sedan like something out of a *film noir*. But this car isn't for driving. It's for taking apart and putting back together. Shirley's father owns a car upon similar principles.

At night, as I lie in bed, I hear an occasional car pass by on Oxford Street. My window is leaded and the sweep of headlights causes the pattern of glass to rotate around the room. This image of the night, silent except for the shush of tyres on the rainy street, is the most powerful one of my childhood.

The absence of cars is reflected in Nellie's language. It, too, is Victorian, retaining many dialect words and old pronunciations, which she loses in later years. She says 'kekkle' for 'kettle' and 'bokkle' for 'bottle'. A street or road is specifically the 'cartroad', because it's carts not cars that use it. A motor coach is a 'sharrabang' or 'sharra'. The name was once used for a horse-drawn vehicle.

It's possible for a child of seven to cross the main road from Oldham to Manchester unsupervised. I often do in order to go to Werneth Park. Children ordinarily play in the street at hopscotch and tag games or swing on a rope from the horizontal bar against which the lamp lighter rests his ladder. Dorothy Mee is my sister's age, has pigtails and big feet, and, when George the Sixth dies in 1952, she tells me so outside the back gate of her father's butcher's shop. One day we play a game of circuses together, leaping off a low wall like acrobats. It counts among the handful of days that are the happiest.

Streets are cobbled. Tarmac is so rare that, when we come across a drop of it in the cracks among the cobblestones, we scrape it up and mould it into shapes. Tarmac streets are a sign of modernity. Cars are objects of wonder driven by grocers and other members of the aristocracy. I ride in one no more than half a dozen times until I am well into my teens.

My house and its area are by no means the worst that Oldham offers. Indeed the house still stands, now occupied by Pakistanis in ethnic dress for whom its resonances must be quite different: for whom it is in no sense Victorian.

Until the great slum clearances of the sixties, Oldham had many miserable terraced cottages in very poor repair. Some of them had inhabited cellar-rooms that were entered by steps from the street. I recall something like them in the film *Hobson's Choice*.

'Ra-ag Bo-hone! Donk-hee Sto-hone!'

Most weeks the iron-shod wheels of the rag and bone cart rattle down the street or the back entry, and Hughie rushes out to shovel up horseshit for his roses. In exchange the rag and bone man gives blocks of pumice stone in a range of colours from cream through honey tones to a light tan. Donkey stone is one of the kinds on offer.

In the Victorian class war, pumice stone is the heavy artillery.

Marx is wrong. For the working class the sharpest conflict is not its opposition to the bourgeoisie. That war is

46

unwinnable, even though one may succeed in an occasional skirmish. The bourgeoisie is rich and clever and the workers know it and decline to fight.

For families like mine, and in particular for women like Nellie, the bitterest struggle is at the boundary between the rough and respectable working classes; for respectability is something that can be lost. Equally, it can be won. More to the point it's a struggle that's easy to conceive of in real terms and for which practical strategies can be devised. The bourgeoisie live in their distant castles (though they may be no more than a mile away), but the chaotic poor are our closest neighbours. Their kids steal our milk and their dogs make a mess outside our front doors.

Nellie wasn't respectable by nature. She achieved the blessed state by a long struggle. She always knew her claim was thin. She'd been brought up in poor circumstances. Her own legitimacy was questionable, her stepfather lived on a war disability pension, and her mother was an alcoholic. She had two half-brothers, Joe and Fred, with whom she was brought up, but there were rumours of a previous family her mother had abandoned. Nellie set up home with a coal miner from Wales, who already had a wife and three children, and in due course she had a child by him. Little Jimmy was nine years old when they slipped out one day and got married.

'Don't tread on the steps, I've just donkey-stoned them!'

A common sight in any street is a row of large bottoms as women kneel to mop and stone their steps, and afterwards, from all mouths, the same cry goes up: 'Don't tread on the steps!' But how can you not tread on them? They're the threshold to the houses.

In Little Jimmy's childhood, respectability can't be measured by money and consumer goods. The 'rough' working class has money. It squanders it on beer and fags. Consumer goods are scarce. A woman can cling to her respectability even if impoverished. But to maintain her claim she must spend the one thing she disposes of: her own labour. Let the lazy buggers match *that*!

If you want, you can pumice the front and back door steps, the windowsills and the area of pavement in front of the door. You can completely mop the step or just the edges. You can do it daily or weekly, or – God forbid! – not at all. Respectability can be exactly measured.

The point of pumicing the steps is precisely that it's pointless by any criterion except respectability. It has no hygienic value. It doesn't last. Within minutes ('Don't tread on the steps!') the effect may be lost by a careless caller whose feet will print dirty patterns on the powdery surface left by the donkey-stone. Only rarely will the result of so much effort outlast the day in its pristine state.

And so it has to be repeated like mowing the lawn: another activity that consumes labour and which respectable people do while their rougher neighbours watch satellite television.

Nellie hated donkey-stoning the steps, but she did it. Then, as affluence provided more material means of demonstrating status, so the custom of mopping and stoning died out, and now it seems as antiquated and barbarous as foot binding. Mowing the lawn may go the same way – the increased use of gravel and decking gives reason to think so. Customs become redundant or absurd that were once seen as essential. So, as I write, young men with earrings and shaven heads wear morning dress for their weddings. The trousers concertina over their Timberland boots and their shirts and bellies show beneath waistcoats that are too short. To win respectability, money is spent instead of labour, but the effect is still ridiculous.

Clogs. The footwear of the Lancashire mills. Black leather with wooden soles trimmed with irons. The tops of men's clogs are enclosed, but women's clogs, though so clearly functional, retain a feminine note and are cut low over the instep and fastened by a strap.

48

A Message to the Children

In the fifties the cotton mills are still in a substantial way of business. The skyline of Oldham is magnificent with its vista of mill chimneys. Each one is emblazoned with its name: the Durban, the Nile, the Royton Ring Mill. I'm placed in their nurseries while Nellie works there. She wears a headscarf but still comes home with clumps of cotton in her hair. At nursery I discover toothpaste – something we don't use at home because Nellie and Hughie, though only in their thirties, have false teeth. The brand is Gibbs and it comes as a tablet in a tin similar to shoe polish.

Old men wear clogs. They clatter over the cobbled street. In Manchester Art Gallery is a fine picture by Eyre Crowe of some mill girls, brazen and swaggering in their aprons, shawls and clogs. In my childhood they're still alive as doddery old ladies, still in shawls and clogs.

I wear clogs.

Shoes are a serious expense for working people. Children mostly wear wellington boots or black canvas plimsolls, but my parents buy me a pair of clogs. I'm five or six years old and have to wear them for school.

The shame of it.

'They're cowboy boots, sirrah,' says Hughie. He's the Last Cowboy in Wrexham and should know. To prove the point he fringes the leather at the ankle, but I still can't imagine John Wayne wearing them.

I cry in real distress, 'Nobody wears clogs at school!'

But I do. Little Jimmy trots off to school in his green corduroy windcheater, knitted balaclava and clogs.

Only briefly, however. My parents relent very quickly. They're ashamed of putting their child into such footwear.

Twenty years later my friends, Chris and Ann Hulbert, have a pair of red clogs made for their little boy, Mark. By then the social meaning of clogs has changed entirely.

Victorian pennies are commonplace. Jimmy comes across them in small change all the time. They remain as live

49

relics of the era until 1971 when the currency is decimalised. Authentic Victorian people also exist in their millions. They form the generation of my grandparents.

John Parry is given a copy of *The Guinness Book of Records* for his seventh birthday. The world's oldest living soldier fought in the American Civil War. There are still a lot of ancient soldiers from the Boer War or the First World War. Mr Hardcastle is a veteran of the trenches. War cost him a foot. He's our neighbour and shares one of the outside toilets with us. His wife is very respectable. She comes from Harrogate, which, so Jimmy understands, is grand (and my Auntie Dilys, who looks like the Queen Mother and has a grand manner, moves to live there, so the story may be true). She has a stick with a gravity-knife that shakes out of the tip. She tells Jimmy she intended to use it to bayonet any German paratroopers who happened to turn up in Oldham. But they didn't. Jimmy hopes they still may.

'Uncle' Walter is also a Victorian and a war veteran. I come across him only when I get myself a paper round in my early teens. He's vaguely related to Nellie and lives a couple of streets away in a house that smells of *Condor* pipe tobacco and is furnished with a grandfather clock and a peg rug. Peg rugs are a common item of working class households. We've got one, though it vanishes early. They're made by fixing strips of coloured rag to a backing of old sacks. Shirley remembers her father making such rugs of an evening while listening to the wireless.

Mats of coconut fibre are also common. They're cheaper than carpet and we have one in our front room. Later they became 'ethnic' and fashionable and their significance as a badge of poverty is now lost.

Beneath the coconut mat the floor is laid with flagstones. They're uneven and very cold.

The Victorian Empire lasts until the sixties and its ethos is visible in books like the Biggles stories which I love.

Empire Day – established in the twenties when the Government scratched its head over exactly what the Empire was *for* – is still celebrated in schools. We dress up as Scots, Red Indians and Chinamen (I also played a Chinaman in the Nativity play and, too, a black cat, which makes me wonder which version of the Nativity we were playing). Mrs Hardcastle lends Jimmy a white shirt to wear with his kilt. Its label reads 'Empire Made', which seems so appropriate that he's stunned. He thinks it has been specially made for the occasion.

The Boy Scouts – admittedly an Edwardian organisation but very much a symbol of Empire – are highly visible. Most Sundays they parade with bugle, flag and drum. Every church has a troop. They decline as the churches and the Empire itself decline.

In time the roads are tarmacked, the mill chimneys felled, the slums demolished. The smogs die out in the early sixties: I'm about 14 years old when the last one occurs. My Victorian world is slipping away and Little Jimmy is fading with it, acquiring long trousers and acne and putting *Brylcreem* on his hair: no longer Little Jimmy at all.

Rationing ends in 1954 and from about that date the changes start. We acquire a television – 14 inch screen, one channel, black and white, and rented from DER. In fact I see the Coronation on television the year before: the Hutchinsons own one before they emigrate to Australia as many people do in those years (Jimmy's pal, Alan Hutchinson, promises to return when he is eighteen – but his Second Coming, like another one, is long overdue). The first programme I watch on our own set is *Prudence Kitten*. That same night the damn thing breaks down during *Life With The Lyons*. These early sets are famously unreliable, as are the broadcasts themselves. It's common for programmes to be interrupted and replaced with a card stating 'Normal Service Will Be Resumed As Soon As Possible'. When this happens we play dominoes and pontoon with my Dad. The wireless also figures as family entertainment rather than background. On Sundays we listen to *The Billy Cotton Bandshow*, which is heralded by a cry of 'Wakey! Wakey!' from Billy Cotton himself. And while we listen, Nellie reduces a joint of lamb to old boots because she never learned to cook from her alcoholic mother. She boils the vegetables to mush while she's at it.

In due course Nellie gets a small washing machine that ties the clothes into a knot. Before then she does the laundry by hand in a possing tub using *Fairy* soap and a brightener called 'Dolly Blue'. It's a tablet tied to a stick and wrapped in muslin and we buy it in shops that smell of paraffin. The clothes are mangled by hand on a cast iron mangle that stands in the yard. The first washing machine still has a mangle, which gives it a hybrid quality like a platypus.

Up until the time I finally leave home at the age of twenty-one, we have no telephone or refrigerator. We do have a vacuum cleaner. Instead of a fitted kitchen there's a form of cupboard with a drop-down front covered in enamelled tinplate. It's called a 'kitchenette'. The galvanized bath is in use until I'm fifteen. In 1962 we leave Warwick Street and Werneth for 32 Estate Street, Hathershaw, a house, which has a bathroom. Because I've got no experience of bathrooms I don't know which is the 'correct' way to sit in the bath, and for years I sit with my back to the taps for aesthetic reasons: so that I don't have to look at them

I'm sixteen before I first use a telephone. It's a callbox and the price is threepence, paid with a multisided brass coin that takes its metal and shape from somewhere in the colonies. The first person I ever telephone is my girlfriend, Kathy Redfern.

Do I remember the knocker-up or is he a figment born from repetition? I can't tell.

A 'knocker-up' makes his living waking-up shift

workers by tapping on their windows with a long stick. He's a walking alarm clock.

Such an occupation is too strange to have been invented.

In Uppermill there's a second-hand bookshop, and Shirley and I are there one day when we come across a collection of postcards. One of them is a picture of the last knocker-up in Oldham. He retired in the nineteen sixties.

It's quite possible that I remember the knocker-up as he walked the damp streets in the early mornings. It's also possible that Nellie told me about him. History reaches out fingertip to fingertip.

The Victorian English are addicted to laxatives.

'Have you *been*?' Nellie asks most days. (Conveying unpleasant details by knowing emphasis is a common habit of speech that now seems archaic. Hence my Latin master, Tosser Thompson, is 'one of *those*'. The meaning of 'those' is understood.)

You must empty your bowels every day. You'll die if you don't.

In Salford Museum is a row of shops set out as they were in the late nineteenth century. Similar shops survived into my childhood, gradually dying under the attack of supermarkets. Contemporary Asian grocers retain little of the atmosphere of these dead businesses: the dust and stocks of mean necessities: fly papers, bootlaces and *Camp* coffee. What's striking about the shops in Salford Museum is the range and quantity of laxatives that are sold with the bread, tea and sugar, almost as a dietary staple.

Nellie's preferences are syrup of figs (delicious as I recall) and liquid paraffin. The first is for emergencies. The second is a daily precaution in her case but only an occasional remedy in mine.

'You've got to keep *regular*,' she says.

As far as I know I'm always regular, but I take laxatives all the same.

Self-medication is probably a permanent aspect of the human condition, but the form is a matter of time and culture. Nellie's remedies lack the gloss of pseudo-science or New Age mysticism. She relies on anecdote, folk wisdom and Victorian quackery.

'I've got a sore throat,' says Little Jimmy.

'This'll cure it,' says Nellie. She produces one of Hughie's sweaty socks. Jimmy is to wear it.

So there goes Little Jimmy to school – the last Victorian – in balaclava helmet and clogs, with his dad's sweaty sock tied round his neck to fix a sore throat. Let's hope he gets there before the laxative takes effect.

NOTES ON "THE LAST VICTORIAN"

This essay isn't concerned with incident. Instead it tries to paint the larger canvas of my childhood, and the details are there only to capture the 'feel', the day-to-day texture of my world.

I was born in 1947 and, at the most obvious level, I'm a child of the fifties and sixties. For convenience we divide history into segments and characterise them as having a unique identity, in some way representing a break with what has gone before. It's an approach that has its uses and even a certain truth. It can't be denied, for example, that the fifties and sixties of the last century differed materially from the Victorian period. Nevertheless history remains a flow of events and even catastrophes like the French Revolution and the First World War, when re-examined at a distance, mask considerable continuity between the worlds either side.

It has come to me only lately how much of my childhood was spent in the world of the Victorians: how it was lived in a physical environment built by them and a social environment that still reflected their economy, their morals and their customs: an age when the working people, schooled in heavy and manufacturing industry, retained much of the culture they created when their ancestors were tipped off the land and forced into the cities. My parents worked in mining and cotton. They were quintessentially nineteenth century industries, and have now disappeared.

As I've tried to suggest, my experience wasn't shared by every child in my age group. Children who lived in council houses or the suburbs inhabited a twentieth century landscape, and many of them no more penetrated my world than I did theirs, which, for me, was represented by bathrooms and indoor toilets and that luxury item, the radiogram.

History is apparently a stream of many currents, flowing at different rates. With this insight in mind (if you think it is one) you may care to look again at your own life and, ignoring such superficial indicators as your date of birth, try to place it. You may be surprised by the similarities with the world of your parents and find them worth exploring.

It's difficult to create a lively sense of the past simply from its buildings. Tower Bridge, from the viewpoint of architectural history, is a classic Victorian structure; but symbolically it's contemporary: still firmly incorporated in our present image of London. When we see ordinary houses in ordinary streets, that's precisely what we see: their ordinariness. They'd have to be pulled down before we began to appreciate their special contribution to the look of things and their social meaning. So it was necessary to demolish the old slums and build high-rise flats before the qualities of the former could be fully understood.

When you come to describe the past, you should focus on ephemera – the fleeting things that go into the dustbin – because they seem to capture it in a special way. More than paintings, we associate advertising posters with the nineteen thirties. Brand names of products, that were once famous but are now gone, are deeply evocative, and jingles are more memorable than most poetry.

Studies suggest that our senses of smell and taste call up the most emotive responses. It isn't for nothing that Marcel Proust embarked on his great re-creation of the past from a memory stirred by the taste of a small cake dipped in tea. The past smells and tastes different.

Two examples from the essay illustrate this point. The first is the grocer's shop of Joe Holden. It was dominated by the smell of unwrapped food, especially coffee, ham and cheese and, on the rare occasions when I enter such a shop these days, I return to 'J'oldens' as a child hand in hand with my Mum. Similarly the house at Werneth smelled strongly of pee, bleach and mothballs. The stink of urine has been eliminated by plumbing, the bleach by new products with artificial perfumes, and the mothballs by the manufacture of clothes from non-natural fibres. Because they've largely disappeared, any of these scents can call up a memory of my old home.

With these indicators in mind, you may wish to re-read this essay, paying special attention to references to ephemera and to scent and taste.

From transient signs such as brand names, it's only a step to consider customs that were once common but have now fallen into disuse. Shirley and I both remember a time when the churches organised large parades at Whitsuntide: when traffic was stopped by the police and the Protestants goggled at the heathen Papists, especially the exotic Ukrainians in their national dress and the florid faced Irish staggering under the burden of a statue of the Virgin. To us as children it seemed an occasion with origins in time immemorial and immune to change. Yet within twenty years it had largely vanished.

The bizarre business of 'stoning' steps belongs to this realm of dead customs. Indeed it's almost impossible now to convey the importance of this backbreaking chore, which hard-pressed women imposed on themselves to prove their status as good, respectable wives. Shirley lived in a house with a front path long enough to hide the doorstep from the street, so there was little public reason for 'stoning'. Still her mother, Ada, did it. Why? For herself, of course: for her sense of her own worth.

If Nellie were to say to one of her contemporaries, 'Edna didn't stone her steps,' the reasons for the failure of Hughie's first marriage would be immediately understood.

To summarise: the feel of the past is determined not only by events but by small points of detail: brand names, advertisements, popular songs, fashions, scents, tastes and patterns of behaviour. Your memory is filled with these trivia. Individually they mean little. Collectively they describe in the most vivid terms a world that's passing if not dead. In the present essay I've tried to salvage this material and form it into a coherent picture around the motif of The Last Victorian. It may help if you can find a similar motif that you think describes you: The Last Teddyboy? The Last Goth?

The clue that will unleash a flood of memory may be hiding forgotten in your wardrobe. Try to convince your grandchildren that those shoes were once a great idea.

You may have noticed that this essay contains a short passage summarising the history of Nellie and Hughie: material, which is expanded in the two essays about my parents. The reason it's there is that the present essay, though it appears later, was written before I knew I'd write the others. So it was necessary to say something about my parents in order to tell a complete, self-contained story. In putting the collection together, I might have cut the passage to avoid repetition. However I decided to keep it as a reminder of how this book has been constructed: that it has grown organically by putting together small pieces which once had an independent life.

This book has its own biography. I feel it as alive. That is part of the excitement.

GENTS AND GYPSIES

Uncle Joe Wright kept a seven feet high luminous Frankenstein in his kitchen. Uncle Joe Williams wore a flying helmet and drove a motorcycle and sidecar. Uncle Joe Burton looked like Goebbels.

Joe Wright was Nellie's brother.

'He had meningitis when he were a kiddie,' she says, adding darkly, '*and mastoids.*'

Whatever the case, Uncle Joe was a strange, lonely man. But I don't think he was unhappy. He could be seen about Oldham in his decorator's white overalls, walking his long, loping stride, self-absorbed except to smile at anyone he knew and say, 'How do, lad! How're you getting on?' He never said anything else much

Nellie says, 'Tommy Jackson promised my mam he'd always give Joe a job, painting and decorating.' And Tommy was as good as his word. The job suited Joe: to be left alone all day with an old radio and an endless supply of *Park Drive* cigarettes. His face was gaunt and lined; his hair was lank and thin; he was tall, hollow-chested and long-legged. Two of his fingers were deep brown with nicotine and he had a horny thumb nail protruding an inch or more, which he used to trim wallpaper.

After his mother died from giving up drink, Joe continued to live at her house in Pembroke Street. It was a dark, smelly place with two rooms on the ground floor and a tippler toilet in the yard. The front room was occupied by a shabby and sinister grey and yellow cockatoo, that swore, bit people and pulled out its own feathers. The back room was inhabited by Frankenstein.

The business of Frankenstein had its origins in a

59

strange talent Joe had. He owned a rusty, pedal-operated fretwork machine and he used it to turn out objects made of plywood. He also had a talent for copying pictures, and he'd paint the wooden blanks using leftover materials from his jobs and give the result to his friends. His problem was a very limited imagination. If you knew Joe, then sooner or later you finished up with an immaculately painted four feet high Donald Duck ashtray in your front room.

Joe made the Frankenstein.

It seems to be the way with bachelors that they can carry on for only so long before suffering a collapse. After sixteen or seventeen years, Joe's diet of beer, cigarettes and Holland's Meat Pies ceased to work its magic. Hughie and Uncle Fred dug him out of the accumulated filth of the house and Nellie tended him until he recovered his health; and then she browbeat the pair of them – Hughie and Joe – until Joe agreed to stay in the spare room at our house. He came for a week and remained about fifteen years. Yet it was a satisfactory arrangement. Hughie was good-natured and Joe was quiet. Much of his spare time was spent in his room, listening to the radio and smoking. For the rest, he stalked from pub to pub saying, 'How do, lad?' to anyone who caught his attention.

On the evening before his sixty-second birthday, he went out boozing, had a pleasant skinful and died in his sleep.

I liked Uncle Joe Wright.

Uncle Fred was Nellie's other brother and a year or two older than Joe. He was a plasterer and, after our move from Werneth to Hathershaw in the early sixties, we lived only a few streets from each other. He was a tall, handsome, cheerful man.

Fred's wife was my Auntie Winnie; his children my cousins Harvey and Christine. The two families were close and went on holiday and spent Christmas together – at least until I was about eighteen when Something

Happened on a holiday to Paignton. I wasn't there and don't know what the Something was except that the women fell out and Nellie nursed a grudge for more than twenty years until Winnie and Hughie were dead. After that, she and Fred and Fred's bachelor son, Harvey, resumed going on holiday together.

Hughie was never a party to the quarrel and would always have a drink with Fred if he felt like it. He was incapable of bearing a grudge

Fred had two weaknesses: he liked his beer and he suffered from nightmares. During the War he'd been in London during the Blitz. Hughie couldn't face Winnie when she was angry and so, on the odd occasion – usually around Christmas – when Fred was legless, Hughie would prop him up against the door of the house in Plymouth Street, give a knock, then run away like a naughty child.

'You're a rotten bugger,' Auntie Winnie complained. 'He was at it all night, screaming about the bombs!'

It was Shiny Jim's children who divided into the Gents and the Gypsies. My Uncle Albert and my Auntie Dilys were the Gents: Hughie, Uncle Joe Williams and Blodwen-alias-Billie were the Gypsies.

The Gents were tall, fair and gifted with grave, polite manners.

The Gypsies were small, dark and looked canny with horses.

Why this should be so is a mystery, especially as far as the Gents are concerned. Albert, after all, was a coal miner like Hughie, but he carried himself with a certain grace: a pleasant, likeable man and a natural aristocrat. Sadly I met him only a few times and not before I was fifteen. I last saw him in 1988, when he called at our house and Shirley met him. The next year he died and Hughie, Denis and I went to his funeral in Wrexham. At the funeral, my cousin Irene, a trained nurse, took one look at my father and said, 'Hughie, you've got jaundice!' He had, and it was a symptom of cancer. By Christmas he was dead.

Everyone agrees: Dilys looked like Queen Elizabeth the Queen Mother – though Dilys didn't have the gambling habit. She married Billie Fisher, an ambulance man. They scrimped and saved and moved into a new-built house on Broadway, Chadderton, which was very respectable. After Billie's sudden death she abandoned Oldham for Harrogate where she lived as genteelly as a moderate income allowed.

Surprisingly, given their difference in outlook and manners, she and Nellie got on well together and, after Hughie's death, Nellie often went to spend a few days with her sister-in-law. Equally unsurprisingly it all ended in a quarrel and an estrangement, but I hold no opinion as to where the fault lay.

Uncle Billie owned a Nazi dagger and a copy of *Mein Kampf*. I used to lust after them as Nellie and I sat drinking tea in the best room. It was served in china cups and saucers: something we never used at home.

Uncle Joe Williams lived in a hamlet near Shrewsbury, a place among the hills called Stiperstones, dominated by some rocks called 'The Devil's Chair' as I recall. The houses had been built just before the War but they had no WC, not even the humble 'tippler'. Instead, at the bottom of the garden, was an awesome thunderbox filled with ashes and newspapers, which was emptied once a week by the honeycart.

Earth closets appeal to every child's spirit of adventure. There's something heroic about using them when they're close to full, smell appalling and attract flies. I enjoyed this one when I was seven years old.

A mist of vague rumours surrounds this second Uncle Joe. Even now in his eighties he gives an impression of being on the run from the police, and when he was younger he was raffishly attractive, while Hughie was debonair. I never dared to enquire and so collected only dark hints about difficulties in his teens under Lucy's regime and mention of a sanatorium where he learned basket weaving.

Joe married my Auntie Doll, a lapsed Jehovah's Witness and harmonium player – so Nellie tells it. Whatever the case, she was as lovely a woman as ever lived. Between them they raised a houseful of kids and then hordes of grandchildren, and they all lived merrily in a raggle-taggle band within a few streets of each other in Shrewsbury.

I stayed at their house briefly in the summer of 1968. I painted watercolours and accompanied my cousins Tony and Pepé when they went fishing, and joked with Barry and Sheila. Tony was full of tales of his precocious sexual exploits. My cousin Margaret – blonde, beautiful and with a sparkling personality – was single and pregnant with her first child.

Concerning the father: 'He was a bus conductor,' she told me in a voice with a Welsh lilt, and laughed. 'He asked me, "How far do you want to go?" I said, "All the way." So we did!'

I met Blodwen only three times in my life, but I loved her very much and she left me all her memorabilia. She was a nurse and married a licensed victualler, Uncle Joe Burton, and after a spell running a pub in Chapel en le Frith and the Swan With Two Necks in Stockport, they took the subsidy and emigrated to Australia when I was very small. They were 'ten pound Poms'.

At first they did well in the catering trade. They returned to England for a holiday when I was five or six years old and annoyed Dilys with their evident prosperity. Later their good fortune ran out. Poor health and medical bills took away most of what they had and Joe Burton died relatively young, leaving Blodwen to face a long widowhood. Fortunately she had a wonderful way of making friends.

After thirty years I saw her again in 1983, and in similar circumstances in 1985. I was working as a commercial lawyer and had business in Sydney. I routed my return flight through Perth where she was living and we met at the airport. There was an immediate chemistry between us and in no time flat we were laughing and joking as if we'd known each other forever. During these trips she showed me the city and Fremantle and I met her friends and thoroughly enjoyed myself. After that second meeting we corresponded until her death. I still keep contact with some of her friends, to whom I'm grateful for the happiness they gave her.

It was Blodwen who had the generosity to recognise the difficulty under which Shiny Jim's second wife, Lucy, laboured as mother to five truculent stepchildren and the foundling Millie.

Joe Burton appears in photographs. He has oiled hair, a double-breasted suit and a huge sickle-shaped smile like a ventriloquist's dummy. He looks the epitome of a cheeky chappie music hall comedian of the nineteen forties – and by Blodwen's account that's pretty much what he was like.

Also – it has to be said – he looked like Goebbels, always assuming the latter had taken up telling risqué jokes with some tap dance accompaniment. I saw the resemblance immediately and it was a little disconcerting to inherit his passport from 1938, which, for wholly unexplained reasons, contained a Nazi visa complete with eagle and swastika. The coincidence seemed too improbable? Was it possible…?

One hears of these things: of Nazi chieftains fleeing to Argentina, Bolivia and Paraguay. An American reader (mad I hope) disliked my first novel, *The Hitler Diaries*, and told me she had it on authority that the Führer had escaped from Berlin dressed as a woman, and would shortly come and get me (which implied the flattering possibility that he read my books). The

Reichspropagandaminister was a man of creative imagination and could certainly have escaped. It's possible to imagine him decamping to Australia with a plump Welsh nurse, to spend the rest of his life in the innocent business of selling beer.

Isn't it?

Frankenstein didn't make it to our house at the time of Uncle Joe Wright's collapse. It's tempting to think that, like the original, he fled to the frozen wastes of the far North, where he spends his days saying, 'How do, lad?' to polar bears. However more likely is that Hughie and Uncle Fred dumped him on Oldham Council Tip. It seems a pity. He would have been a talking point in our front room, where – come to think of it – I now keep a six-foot statue of Humphrey Bogart bought for me by Shirley as a present on my fiftieth birthday.

Even so, Frankenstein didn't vanish without a swan song – though to understand this you must know something of Joe's sense of humour. Born of tongue-tied loneliness, it was unsophisticated and direct.

Joe had a habit of slipping goldfish into other men's beer.

When one of his friends became impotent (and apparently advertised the fact), Joe sent him a plaster penis in a cardboard box.

Joe tells me the tale of Frankenstein like this. Though his face is normally lugubrious, his eyes light and he has a magical smile when something pleases him. He says:

'Me and Tommy Jackson went out for a drink, you know? And at chucking-out time it were raining cats and dogs, and we got some bottles and went back to my house, see. So we drink the bottles and Tommy says he wants to pee. The toilet's at the bottom of the yard; it's pitch bloody dark; the grass is up to your knees; and it's pissing down – but Tommy says he has to go.'

'But what has this to do with…?'

'Frankenstein were in t'yard,' says Joe.

'Oh.'

'It were there – hiding in the grass – in the dark – rain streaming down it – *and glowing!* But I'd forgot to mention it to Tommy,' he adds.

'Ah!'

'Any road, Tommy let's out this yell. He lets out this yell, and I asks, "What's up, lad?" and he points at Frankenstein. "Oh, that," I says and tells him what it is, which he's seen before. "Oh, bloody hell, Joe!" says Tommy – and you have to laugh, eh? – he says, "Oh bloody hell, Joe – *I've just shat myself because o' thee!*"'

NOTES ON 'GENTS AND GYPSIES'

I enjoyed writing this essay because I was fond of my aunts and uncles. If you decide to write your own autobiography, enjoyment is an important consideration, especially at the beginning when you're still wondering whether you're up to the task. At this stage you should focus on subjects that give you pleasure – which, as it happens, are also the ones most likely to please your readers. Once you're firmly committed to essay writing, the miserable subjects will come in their own time.

The topic of my relatives deviates a bit from the main thrust of describing my life. However, I've set the rules for this book, just as you'll do for yours, and if I feel like writing about my various Uncle Joes or anything else, then so be it. For an autobiography that wanders all over the place, read Montaigne. In any case, there's a certain relevance because we are in large measure a reflection of our families, though, if I were a different person, it might be a problem since, excepting the 'Gents', my relatives seem to be a vulgar lot – '*dead common*' as Nellie would say – but good hearted, I hope. Whatever the case, I'm happy to be numbered among them.

My main audience is my children. (As I write these notes, I've no idea if anyone else will be interested). I think it's important that they should feel in some way grounded: placed in an understandable context, against a background that will help them grasp why their own lives and characters are as they are – which includes an understanding of why their embarrassing father is who he is. Despite the fact that, on any view, my family is a humble one, it isn't without its heroes and its comics (Nellie to my mind is both), and by telling their stories (if only as brief sketches), I hope my children will have a sense of its human richness far beyond what can be gained through putting together a family tree only to discover the mundane fact that an ancestor in the eighteenth century was a grocer. I want my children to be glad to be members of this family.

If you want the same for your children, you should press on.

To repeat: I'm fond of my aunts and uncles; yet, as far as I know, none of them has left anything much in the way of autobiographical material except for my brother Denis. I've got little except a few photographs and letters from Blodwen, and, if I do nothing with them, they'll disappear in a house clearance some time when her name has no meaning for anyone: a time which isn't so far off. This seems to me a shame. So a part of my motivation is to give a voice to the voiceless and leave a little echo of their passing.

To put it bluntly, I couldn't pass the chance of telling the tale of Uncle Joe Wright and his Frankenstein. Who could?

You may want to reflect on the following technical points for what help they give. None of them are original, but they're characteristic of my approach to this book.

(1) The first sentence ("Uncle Joe Wright kept a seven feet high luminous Frankenstein in his kitchen") is known in the business as 'an arresting opening'. Its object is to grab the reader's attention, and it does so by provoking shock or mystification or some other strong emotional reaction. In this case, I've tried to strengthen the effect by repetition in each of the first three sentences. I've relied on the incongruity of the images to draw the reader into seeking an explanation.

An arresting opening doesn't require its impact to

be in the first sentence. It can be effective to deceive the reader with an apparently nondescript introduction leaving the killer blow to the end of the paragraph or section. Neither is it compulsory. A reader may be seduced imperceptibly into a book by artful blandness – but, frankly, unless you're a good writer, this is a difficult trick to pull off. In most cases I've gone for a direct and fairly brash opening, which I also think appropriate to my material and general treatment. In contrast, if my inheritance had been, say, a faded noble family in a decaying ancestral home – *Brideshead* perhaps? – or if I had a less acute sense of my own foolishness, the tone of this memoir might have been lyrical. Certainly it would have been different.

(2) I've tried to use *loaded* images and descriptions. By that I mean they have a richer sense than appears on the surface: usually in the way of an implicit emotional or social reference. If you return to the first paragraph of the essay, you'll see that the images included in the thumbnail sketches of my gaggle of Uncles Joe go beyond simple description to give a clue to their characters, which are then elaborated in the longer sections. In the passage concerning my Auntie Dilys, I mention that she served tea in china cups: a custom that is suggestive of her genteel aspirations. I might equally have said that there was a red carpet on the floor; but, though true as a matter of simple description, its lack of strong social significance would have left it meaningless as a clue to her character. The use of loaded description (tea cups rather than carpets in this instance) allows the writing to be economical with words yet rich in meaning. It shouldn't be confused with a desire to be clever or especially subtle. In fact, in the matter

of the china teacups, I drive my point home by explicitly contrasting their use by Dilys with the custom at home where, at this date in the 1950s, Nellie was still drinking from a chipped enamel mug. I might have gambled on the reader interpreting the meaning without further help, but I confess I wasn't sure that after the lapse of so many years the significance of china cups would be evident.

In writing you'll often have to make this kind of decision – and sometimes you'll be wrong. Don't agonize over the problem, particularly in the first instance. When you come to editing your essay, you can review whether a more telling image is available. You can also cut out the parts that don't earn their keep by contributing something of substance – the red carpets for example.

(3) The essay is organized around individual character sketches, loosely grouped according to the two sides of my family. There's little attention to dates and the chronological structure is ill defined and subordinated to the theme. In each sketch I've combined general material as to history and character with an anecdote that illustrates the keynote of the sketch. Again I've used a story – in this case Uncle Joe Wright and Frankenstein – to frame the entire essay. Knowing in advance that I intended to close in this way helped prevent me from digressing too far from my theme.

(4) As with my grandfather, Shiny Jim, the portrait of Uncle Joe Burton is largely drawn from photographs. In fact, without them I'd have had almost nothing to say. It seems to be a quality of photographs that they provide a record of people on the edge of our awareness, who function like film-

extras in our lives, as no doubt we do in theirs. Yet such people do have importance in adding to the density of experience (imagine a film without the 'extras' – the strange emptiness), and, once we've recalled who they are, we can usually find a little to say about them which will add life to a scene that would otherwise be flat.

The use of photographs in this essay develops a point I made earlier: that they provide an alternative route into your autobiography, one that can be used with or instead of essays. I've called this a 'scrapbook' approach without meaning in the least to denigrate it, and it can be taken further by blending other kinds of ephemera into the text. By way of illustration, do you remember my mentioning Joe Burton's passport with its Nazi visa (which I still have)? I could have begun my narrative with that as a starting point and pasted it – the original or a photocopy – into my book.

The scrapbook approach has a lot to recommend if you want to construct a family rather than a personal history: in particular it allows children to participate and the effect will be to hear several voices instead of one. If you go down this road while your children are small, I guarantee you'll value the result. I've got more to say about this in relation to the essay *My Holidays*.

LITTLE JIMMY'S CHRISTMAS

Auntie Lottie suffers from deafness, senility and badly fitting false teeth. She's a relative of Auntie Winnie, my Uncle Fred's wife, and already a million years old when Little Jimmy is born. I only ever see her at Christmas. Except when liberally plied with gin and orange – at which time she can be induced to sing – all she ever says is, 'Nyaga nyaga nyaga.'

'Lottie, put your teeth in!' says Winnie in a loud, patient voice.

Until the fatal holiday in Paignton in my late teens, when Something Happened and Winnie and Nellie stopped talking to each other, our two families always passed Christmas together. On Christmas Day Uncle Fred's family would come to our house in Werneth, and on Boxing Day we'd go to theirs in Hathershaw. The children usually stayed overnight, and Harvey, Christine, my sister Anne and I bunked together, top to tail, in the double bed I once shared with my brother Denis. I loved those Christmases because I liked my cousins but couldn't play with them as often as I wanted.

Once – when I was five and Nellie had her operation '*down there*' among the unmentionables – I spent the whole holiday at my cousins' and it was bliss. I was given a present of some Roman soldiers made of polythene, an uncommon material in 1952. My other soldiers were made of lead alloy.

Presents comprised comic annuals such as *Beano*, *Dandy* and *Film Fun*, games like Ludo and Snakes and Ladders, cowboy outfits, footballs, boxing gloves, soldiers, toy cars and stupendous quantities of sweets and chocolate. They were cheap but plentiful and I never had a sense of being deprived of things I desired.

Electrical toys barely existed. Model cars were clockwork or friction-powered and so were trains until I was nine when Hughie bought me a *Hornby* electric train with a *Coronation* class locomotive and cream and maroon carriages. My brother Jack made me a station platform at his school woodwork class. I still remember the damp winter evening when Dad and I bought the train set in a shop near the town centre. The street was dark and rainy, but the shop window was brilliant with light and crammed with wonders.

Later I collected plastic aeroplane kits until Jimmy Hall, the Parrys and I shot them to pieces with an air gun in the back yard. That was typical of Jimmy Hall. He and I once passed a very enjoyable hour boiling centipedes and wood lice in a tin can full of pee on the waste ground behind his house among the old gas masks and discarded prams. He had the face of an angel and the aspirations of a gangster until he and David Parry were killed in a motorcycle smash at the age of seventeen.

I believed in Santa Clause. We have a photograph of Anne and me on his knee in a 'grotto' somewhere on Manchester Road. Then Anne, out of spite, blew the whistle on the old geezer when I was six.

But when exactly *was* Christmas? I had an idea that it was synonymous with snow and one morning, when it had snowed overnight, I roused Anne and persuaded her that it was now! – yes! – today!

'Go back to bed, you silly buggers,' said Nellie, who was doing her chores in the kitchen.

My parents' ideas of fine food were limited to their experience of children's parties. So our Christmas meals with Fred, Winnie and my cousins were in this vein, with cold meats, beetroot, lettuce, trifles and tinned oranges with *Carnation* evaporated milk, all accompanied by white bread fingers (which we called 'bunnies') and cups of sweet tea. Certain foods have become so associated with the event – piccalilli and dates in particular – that I find it difficult to imagine eating them in any other context.

After tea we retired to the front room. Hughie, Fred and Uncle Joe Wright went through a bottle of *Johnnie Walker Red Label* scotch, though they were all beer drinkers and wouldn't dream of touching the stuff at any other time of year. The women – Nellie, Winnie and Auntie Lottie – drank gin and orange. While they chatted the men played cards: three-card brag or pontoon for matches; and the children played with them as they grew older.

My most vivid memory is of a Boxing Day evening when I was eleven. My cousins, Anne and I watched the terrifying *Quatermass and the Pit* on TV and played a horseracing game, *Escalado*. It was one of those perfect moments that life occasionally offers.

One of Nellie's most endearing qualities is that she's willing – even eager – to laugh at herself. Show her a photograph in which she's in any way comic (even unintentionally) and she'll hoot with pleasure. 'Eee, look at me!' she says. 'Would you credit it? What a silly woman I am!'

My daughter Hannah has videoed and photographed her in old age. These pictures capture a beautiful sadness and Nellie is entranced by them. 'Oh, you must keep 'em!' she says and kisses Hannah on the head. 'People'll say what a silly old grandma you have!'

When I was fifteen, my parents bought me a tape recorder so I could record French lessons from the wireless. The gift was a measure of their interest in my education.

At Christmas out it came. It was a novelty for the adults to hear their own voices; so, once they'd put themselves into the mood, they'd sing and talk to the machine and giggle and squeal.

'Hey!' cries Nellie. 'Is that me? Ooo, listen to me!

Don't I sound *common*!'

'Pipe down, you silly woman!' says Hughie, but he's laughing with everyone else.

By now the childish days are passing. In my teens I get religion and go carol singing on Christmas night. I find myself in Glodwick, near the park, on a frosty evening when the sky is clear and the stars are glittering. In Oldham it's usually cloudy and the nights are drenched in yellow sodium light so that stars and the phases of the moon pass to no effect. But tonight, like the star that guided the Magi, Sirius appears in multi-coloured brilliance. I'm stunned. I had no idea of its existence and don't know its name.

But now I do. And it'll be forever mine – once this night is over. But for the moment I have to return to Uncle Fred's where the party has got slightly out of hand and everyone is more or less drunk, though very cheerful. Nellie has been singing *Edelweiss* from *The Sound of Music* – which is a Bad Sign as far as common-sense is concerned. Still she's very biddable, and so Hughie and I take her by the arms and walk her home. It's two in the morning as we pass along the respectable streets of the Coppice.

Nellie giggles and sings *Edelweiss* at the top of her voice.

Lottie is as old as the Ancient of Days, a small brown thing barely four feet tall.

LITTLE JIMMY (*loudly*): Merry Christmas, Auntie Lottie!
LOTTIE: Nyaga nyaga nyaga.
LITTLE JIMMY (*louder still*): How are you getting on?
LOTTIE: Nyaga nyaga nyaga.
WINNIE: How many times do I have to tell you? I say: how many times? PUT YOUR TEETH IN, LOTTIE!!
LOTTIE: Nyaga nyaga nyaga.

And so forth.

Lottie has a house somewhere near Pembroke Street, where Uncle Joe Wright lives with Frankenstein and Polly, his sinister cockatoo. She 'takes in lodgers', which seems an old-fashioned expression referring to something disreputable engaged in by Irish washerwomen in Queen Victoria's time. They're men in their sixties – sprightly by Lottie's standards – who have red faces and wear sports jackets, twill trousers, cardigans, suede shoes and small hats made of tweed with feathers in the band. I know because one of them turns up one Boxing Day evening. The occasion goes something like this.

SCENE The sitting room at Uncle Fred's. The men are drinking Scotch and playing cards with the children. The women are gossiping.
WINNIE: Will you have another gin and orange, Lottie?
LOTTIE: Nyaga nyaga nyaga.
WINNIE: Gin and orange? Will you have another?
LOTTIE: Nyaga nyaga nyaga.
WINNIE: I wish you'd put your teeth in. Are they sore? Your teeth – are they sore?
She pours the drink without waiting for an answer. At this point someone proposes a singsong, and the men break off their game of brag. In turn Nellie delivers a raucous rendition of 'Edelweiss', Hughie sings 'Danny Boy' in a fine baritone, and Little Jimmy is prevailed on to do his party piece, 'Jerusalem'. Winnie turns to Lottie.
WINNIE: Are you going to sing now, Lottie? Sing? You know "Little Wooden Hut". Go on, you know it.
And – astonishingly – Lottie sings.
LOTTIE: Nyaga nyaga nyag-I wouldn't change my little wo-oden hu-ut fo-or yoo-hoo!
WINNIE: That's it, Lottie!
LOTTIE: Nyaga nyaga nyaga.
WINNIE: Oh, I do wish you'd put your teeth in!

A knock comes at the front door. Winnie answers it and returns with a bleary-faced character, obviously the worse for wear.

WINNIE: It's your lodger, Lottie! Your lodger! [*to the Lodger*] Will you have something?

LODGER: I wouldn't say no to a pale ale. I've come to get her. [*He puts his mouth to Lottie's ear and yells at the top of his voice.*] I say I've come to get you, Lottie!

Even so, the Lodger is in no rush to go but settles down with his pale ale and joins in the general merriment. In fact he's so far gone that the others begin to feel sober and virtuous in contrast, as well as concerned that he goes home with Lottie before he passes out.

FRED [*casually*]: So how did you get here? It's cold out. Are the buses running?

LODGER: I drove.

FRED: Drove?

LODGER: T'car's out front.

FRED: And how are you getting home?

LODGER: I'll drive.

FRED [*concerned*]: Don't you think you'd best leave t'car and walk.

LODGER: Walk?

FRED: Aye – walk.

The Lodger is touched by this. He puts down his glass, leans toward Fred and pats him on the shoulder.

LODGER: Ee, Fred, you're a grand feller – but I think I'd best drive. Ha Ha! I'm too bloody drunk to walk!

77

NOTES ON "LITTLE JIMMY'S CHRISTMAS"

Uncle Joe Williams has died. The news broke a half hour ago in a call from my cousin Margaret. It happened between the writing of the essay and the writing of these notes. He was alive when I wrote about him in *Gents and Gypsies*, but now he isn't. I mention it not in the specific context of the present essay but the broader one of the process of writing an autobiography. It illustrates compellingly that it's a *dynamic* activity, always incomplete and liable to be influenced by events. In other words what you're reading is as live as its subject matter.

I liked Uncle Joe for his swash-buckling dash and I'm glad that I wrote about him, the last of Shiny Jim's children. I'll go to his funeral if I can, and afterwards I may write some more.

My Christmas is one of the essay titles beloved of teachers, and it was this thought that gave me the idea to write about my own Christmases. It seems a straight forward subject and fairly self-contained, and – unless your Christmases are particularly fraught – I'd recommend it as a beginner's topic. I have in mind several other titles for the same purpose and I'll mention them as I come to them.

By now you should be familiar with my general approach, particularly my use of a motif or anecdote to act as a frame for the whole essay: in this case my memories of Auntie Lottie and the time when her lodger turned up at a Boxing Day party. Now that the trick has been explained it may seem a little formulaic from a technical standpoint, but you'll recall why I devised it: namely against a background of each essay being, potentially, a stand-alone piece. In other places such as *Fabulous Freddie Teaches*

Poetry and *Parlez Vous Williams?* I ring the technical changes so you can consider if there's anything in them of use, and, in fact, there's an example in the present essay, which is explained below.

In this essay I've used a lot of 'direct' speech, i.e. I claim to set down the exact words spoken, emphasised by laying out the text in part like the dialogue of a play. All the passages in quotation marks are direct speech.

The alternative to direct speech is 'indirect' or 'reported' speech. Typically indirect speech is introduced by expressions such as: *Nellie said **that** we should go back to bed* (an example adapted from a direct speech in the actual text). The word 'that' is a common clue to indirect speech. What follows delivers the sense of what's said, but not necessarily the actual words used or the voice of the speaker. I've largely avoided it.

The general opinion of writers – which I share – is that direct speech is more vivid than indirect speech and more interesting for the reader, who can hear (and see!) the person speaking. Think over Nellie's speeches and how much they contribute to your image of what she's like.

Nevertheless, it should be obvious – and I freely admit – that I can't remember every single word that was said forty and more years ago. In fact, as you've probably guessed, many of the scenes in my essays (not merely dialogue) are reconstructions: a re-imagining of events of which I remember only essential elements with real clarity. The clothes worn by Auntie Lottie's lodger on the night of the party are typical of those worn by the sort of men who rented a room with her. But were they worn by *this* lodger – or indeed by any *actual* lodger? I can't truthfully say.

So, you may be thinking, this autobiography isn't an accurate account, and from a certain perspective you're right. However, you ought to consider the alternatives and what they do for whatever truth it is that you're trying to convey. Direct speech – reconstructed in the manner I've explained – is flagrantly untruthful if it claims strict accuracy. Indirect speech, by making a lesser claim, is in this respect more truthful – though in fact it still takes quite a feat of memory to recall the sense of each exchange in a long conversation, so that a report even in indirect speech may still be inaccurate.

The problem with indirect speech is that, by refusing to commit to the exact words used in a conversation, it loses the voice of the speaker – think of Nellie again and her verbal tics. Yet there *is* a speaker and he or she has a distinctive voice, which is necessary for a complete and truthful account.

In short there are pitfalls in both approaches. Direct speech departs from the truth by making a spurious claim to accuracy. Indirect speech departs from the truth by omitting material parts of the scene. And a similar point can be made in respect of matters of description. Auntie Lottie's lodger wore clothes, and one can either ignore them and omit that part of the scene, or hazard a description that won't be correct in detail but will convey a sense of what he was like.

Clearly I've got no problem with using direct speech. It's anchored in a very lively feeling for how Nellie and my other relatives speak, and I want the reader to hear it because it's such a powerful contributor to any understanding.

On the other hand, setting out dialogue in a play format – for example in describing the visit of the lodger – is quite another matter. It's simply a technical device that appeals to me and which I've used in writing novels precisely because it's unusual in a narrative and I like to liven up the text. Lots of very good writers wouldn't use the technique in the present context (or at all) and I offer it simply as something for you to study without making a recommendation one way or the other as to whether you should try it. I draw attention to it only to emphasize that I don't have a set formula for writing (not even my framing device): only a number of suggestions that you may be able to make work for you. The play format, like the photograph and scrapbook approaches mentioned elsewhere, is just another method of dealing with parts of your material.

MY HOLIDAYS

Waterside was a caravan park by a rocky cove. The railway line ran next to it, taking trains to Paignton and Torquay. At the age of eight I sat on the grassy embankment and watched the Great Western engines. They bore the splendid names of kings, castles, halls and granges, and pulled cream and brown carriages. Oldham was overcast and dreary, treeless and rainy, with black sooty soil. It couldn't compare with Devon, where the sun shone, the sky and sea were blue and the earth a rich red. The muted greys of the town were so dreary I hardly noticed them. But, at the caravan site, the saturated colours and sharp shadows gave objects solidity, a hyper-reality. The very signs by the railway, which warned off trespassers in high-flown language, remain in my mind as things of wonder because they seemed to exist more convincingly – they were somehow *harder* than the furniture of the ordinary world.

Rationing continued after the War. Hughie and Nellie didn't have a stick of furniture, or a roof of their own, when they took on the task of feeding and clothing four children. In those first years there were no holidays, only two day trips to Blackpool by charabanc, the second time with Alan Hutchinson. We spent our time on the beach making sandcastles, and Hughie took me on a magical ride through the realm of Snow White, which was close by the Tower. Later it converted to a freak show, "KAP DWA! THE TWO-HEADED PARAGUAYAN GIANT!"

By the time I was seven, prosperity was returning. We got a rented TV the year after the Coronation, and we stayed for a week at Mrs Povey's Guest House near the

South Pier. For the most part I still played on the sand, and there was a steady traffic of people across the promenade to the small cafés where, for a deposit, you could carry off a tray of tea in a pot, the shiny white crockery accompanied by slices of *Mother's Pride* bread spread with margarine.

When it rained, Hughie took me to a cinema that showed non-stop cartoons. As for Kap Dwa, he lay motionless in a glass case labelled: *Not to be opened without the authority of the curator of the National Museum of Paraguay!* Alas, the address of the curator wasn't given and so the lonely two-headed giant continued to look as he might have done if some dishonest fellow had made him out of *papier maché*.

Hughie bought me a present: a toy aircraft carrier, battleship, destroyer and submarine, each nestling inside the other. They were made out of grey polythene. That night I played with them in my bed (it had a luxurious red eiderdown), while Hughie and Nellie went out to the pub.

That same year – in fact the next week – we went to stay with my Uncle Joe Williams and lovely Auntie Doll at their house in the hills by Shrewsbury, the house with the stupendously smelly thunderbox at the bottom of the garden. Uncle Joe turned up for us riding his motorbike. It had a sidecar that looked like a crate covered in tarpaper and how we all got to Stiperstones I forget. What I remember is scrambling about the hills where the bilberries were in season – though we called them 'wimberries' – and we picked them on the principle of collect-one-eat-one.

Next year we began the custom of holidaying in Paignton with my Uncle Fred's family. We travelled overnight by *Yelloways* coach from the Mumps bus station in Oldham: Hughie toting two suitcases, which miraculously held enough clothes for four of us for a fortnight. He had fifty-three pounds in cash from which he paid for the caravan (nine pounds a week), fed and

83

entertained us.

And so we came to *Waterside*.

We rented a small, pink, caravan. I loved it and have enjoyed caravans ever since. Even the absence of a shower didn't worry me, since washing wasn't a habit I was addicted to and I was content to make the occasional trip to the brick washhouse. No, what I loved was the soft gas light with its *"pop!"* when lit, its hiss and slight sweet smell. I read by it or tried to make scenery for my soldiers by cutting up empty cigarette packets to make simple models: trying and failing to capture the sensuousness of this holiday world.

We hired a beach hut nearby at Goodrington and stuffed it with swimming costumes and boiled sweets that were soon covered in ants. Behind the beach was a stretch of grass where children and dads would play ball. Hughie was ungrudging of his time when engaged in a vaguely sporting activity like ball throwing.

We had our photographs taken. Hughie owned a *Brownie* which took tiny black and white pictures, but these were also the last days of the beach photographers, who snapped people on the fly, tipped their hats and handed out cards with details of prices. On the front at Goodrington was a stuffed horse, and we all had our pictures taken on it, and Nellie and Winnie were caught by one of the photographers, strolling by in their costumes, looking plump and pretty. What the photograph doesn't reveal is that they smelled of *Nivea*.

That and vinegar. Nellie covered us with vinegar on the principle that tanning people and tanning boots were much the same thing.

Having no car, we got about by bus. We went to Babbacombe with its pebble beach and funicular railway, and Cockington where Fred and Hughie sat in the village stocks and looked mournful for the camera. We even made it to Plymouth.

Above all we loved mackerel fishing. Once or twice

every holiday we went out on one of the small boats and fished with reel and spinner and always hooked several fish, though we weren't a fish eating family. The mackerel came inshore with the tide, following the shoals of sprats. One night we were on the front at Paignton and the sea was in. With it came the sprats, then the mackerel. They passed from right to left, and then the shoal turned and passed from left to right, until, when the mackerel caught their prey, the sea foamed white and was flecked with silver in the moonlight.

In the main street was an arcade of slot machines, all of them mechanically operated: nary an electronic one except a shooting game that ran a continuous reel of black and white film of German fighters, taken from wartime footage.

In the same street was the *Igloo* ice cream parlour that served the new soft ice cream, which I loved then and loathe now.

In the small village of Brixham an artist pointed out to me that the colour white looked bluish at a distance – that, in other words, colour wasn't a stable property: a key discovery in my aesthetic education.

On the front at Paignton we went to a 'Summer Variety Show' held in a grand marquee, where the tradition of music halls and end of pier shows was fading.

And then I grew up and no longer went on holiday with my parents. Something Happened, which put an end to the friendship of Nellie and Winnie. I don't know what it was, but feel sure it was trivial, which is why it's sad.

In due course I married Shirley and became a father, and the pattern of family holidays resumed, but this time I had the role once so admirably filled by Hughie.

In the early years we needed to be careful with money – though I have to say we were well off by most standards – and we had fairly modest holidays. When our eldest, Tom, was two, we took Shirley's nieces to Fishguard in Wales.

There, for the only time in my life, I went cockling. On a drizzly day, Tom and I scraped shellfish out of the sand with our fingers and gathered them in a child's bucket. The following morning I washed them and ate them for breakfast. It was one of the most wonderful meals I've ever eaten and when I close my eyes I can still catch that faint briny tang.

The holidays are too many to recount them all, but three are distinguished by the fact that we kept a scrapbook. Here's Shirley's account of a day spent in Laval in 1983. It doesn't show me in an especially good light.

> Saturday 28th August 1983
>
> Today we shopped in Laval. We had a bad start as Jim left me with no money etc. when he whipped off to find a parking place and I didn't know where he had gone. I have not felt so desolate for a long time – I burst into tears when he reappeared 15 minutes later.
>
> Laval is a pretty place and we walked through the market – full of the usual cheap crimplene frocks and bric-a-brac, but also with small local farmer run stalls with one fly-covered plucked duck or hare for sale and a few vegetables. Alex was upset because the fish stall was closed before he could buy any.
>
> I met a very elegant old French lady in a cake shop. She spoke beautiful BBC English, though she didn't know what the French word for "ice lolly" was! Bought some delicious pastry slices and more sugared almonds – fearfully expensive but good and very pretty!"

This scrapbook has a picture of Jon Pertwee and Una Stubbs as Wurzel Gummidge and Aunt Sally on its cover. Inside it is a treasure of ephemera: photos, sketches, tickets, bubble-gum wrappers, a coin of Napoleon III, a Painted Lady butterfly. There's even a small flyer for a fortune-teller: *Mr Khalifa – Grand Médium et Marabout Africain.*

It was on this holiday that we visited the nondescript village of Port Brillet, where by chance, in a working man's restaurant, we ate a *prix fixe* lunch of ham, melon and braised steak so tasty that Shirley and I recall it after more than twenty years. Here too, in the small lake – which I sketched – Shirley saw her first otter. At our cottage Hannah took her first hesitant steps.

The following year we passed a rainy week in May on the Isle of Wight. It generated comments like these. On the twenty-eighth: "Hannah throws up her breakfast. Day overcast. Dad and Tom play cricket briefly and the rain begins to fall." And the following day: "Hannah does *not* throw up her breakfast as she refuses to eat any. Alex wets the bed. Dad and Tom and Sandy play cricket, which is becoming very popular."

Apparently we played crazy golf: "Tom claims six holes-in-one but no one believes him".

I made a sketch of Shanklin pier and inserted it in the scrapbook and we saw a partial eclipse of the sun: "The diminution of light was not noticeable and a brief glance at the orb wasn't revealing since it was too bright. But, if one masked the sun just *so* with one's finger, for a second one could see a piece taken out."

Shirley's view of the cricket is expressed in this entry. "Tom has made a good friend and they are playing a board game. We played cricket with him and his dad this morning – it was nice to see they were as useless as we were!"

Having re-read the lively record of this holiday, I'm sorry Shirley and I didn't keep one when we went cycling in Burgundy in August that year. This event gave rise to an amusing incident when a work colleague, Dr Ruhemann asked me what my holiday plans were.

'Oh, I'm cycling in France,' I said loftily, thinking it held a touch of adventure. 'And you?'

'I'm going to Samarkhand, Bokhara and Tashkent,' he said. 'I always wondered what the Soviets had made of them and I wasn't able to go there in the thirties.'

At the time Martin Ruhemann was eighty-four years old. Next year he went walking in the Alps and when he was ninety he visited Cuba out of curiosity. I believe he took his girlfriend with him

Martin was both impressive and modest. A Jew and a Communist, after whom a building in East Berlin was named, he explained, "I went to the Soviet Union as a German and came out as an Englishman." Sadly he never explained how this trick was done. He died when he was ninety-two. They said his life was cut short by smoking.

We moved house in 1988 and the following year went to Crete where we kept another scrapbook. I seem to have spent time sketching passers-by and noted: "In the cafés the posers gather in shoals. They come past in pairs, driver and pillion passenger, on small motor scooters. The American sailors, in tattoos and dog tags, sit in a row of deckchairs and ogle the topless females."

On this holiday, Hannah, aged seven, swam for the first time in the hotel pool and on one of our walks found a skin sloughed by a snake, which we dutifully stuck in the book, where it still remains. My younger son, Alex, was twelve and one day we walked the twelve-kilometre length of the superb Samaria gorge to the sea where it ended at a windblown village crowded with Germans. The gorge was full of oleander, yellow butterflies and dragon arums, but what I remember most is a change in my relationship with Alex from spending the whole day in his company. I realised just how much I loved him.

From this holiday comes a scene, which has stayed with all of us. At Knossos a plump guide in a straw hat shaped like a pith helmet treats us to his archaeological knowledge.

'The ancient Minoans,' he informs us, 'burned olive oil in their lamps. Now why do you suppose that was?'

Search me, guvnor – you tell me.

'Because' – he says, and his voice rises with self-satisfaction – 'olive oil burns with *no smoke!*'

Cripes! You don't say! We are prostrate in admiration.

Hannah found the snakeskin near Gouvernetos monastery. There we encountered an odd character who reminded us of our friend Lionel Trippett, who took up writing pornography. I wrote: "A queer old Englishman of seventy or so ran the place and chatted in a lilting voice, taking an interest in the text of our guidebook. I was reminded of the fate of Sebastian Flite in *Brideshead Revisited*, as a charitable pensionary of a monastery in North Africa."

This same scrapbook also contains entries for a holiday we took in Kent that year. I've always regarded 1989 with affection because it left such vivid impressions, no doubt helped by the scrapbook. I still have it when the monstrous sandcastles I used to create have long surrendered themselves to the sea.

A few years later this phase of holidays ended when Tom took himself off to university.

As Shirley and I have grown older, our holidays have turned into two kinds. After a gap of seven years, Tom resumed accompanying us, mostly on trips to Dolgellau in Wales where we love to stroll in the mountains and along the estuary to Barmouth. Only occasionally have we managed to get all the children together – Hannah frequently doesn't come – but there's a feel of the old holidays when they were small and I enjoy them.

That aside, Shirley and I often go away on our own, whether for a weekend or a week. We spend our time quietly, mostly walking in the day and reading in the evenings, or, if we're in a city, we visit galleries and the theatre. We dance at every opportunity.

Our friends, the Sheltons have a cottage in the foothills of the Pyrenees, which we've visited several times. Here's part of an account of a holiday there in 2003. I included it in a Christmas letter.

It was Whitsuntide and the villages were *en fête* with people banqueting under the open market arcade. In our village there was a dance to the music of a keyboard, an accordion and a singer. We stumbled across it and sat in a group with the party of English lesbians and a jolly Dutchman in socks and sandals who had wandered over from the campsite. The villagers were out in force, all sorts, including Yvan the *magnetiseur*, who owned a windmill and was very taken by Shirley, and one of those young men who can only exist in France: rakishly thin with hair in black ringlets and smoking unfiltered *Caporals*. They were an unstuffy lot and bounced about the dance floor doing a very merry waltz, and Shirley and I (in best shorts and sandals in my case) did the tango.

The following day we were walking through the village when we came across Yvan the *magnetiseur*. Shirley made some remark about discomfort in her leg, and, taking no refusal, Yvan whisked her off the road into the home of his cousin, sat her down and proceeded to make "magnetic" passes over her leg until it felt better. And indeed it did get better!

The *No Trespassing* sign by the railway at Waterside Caravan Park truly existed and it ranks with my childhood dream of red tulips as a key image that seemed to lead me into a new mode of experience. In the case of the metal sign, its hyper-reality, gave me a consciousness of the beauty of ordinary things and their simple *otherness*, so that almost fifty years later I find myself pausing in the street to stare at something of no particular distinction because of an indefinable quality that makes me think: "Yes, it *is* there. It *does* exist."

My holidays are important partly because they refresh this receptivity. When Shirley and I are strolling, I take in shape and colour and fix pictures in my mind. Shirley says I have a habit of staring at people too, and this is the reason.

Along the estuary near Dolgellau we catch a faint whiff

of vanilla from the gorse. On a hillside across the river from Mirepoix we're made dizzy by the scent of broom. Sollér in Mallorca is remembered for the heady perfumes of orange blossom and the stink of gunpowder in the main square, where firecrackers are let off to celebrate an ancient victory over a Moorish raid. In an old-fashioned dance hall in Paris, in a cellar whose ceiling is supported by Egyptian columns, louche middle-aged men with moustaches and brilliantined hair cast their eye over Shirley because she looks so beautiful and dances so well.

Holidays are also important because they provide a reference point by which I structure Time, which allows me to see my life as a whole. Yet the content of a holiday isn't especially important and can be varied or simple and the weather fair or foul.

Shirley and I have a joke that, provided we're together, we could enjoy "a wet weekend in Wigan".

My Uncle Joe Williams scattered Auntie Doll's ashes by the caravan where they'd holidayed so happily together. He felt an urge to go there a day or so before his death, and it's in that caravan that he died peacefully.

NOTES ON "MY HOLIDAYS"

I recommend beginners to tackle *My Holidays* as an early subject. It has a number of features, which, taken together, make it very suitable. For simplicity, I'll number them:

(1) It breaks down into components of individual holidays and you can cover as few or as many as you wish. In this respect it follows my basic plan of abandoning large-scale narrative for self-contained segments. Why not begin with one holiday and see where you go? You can always return and build on your earlier efforts.

(2) The subject is vivid and, for most people, will call up relatively uncomplicated memories of happy times. If it doesn't, you should consider one of my other suggestions. In your first essays you should aim for something that's short, straightforward and descriptive.

(3) You probably have a lot of supplementary material in the way of photographs. They should aid your memory and fill in details of how things looked. If you take up my suggestion of a "scrapbook" approach, you could organise your essay around explaining some carefully selected snapshots

(4) Holidays provide a panoramic view. If you re-examine my essay you'll see it covers some fifty years from stumbling in the sands of Blackpool to dancing in a French market. It follows the changing patterns and rhythms of my life. I haven't tried to philosophise at length about what it all signifies, but this essay gives in a short space an overview which is full of implicit meaning. I'd be glad to have written it, even if I wrote nothing more. The

fact that Shirley enjoyed it when I read it to her (in the bath, if you must know) underlines the point.

If you look at the essay, this time with an eye to style, you should be struck by an attention to description, colour, light and smell. This is particularly emphatic in the final section where I put together a series of quite unrelated vignettes for no other reason than their intense sensuousness. So the scent of gorse in Wales, of orange blossom and gunpowder in Mallorca, and sight of the brilliantined dancers of Paris are all lumped together.

My reasons are two-fold.

The first – more obvious one – is to evoke the scene as powerfully as I can: particularly by the reference to scents, which research (and Proust as it happens) shows to be a key to memory. I've mentioned this point in *The Last Victorian*.

Less obviously, the essay has, as an underlying theme, the awakening of my sense of how beautiful even ordinary things can be. This sense – which in due course was to lead to my interest in the arts – was partly generated by trying to get to grips with the "reality" of the signpost by the railway at Paignton. I was always vaguely aware of the connection between this event and the broader theme, but writing the essay has helped to crystallise it; and also to establish a link with the similar incident of my childhood dream of red tulips. Your connections will be different from mine, but I suspect you'll make them as you develop your taste for essay writing. I hope this essay encourages you.

Scrapbooks – it was Shirley who first proposed them and, in my superior way, I went along with the idea (just to humour her, you understand – ho hum). They've proved to be among the happiest things we ever did. They're dirty and scruffy and filled with old rubbish and bad drawings, decomposing butterflies and yellowing *Cellotape*, but they give immediate access to the time when our children were young. A ticket or a bubble-gum wrapper is not so much a souvenir as a piece of the day itself, without any of the artificiality implicit in souvenirs.

If you have young children, I do recommend that you make up a scrapbook when you go on holiday. Let the kids participate. Include pages from their colouring books, shells, bits of seaweed – whatever. Throw in the contents of your pockets, and your snaps, and finish with a few words. There are no marks for artistic effort. This is just for you!

Shirley and I kept scrapbooks, and now, years later, I've used them to write this essay. I've also used diaries and letters as source materials. Among their advantages is that of directness: they stem from the time they speak of. They also help vary the uniform tone of voice that's a risk of writing. The author of the letters and diaries is different from the man who writes today. Even his voice is subtly different.

JESUS WANTS ME FOR A SUNBEAM

Hughie is sceptical about God and evasive as to his existence.

'I stick to my Principles,' he says. 'That's enough.'

He's too inarticulate to explain what his 'Principles' are, but it isn't difficult to guess. My Dad believes in honesty, hard work, kindness, and generosity. Conversely he has no high regard for ambition or accumulating material wealth and he isn't envious or status conscious.

Taken as a whole, he's true to his Principles. Granted he is, by today's standards, mildly racist, but his racism excludes all foreigners he ever actually meets. Essentially his good nature defeats every ideology and he's even-handed in his prejudice. Born in Wales, he doesn't even like the Welsh.

Nellie regards herself as a Christian but never darkens a church. Her theology is rudimentary. She thinks Jesus is 'the best person who ever lived', but any more elaborate description of the Christ is beyond her comprehension. Her theory of salvation is that 'a good woman will go to heaven', and she tries to be a good woman. Unfortunately she has occasional doubts.

Nellie's doubts about her state of grace originate in the old business of Hughie's split with his first wife, Edna, and the struggle to raise her inherited family. She confesses: 'It were duty that made me do it. It weren't love. They weren't my flesh and blood.' In her old age, when she's more self-obsessed, she blurts this out to Denis and Anne. She's looking for forgiveness but only causes distress. Fortunately my brother and sister take after Hughie in their fundamental decency and put up with this. But in fact Nellie does herself a wrong. She does love

95

them – if not as much as she loves Little Jimmy.

My parents may not practice religion, but they insist I go to Sunday school. There are two churches within a quarter of a mile of our house in Werneth. Christ Church is gothic and Anglican. Edward Street Chapel is neo-classical and Methodist. Little Jimmy is sent to the chapel because Hughie's residue of Welsh non-conformity and vague radicalism means he regards the Anglican church as a home for snobs – the people responsible for Tonypandy (whatever that is).

For ten years I traipse wearily to Sunday school of an afternoon. Afterwards, as evening wears on, I bathe in the kitchen in the zinc bath filled by kettles, and am warned by Nellie not to 'touch' myself. This makes me diffident about washing in intimate places and I probably stink for most of my childhood. Afterwards we watch TV, except that sometimes adult horror serials are shown such as *Dr Jekyll and Mr Hyde*, *Quatermass,* and *The Trollenberg Terror*, in which case Anne and I are banished to the kitchen to play cards or dominoes.

At Sunday school we sing.
> *Jesus wants me for a sunbeam*
> *To shine on him each day;*
> *In every way try to please him,*
> *At home, at school, at play.*
> *A sunbeam!*
> *A sunbeam!*
> *Jesus wants me for a sunbeam!*
> *A sunbeam!*
> *A sunbeam!*
> *I'll be a sunbeam for him!*

Or perhaps:
> *I am H-A-P-P-Y!*
> *I am H-A-P-P-Y!*
> *I know I am, I'm sure I am!*
> *I am H-A-P-P-Y!*

> *I am S-A-V-E-D*
> *In J-E-S-U-S!*
> *I know I am, I'm sure I am!*
> *I am S-A-V-E-D!*

And finally:

> *Now Zacheus was a very little man*
> *And a very little man was he.*
> *He climbed up in a sycamore tree*
> *For the Saviour he wanted to see.*
> *For the Saviour he wanted to see!*
>
> *Now, as the Saviour passed that way,*
> *He looked into the tree,*
> *And said, 'Now Zacheus, you come down,*
> *For I'm coming to your house for tea,*
> *For I'm coming to your house for tea!'*

When everything else has gone and I no longer recall my children's names and even Shirley is forgotten, whom I love so much, I shall probably remember these songs and sing them in a shaky voice. By then the man I've become will have gone, and the voice will be Little Jimmy's, and they will be his swansong.

We sing these children's songs and learn our first hymns. Many of them have precious little to do with religion, or, if they do, they suggest the British Empire was lending Jesus a helping hand in sorting out the benighted heathen. In the late fifties, the colonial empires are still unwinding: one of our teachers fought as a mercenary in the Congo before seeing the Light.

We also draw. We're given paper and wax crayons with which to sketch Bedouins, donkeys and camels we've never seen, in illustration of Biblical stories.

Scene: Sunday school. A bare wooden floor, bentwood chairs and a scent of dust and lavender polish. TEACHER is holding up a drawing of an aeroplane with a Roman centurion in the cockpit and various characters in Arab dress in the back.

TEACHER: And what's this a picture of, Jimmy?

JIMMY: It's the *Flight to Egypt*, Miss.

TEACHER: *(confused)* I see…and this? This man in the front?

JIMMY: That's Pontius the Pilot, Miss!

I'd like to claim the credit for this story, but I think it's something I heard. Yet it illustrates a truth. Along the road between Wythenshawe and Altrincham stand a number of houses built between the wars in a suburban *Bauhaus* style. Shirley and I call them 'Jews' Houses' because Jewish people live in them. And how do we know this? Easy – they have flat roofs! We've learned at Sunday school that Jews live in houses with flat roofs. They sleep on them. So do their camels.

The Jews of Wythenshawe and Altrincham, however, have no feeling for tradition and don't sleep on the roofs of their houses – with or without camels.

But we still keep looking in case they change their minds.

My Sunday school years end as organized religion itself goes into a steep decline. Churches and chapels close and the one at Edward Street is demolished and a block of sheltered housing for elderly people is built on the site. Before that, however, I become, briefly, a Sunday school teacher. I also collect a stack of book prizes for attendance. I think standards must be slipping. I choose *German Aircraft of World War Two* and it's given to me without any sign of misgivings.

As I move into my teens I go to the youth club, play table tennis while listening to records by The Beatles and

The Beach Boys, and moon over Ethel Ashton and her sister Margaret. My best friend, Mick Mills, lives in Glodwick and I move my allegiance to Trinity Methodist Chapel, near his home.

It's there one evening, during the height of the Cuban missile crisis, that a girl is overcome by the prospect of nuclear holocaust. In the chaos, I'm torn between naked terror, a desire to comfort her, and a longing to squeeze her tits – perhaps my only chance of carnal knowledge before universal incineration. I'm too shy to take my chance and would have died a virgin if Kennedy and Khruschev had been bigger fools than they proved to be.

The vicar of Trinity is called Eric Foster (known as Reveric), a man of charm and humility like most clergymen. It's during his tenure that a young, charismatic cleric preaches one evening and issues a call to be saved. I go down to the altar rail and am converted. I'm fourteen years old.

These days I'm no longer a Christian, but I don't treat this experience lightly and never mock it. I recall it vividly and felt it with entire sincerity. It lasted for about five years and during this period I studied the Bible avidly, prayed and attended church zealously. And I don't regret a moment of it.

Two lessons have remained with me. I'm by no means convinced they're true, but they've served me well enough and I'm prepared to run the risk that they're false. The first (which I think was a particular belief of John Wesley) is a faith in Man's capacity to be better. And, related to that, is a belief in redemption and forgiveness, even if it's the redemption we must earn for ourselves and the forgiveness we must extend to others. I think it's better to forgive and have faith in another and be punished for that error, than to be prudent and lose someone from a failure to take a generous step. I don't claim to live adequately by this ideal. But at least I know what it is.

In particular I believe in the redemptive power of love.

I have reason to because I've been well loved.

I lost my faith during my first term at university, though the timing is merely coincidental. The cause was a conflict between my religious instincts – which were and remain profound – and my rational mind, which found the entire theistic scheme (not just Christianity) unsustainable on grounds of logic and evidence. In short, religion ceased to make sense and I was faced with a number of unpalatable choices. I might compartmentalise matters and apply different criteria to religion and general thinking, ignoring the conflict. Then again I might recognise some of the difficulties and take refuge in the assertion that religion is a 'mystery' that at some level reconciles and explains everything in ways beyond the grasp of intellect. Or, finally, I might conclude that religion – in the dogmatic sense at least – is essentially false.

I decided that the last was the only honest course, and ever since I've considered myself an atheist.

The notion that belief in a particular creed is a condition of true religion is largely a feature of Christianity. Other religions suggest that ethical and ritual practice (supported only by general religious sentiment) is enough. Indeed I understand some rabbis hold that the key obligation of a Jew is to act in accordance with the Law, and his beliefs – including a belief in God – are a matter for his own conscience: God, being understanding and loving, has broad shoulders and can put up with pious atheism. While not going so far, Islam has also been generally tolerant of other faiths. Though quite prescriptive in its practices and its demands for honesty and social justice, it's undemanding in its beliefs beyond an acceptance of the one God.

I mention this because religious feelings and intellectual beliefs are quite different matters. Some clerics, I'm told, prefer to debate with atheists and find them more sympathetic. Their beliefs are held with more essential honesty and their religious inclinations are purer and more authentic. In comparison, believers are either indifferent to the foundations of faith or hold doubt at bay with barriers of rationalization and nonsense.

I applied to religion the same tests of reason and evidence I'd apply to any other matter, and found it wanting. Towards the end of my time as a Christian I read a book by C. S. Lewis: a justification of Christianity for the general reader. It seemed to me to have been written not as an open-minded enquiry leading wherever it might go, but a completely tendentious argument to support a position that had been reached on quite other grounds. I thought this approach thoroughly dishonest and that, if it was the best Christianity could come up with, I'd have nothing to do with it. I've never regretted my decision.

None of this means I'm right. I've no interest in persuading anyone to agree with me. I no longer find it important.

Some of the fancier proponents of religion pitch their case on ground that can neither be proved nor disproved. Their arguments are ultimately unanswerable one way or the other. I'm reminded of a conundrum in which one is faced with a choice between two doors, one of which leads to life and the other to death, with no information to select between the two. On its surface the dilemma seems critical, but in fact it's trivial once it's recognised that no amount of reasoning will resolve it and that tossing a coin is as likely to yield the truth as any other method and anything further is a waste of time.

Having satisfied myself that the existence or not of God is an unimportant question because it's unanswerable, I'm no longer troubled by issues of belief. On the other hand matters of practice – of how to behave – do concern me. The question of God can be put in terms other than those of belief in his reality or otherwise. Ignorant of the truth, one has to choose whether to act *as if* God exists – or not.

In my case I choose to act as if God does indeed exist.

But I'm clear that he exists, for me, only as a metaphor or point of orientation. The other God vanished years ago and I don't miss him. If he turns up after my death, so be it. I'll have to hope that the liberal rabbis are right and the Divinity isn't too fussy about imponderable matters of theology.

Shirley and I often go to churches. We slip into them all the time, especially when on holiday.

Our preference is for simple chapels with spare, rustic furnishings. Among our favourites is one on the links overlooking the sea near St. Davids; also a seventeenth century Unitarian meeting house near Wilmslow and a church with modest *art nouveau* decoration that stands in the village of Brithdir. These quiet places, where God hides in the dusty shadows and coughs politely to attract attention, exist in their hundreds and each offers something to remind us of the numinous quality of everyday life.

By the shopping precinct in Salford, among the high rise flats built on the site of industrial slums, a Victorian chapel has escaped the ruin and its interior has been painted in the most jolly and inspiring colours. Here, in two thousand and two, Shirley's niece Lynne re-affirms her vows twenty years after a shotgun wedding, when, as the saying goes, she and Malcolm didn't have a pot to piss in and everything was done in a rush.

Now he stands beside her, grinning sheepishly, all six foot four of him. He has a shaven head and wears gold earrings and black boots. But he's put on morning dress for the occasion because these days he's respectable in his own way and he's happy to make a fool of himself.

It seems I'll never be done with Jesus, though Little Jimmy and Edward Street Sunday school are long behind me.

In two thousand and two Shirley and I holiday in Verona and spend a day at Padua. Here we visit the Cathedral, the one St. Anthony made famous. It's gorgeous – in fact stuffed to the ceiling with gorgeousness – but this sort of religiosity is cloying and doesn't appeal to either of us, not after all our chapels. Here there are saints and virgins, nuns, incense and inscriptions in Latin. But in the church in the hamlet of Macclesfield Forest there's a hassock embroidered in wool with the dedication: "Leslie Lewis – priest, pianist, magician and lover of dogs". And we know which we prefer.

In Padua we emerge blinking into the sunlight and wander up a street full of shops and stalls selling gimcrack religious souvenirs to tourists. I don't mind this stuff. Its honest vulgarity tickles my sense of humour and half way tempts me if I can find something outrageous enough that it will count as 'post-modernist irony' – whatever that may be. And I come close. Indeed I do!

Here it is. A portrait of Jesus: the head only – very lifelike – the face torn in an authentic expression of agony. Quite enough to make its point, one might think, but its creator did not. So, instead of one Christ, we have two: almost identical and laid over and against each other so that first one and then the other appears according to how you look at it.

Stand here and the Christ's eyes are shut in pain. Stand there and they are open in recognition.

And stand here....

One eye opens and closes slowly. Jesus is...he is...

"Shirley! Shirley! Look!"

I grab Shirley's arm and drag her to the stall and pick up the picture and turn it through its different angles. Shirley peers – then sees – then squeals:

"Oh, my God. *He's winking!*"

Yes, he's winking.

Jesus is winking at me! There's no question of it! He's giving me a long, slow wink that's full of meaning. And I'm stunned – stuck somewhere between hilarity and revelation.

103

After all these years, does he *still* want me for a sunbeam?

NOTES ON "JESUS WANTS ME FOR A SUNBEAM"

In the natural course of things, everyone forms views about the world. Some are of a general character: conclusions as to the meaning of life, the existence of God and so forth. Others are more specific: for example opinions about the destruction of the rain forests, membership of the EU, or whatever. For convenience I'll call them our 'philosophy'. Though your beliefs may be abstract and on its face have nothing to do with you, they nevertheless reflect who you are. You came to them in the course of your history and they have an influence on your conduct. So they are a proper subject for your autobiography.

This topic poses a number of difficulties and it isn't one I'd recommend to a beginner – particularly if you intend to set your philosophy down in any detail.

In the first instance you should bear in mind that it's extremely unlikely you have anything original to say about anything. There seem to be only a handful of basic ideas about how the universe works or arguments for the existence of God – or for staying in or leaving the EU or supporting Manchester United for that matter – *and they've all been voiced by someone else and probably better than you can do.* Originality largely consists of detail and the way you set your opinions down. And, unless you're particularly talented, your contribution won't be especially enlightening. The same rules apply to me.

Another limitation is that you may discover – to your surprise – that you're uncertain exactly what it is you *do* think about a particular subject: certainly when it comes to the degree of clarity necessary to write it down. Human beings are confused thinkers and their opinions are often contradictory, illogical and unsupported by evidence, and in many areas amount to no more than a vague feeling.

Bear in mind your objective. In the first instance it's to explain yourself before your readers: simply to tell them *who you are and why you did what you did*. Only secondarily, if at all, are you concerned to make converts to your point of view.

If you go back now to the present essay, you'll see I haven't tried to explain in any detail my reasons for losing faith in the existence of God. I've simply indicated that I found logical and evidential objections, without elaborating what they are. The reasons for this reticence are that my objections are very unoriginal; I haven't the slightest desire to convince you that I'm right, and I don't want to bore you rigid with an argument that would be even more badly written than the rest of my essays. Also I strongly suspect that my opinions about most things are erroneous or deluded in important respects – I just don't know which ones.

The upshot is that I've set down my 'philosophy' only for its biographical interest. Feel free to consider it nonsense.

With the primary object in mind, let's turn to the structure of this essay. It comprises the following elements in order:

(1) My parents' beliefs.
(2) Stories relating to my religious education before my conversion.
(3) My loss of faith.
(4) Reasons for my loss of faith.
(5) My present beliefs.
(6) Stories with a religious theme from the period after my loss of belief.

You'll see immediately that the 'philosophical' material (points 4 and 5) is sandwiched between biographical material, of which the first section explains how I came by my beliefs and the second hints at their lingering consequences. Without that context, I'm sure they'd be of negligible interest to anyone except myself. It's the human, not the abstract content that provides the interest, and that's a point you should always keep in mind.

Although the essay is structured around explaining the history and general content of my 'philosophy', it also contains details unrelated to the main subject, which could be cut out without altering the structure and thrust. These include:

(1) My childhood bathing habits.
(2) The incident during the Cuban Missile Crisis
(3) Lynne and Malcolm's wedding.

I included these elements to increase the narrative interest – the 'colour', if you like – and because they link the subject in hand to other aspects of my life dealt with elsewhere. Use of detail in this fashion provides the large-scale weave of the essays, ultimately binding them together as a coherent whole, even though they should each be sufficient in themselves.

The essay ends in the *pericope* concerning the Winking Jesus, and its conclusion is left open: a reminder that my life isn't ended and that a Damascene re-conversion isn't excluded, even if it's unlikely.

It means that, because this book doesn't have a plot, it has no predictable ending. Even I don't know how it turns out.

MY SCHOOL

Shortly after his fifth birthday, Little Jimmy goes to school, trotting down the street hand in hand with his big sister Anne. He bursts into tears, but they quickly clear up, and on that first day he learns to use a knife and fork.

My primary school, Freehold School, Werneth, no longer stands. It was built in 1895 or thereabouts and comprised two buildings: a single storey infants' school, and a two storey juniors'. The classrooms on the upper floor opened onto a balcony over the central hall, which rose the full height of the building like an atrium, and the teachers played badminton there at lunchtimes.

Nellie never took me to school. In those days parents didn't. Traffic was light and child molesters were unheard of. A five year old wandering the streets, even in the evening, was thought perfectly safe. When Stephen, who lived two doors away, turned up with his mother, the other children called him a sissy.

My first friend was Dilys Langhorn. Together we stole empty pop bottles and returned them to the chip shop for the deposit until Hughie put a stop to it and Dilys moved. My future as a career criminal never recovered from this set-back.

For the rest I remember learning to write using chalk and a slate and much fooling around with Plasticine and climbing of ropes in the hall, which also served as the gym. At primary school I was hauled before the headmistress for peeing in the play yard. The truth is that to this day I've a penchant for an *al fresco* pee and suspect it's the remains of an ancient instinct for marking territory.

When my class moved to the junior school we were provided with pens. They were simple sticks with steel nibs that had to be dipped into white pottery inkwells filled by ink monitors. The inkwells were also stuffed with blotting paper, which dissolved and clogged the nibs, adding to the natural tendency to leave smears and blots everywhere.

In the hall stood an upright piano. Teacher gave us drums, tambourines and triangles, and we got up a storm of noise to accompany folk songs and sea shanties.

Boney was a warrior – weigh hey ah!
Boney was a warrior – John François!
and
Twanky-dillo! Twanky-dillo!
Twanky-dillo-dillo-dillo-dillo!

And so forth – I think I could sing the lot if necessary. They belong with the early Sunday School songs indelibly etched in my memory; so deep as to be different in kind from ordinary recollection; as much a habit as walking. But I do wish Teacher had let me bang that drum! All I ever seemed to get was the weedy, girly triangle, which I hated.

It was in primary school that one night I had the dream of red tulips that would years later set me on this task of compiling this book, much as Proust (with more skill, admittedly) was provoked to write by the taste of a *Madeleine* dipped in tea. At primary school, too, I was introduced to King Arthur and the Norse myths. My love of history began on that day and has never left me.

I was small and dark with a puckish face and a straight fringe of hair. I wore corduroy 'wind cheaters' and balaclava helmets and a navy gabardine mackintosh tied like a cloak so I could be a knight or cavalier. I was shod in plimsolls, Wellington boots or clogs until prosperity came and I got my first pair of shoes.

My looks meant I was typecast for villainous roles in any bits of drama that might be going. In turn I was Hitler, King Herod, Sweeney Todd the Demon Barber, and Judas Iscariot. These blood-curdling parts made up for the business of the triangles.

I was happy. Perhaps being among the eldest in my class gave me confidence. My position was fifth in the top stream and neither my parents nor I had any expectation or aspiration to doing better.

Twice a year for the whole four years of junior school I sat an exam comprising arithmetic and an English comprehension paper. They were always the same papers – presumably to measure progress over time. Accordingly I knew some of the answers as a matter of memory rather than scholarship. For example, I discovered that 'source' and 'origin' had the same meaning. But what that meaning actually was remained a complete mystery for several years.

Our schooling was formal and involved a lot of rote learning, but we made great progress. By the age of eleven I knew decimals and algebra and I could analyse a sentence according to the rules of formal grammar. I understand this skill has fallen out of the curriculum, but I've always found it useful in learning new languages and understanding why a word or sentence construction is ungrammatical – though it doesn't mean I avoid all errors.

The most curious aspect of education in those days was the necessity of learning how to calculate amounts in the old currency of pounds, shillings and pence. Because it required counting in base twelve and base twenty, it formed a separate branch of arithmetic and tiny children slaved for hours at it.

In the days before decimalisation and calculators, those who had to do with money had small books called 'Ready Reckoners', which contained pages of tables to allow haberdashers to buy a gross of nylons at three and sixpence a pair. Once they fell out of use, these substitutes for computers had an enchanted half-life, turning up on stalls and in second-hand bookshops.

They also put in an occasional appearance in the Magistrates Court if the Bible went missing. Many a witness has unwittingly hazarded his soul and sworn by God and a Ready Reckoner to tell the truth, the whole truth and nothing but the truth. By a quirk of English law, it seems such an oath is valid.

I went to school with Hazel Hunt (winsome and round face), Jaqueline Holt (blonde and beautiful), Dennis Price (curly-haired), Jimmy Hall (tiny and angelic with hair so fair as to be almost white). Dilys Langhorne was a fellow conspirator, but Hazel Hunt was my first girlfriend. I appeared with her on Nellie's doorstep scrounging biscuits within a few days of going to school.

I can remember the names and faces of children I went to school with fifty years ago. People I met last week – or even more recently – are as often as not forgotten. Sidney Jolly was a sparky character who looked as though he'd come to a Bad End. He came from a home even poorer than mine and wore pullovers with large holes in them. He was cock of the school, but, strange to say, I won both the fights I had with him. I clocked him in the face as he was squaring up, and cleared off pronto before retribution came.

We were a class of bright children and beneficiaries of the 1944 Education Act. I was spared the fate that befell Nellie. Two boys in my class passed the entrance exam for Manchester Grammar School while in the third year of junior school. That left me top of the class, and, when five of us sat the exam the following year, I confidently expected to pass: indeed I had no difficulty with the papers.

I failed.

The four slightly duller boys all passed, but I failed. I've no idea why, and it never occurred to Nellie or Hughie to challenge the assessment as any thrusting middle-class parent would have done. Why should it? They had no expectation that I'd pass and no sense of a proprietary right to a place at a good school. Their world wasn't in the least disturbed by an event whose meaning they couldn't interpret. In any case they'd no idea the result of an exam could be appealed or how to go about it.

Nellie's grasp on the entire business of Manchester Grammar was unsure. All she could think to ask my prospective teachers was, 'Will Jimmy 'ave to talk posh?'

If so, then I was lost because she hadn't a clue where I'd learn such refinement.

With relief she told me, 'They said, "No. 'E'll just 'ave to learn not to drop 'is *h*aitches."'

But I didn't have to learn not to drop them.

It was a bitter disappointment for me and a mystery, and the feeling remains. Yet to wish things had been otherwise is to wish not to be me: to wish for another life in which I wouldn't have met Shirley and wouldn't have had my children.

I don't wish these things in the least.

Greenhill Grammar School was a small mixed-sex local authority school dumped among poor terraced houses, a railway and a flourmill. Opposite the boys' entrance was a reputed brothel run by a lady called Poison Ivy.

It wasn't prestigious.

On the other hand it had a dedicated staff of traditional teachers, most of them men who'd returned to teaching after the War and still wore double-breasted 'demob suits' a decade and more later.

I have a great admiration and affection for them, even for Fred Sedgley, who gave me a belt several times over the years. He was the deputy headmaster, a beefy, red-faced man who had us reciting French irregular verbs in a singsong voice like a Gregorian chant. He was a holy terror, ruling by violence and awe. But the kids liked him for all that, because he was generally good-tempered and scrupulously fair so you knew exactly where you stood. He had a genuine affection for us all and a stupendous memory for our hundreds of names. We were never anonymous.

Fanny Kuler also taught French. She first appeared, screeching and arm-waving, like a manic Cruella de Ville, and reduced us to silence by her hysterical presence and withering scorn. Five years later, the survivors loved her. She was a witty, cultivated woman and did much to develop my interest in literature and language.

One observation made by Ku has remained with me. She said I was "intellectually honest". The remark stuck because I'd no idea what she meant. I didn't know the difference between "intellectual" honesty and the run-of-the-mill kind and supposed it was just a fancy way of saying I wouldn't steal the spoons. In retrospect I can't imagine what opportunities a seventeen-year-old boy would have to display this particular trait, but something evidently led her to this conclusion. As to whether it's true – that I am in fact intellectually honest to a notable degree – I can't say. I'd like to think so, but it seems unlikely.

Harry Martin was a figure of horror. His face was lean with dark jowls in need of a shave and he had a reptilian smile with a glint of gold somewhere among the teeth. He looked like one of the Undead, given up by the grave to teach us German. Four decades later, when he was old but keeping his mind in trim by learning Japanese, my friend Isabel and I used to visit him once or twice a year and take tea and go over ancient school photographs. He still remembered the names of the pupils he had taught. Isabel and I attended his funeral, and this paragraph is a small memorial to a fine man.

Anthony Buckeridge died this year [2004]. He was the author of the *Jennings* books, which I devoured when I was twelve or thirteen. His schoolboy hero was a precursor of Harry Potter and those of us who could only imagine what a boarding school was like were beguiled by his account.

Greenhill and other places like it were modelled on the public school and we were organized into 'houses', largely

113

for the purpose of games. My house was Lees and our colour was blue. The housemaster was a hairy, simian character with a missing finger: a history teacher named George Wright, but known as 'Judd'. He was another returnee from the War.

The resemblance to public schools was only pretence of course. Our playing fields were a mile away: a patch of grass and cinder by a polluted stream and a rubbish tip. Our swimming pool was the decrepit Central Baths in the middle of town, where we had to change immodestly in view of each other on the stone benches that rose in tiers by the poolside. For those of us going through puberty, whose penis size was for the moment greater than our chest size, this was a particular embarrassment. Nellie bought me a jock strap so I could control the damn thing until the rest of me caught up.

Until the sixth form we were required to wear a uniform. The ferocious Fred Sedgley policed the rules. There was a black blazer with a badge, but the compulsory elements (bearing in mind the small means of most parents) were limited to a cap and tie. The cap was a particular humiliation because it was in a style that had been around since Victorian times and was going out of fashion. In protest the boys allowed them to fall apart: the stiffening was taken out of the visor, the button was removed from the crown, and the cloth was peeled back, like segments of a banana skin, to reveal the lining. To his credit, Fred stuck by the rules and never punished a boy whose cap had been reduced to this shambles, as long as he was prepared to wear it.

In the sixth form, at the age of seventeen, I affected a waistcoat.

It turned out I was bright. I was as surprised as anyone else. Intelligent, middle-class parents have an expectation that their children will be high achievers. Nellie and Hughie didn't. They were pleased, but wary in case I got 'above myself'. They supported me but had little idea of what to do, and neither did I. On a couple of occasions they bought me encyclopaedias from plausible salesmen who hawked them from door to door – a breed long vanished. They also came by a second-hand tape recorder so I could record French lessons broadcast on the radio, but for the most part it was used only to listen to Nellie singing *Edelweiss* at Christmas. When I went to university, Nellie never got out of the habit of calling it 'school'.

I scooped most of the prizes in my class and, finally, all of them. Prize giving was held in the autumn in the dance hall at Hill Stores. For this event Nellie and Hughie waived their usual aversion to any contact with teachers and turned up to beam at me.

Hill Stores was also the venue for a dance organized by the sixth formers, featuring such acts as Johnny Dean and the Graduates, and Shedd Vandelle and the Ravens. Shedd Vandelle held no glamour for me. I'd gone to primary school with him and knew him as 'Tatty' Shaw.

At last I became Head Prefect and did absolutely nothing of any note.

Through all of this my best friend was Mick Mills. At lunchtimes we avoided the watchful eye of Fred and, in an alleyway next to the chippy, scoffed penny loaves washed down on at least one occasion with whisky nicked from Mick's dad.

We had an ambition to write an opera – Mick had taken a few piano lessons.

We tried to embark on our own space programme. I drew plans for a craft that would carry a payload of frogs and Mick had a small rocket that was powered by a tablet of chemical fuel. We took it to the top of the quarry in Glodwick but could never get the fuel to ignite.

My childhood school friends had been the Parry brothers and Jimmy Hall, but John Parry and Jimmy were among those who went to Manchester Grammar and so our contact gradually diminished and stopped once my family moved from Werneth to Hathershaw.

Despite his appearance of a faeries' child, Jimmy could have been an enthusiastic gangster. He specialized in making simple but workable guns out of rusty piping, operated on the principle of lighting the powder and praying. When he and David Parry died in a motorcycle crash at the age of seventeen, the armed robber community lost a potential star.

I was spending a month on a farm in France when this happened and Nellie announced the event on my return. Her notions of psychology were simple. She wanted me to visit Jimmy's mother.

'She needs a good cry,' said Nellie.

Well, perhaps. But not from me.

I didn't visit Mrs Hall and I didn't contact John Parry who'd lost his brother. Then, two years later, I spotted him in the public library. Or perhaps it wasn't him. We were changing so fast that even such a short span of time made his identification uncertain. He also saw me but, whoever he was, we never spoke.

As far as I know, none of my schoolmates have won the world's glittering prizes. Many became teachers, librarians and clerks in council offices. I doubt they expected more. They weren't so different from me, nor their parents far removed from Nellie and Hughie.

However one can never tell how other people interpret their experiences or what value they put on their achievements.

A couple of years ago a dozen of us gathered for a reunion at a restaurant called The Smoke Pole. Councillor Jeremy Sutcliffe was ahead of me at school, but I knew him despite the lapse of forty years. He'd become a deputy head teacher at a primary school and taken early retirement. At school he had a prissy manner and a 'refined' accent, but now he found it more politic to speak in a man-of-the-people voice. He was wistful that his best years were behind him. Yet he had something to look back on.

'I had my moment of glory,' he said. 'For a while I was Chairman of the Planning Committee.'

NOTES ON "MY SCHOOL"

Unless your schooldays were particularly hard, this subject is one to tackle early on. It lends itself to a straightforward narrative of events in the order they happened, and I've adopted that approach as the basis of my own effort and hung various other bits and pieces on that frame.

One method of analysing essays is to break them into three elements. The first and most fundamental is the storyline: the main topics around which everything else will be constructed – and, in this case, I suggest you could take my outline and use it with few changes. The second comprises key details, which fill out the story with life and colour. The third is the commentary or theme. The last element may amount to no more than the way language is used, the tone of the essay and the selection of material, but it may also include explicit comments or interpretations.

Schematically it can be shown like this:

Storyline	Detail	Theme
Infants' school	I go to school with Anne Dilys Langhorn Peeing in the yard	A world where children were thought safe.
Junior school	Writing with a pen Singing shanties My clothes Hitler and other villains Teaching methods Counting old money Some friends	The historical remoteness of my childhood: its quaintness from today's perspective.

Storyline	Detail	Theme
Failure to go to Manchester Grammar	Nellie and Hughie's reactions. "Talking posh".	First encounter with disappointment. Poverty of expectation and my parents' innocence.
Secondary school	The brothel; the playing fields; the swimming baths. School uniforms. The "house" system. Help from my parents. My academic success.	My advantages relative to my parents. State schools very different from public schools. My parents' ignorance hinders their ability to help.
My teachers	Fred: violence and awe. Ku: a manic Cruella; intellectual honesty. Harry: the Undead; his funeral.	The kindness and decency of my teachers. Their old-fashioned virtues. Am I intellectually honest, and how can I know?
My school friends	Mick Mills: whisky, opera and space travel. Jimmy Hall: his "guns"; his death. The Parry brothers: death of David; last sighting of John.	Teenage interests. The loss of childhood friends and childhood itself.
What has become of us?	Reunion at the Smoke Pole.	Limited expectations and life-chances. The difficulty in understanding how someone else interprets the world.

You can also use this analysis in advance to organise and plan an essay. However you should understand that the elements are interactive. A broad topic, such as 'junior school', may remind you of some forgotten details. But it's

119

just as likely that a remembered detail will lead you into a broader theme; and also possible that a general insight into how the world works will make you search for stories or details to illustrate it. You could proceed from left to right, setting down the major topics, then listing the supporting detail before finally arriving at some conclusions as to what it all means, which is the approach I'd adopt if I intended to sit down to a formal planning session. However, if you find the idea of a formal planning session rather chilling, you'll probably find it easier to proceed on all fronts simultaneously by jotting down notes in whichever list seems appropriate according to how the ideas come to you.

In the beginning you shouldn't be too rigid in your choice of subject. You may dry up quickly on an idea that at first seems a good one. Start with a number of suitable topics: *My School* and *My Holidays* are candidates. Next draw up sheets in blank except for the three headings and the essay title. Then make notes on all or any of your potential subjects until one of them comes to be front-runner. Finally see what you can make of it. If you get stuck, turn to one of the others. There's nothing to stop you from keeping two or three essays in play, working on each one as the mood takes you.

Remember that writing is an iterative process. Your first pass should be concerned with simply getting through the essay and not with whether it's good, bad or indifferent. In later revisions you can reorder the material, add and omit stuff and tidy up the style. For that reason you should treat your initial plan as a 'live' document: pin it to the essay and continue to note it up with ideas to use in the next version. If you're not happy with the text, don't worry. Go on to another subject as I've just suggested and come back to it later. As you get more practised in writing, and especially if you have some form of plan and notes, you'll find your thoughts clarify and your next effort will be an improvement. If the final result doesn't live up to your aspirations, the only lesson is "don't give up the day job". You'll still have achieved something worthwhile. Your voice will still have been heard, however imperfectly.

I could have added a fourth column to the above scheme (though it would have been empty in the present instance). It would be headed 'Sources' and list any photographs letters or other documents I intended to refer to or quote, especially if I proposed to use the 'scrapbook' technique.

Our schooldays offer source materials that are likely to have survived since childhood no matter how long ago it was. I'm thinking of school photographs and reports: the stuff kept by proud parents. Photographs can form a starting point for a discussion of teachers and friends, and report cards provide amusing quotations. Both can act as a spur to recollection of other things that don't appear on the face of the material.

I guess this is a call to go rummaging in old drawers and tins.

That said, in my case I haven't used any material beyond my own memory. Very little exists other than one or two photographs. My school reports seem to have vanished. With her lack of sentimentality, disdain for material things and desire for a simple, stripped-down life, Nellie has got rid of the lot.

I don't mind.

This essay recounts an important incident: my failure to win an expected place at Manchester Grammar School. It was a bitter disappointment, and very confusing for an eleven year-old. It was the first major turning point in my life. If you proceed far with the exercise of writing your autobiography, you'll find yourself facing similar painful issues and you'll have to make of them what you can.

There's a theory of popular psychology, which holds that confronting issues leads to some sort of catharsis and

121

'closure'. I treat it with caution because I don't think it's true for all people and all issues. What makes me cautious is that it's only possible to engage constructively with problems if you have the means of understanding and overcoming them. A defiant assertion of your own righteousness is a form of confrontation, but it won't do if a solution requires humility – as it so often does.

Speaking generally, I'd encourage you to write about all areas of your life, even the difficult ones. Honesty requires it. However I do recommend exercising common sense before dealing with topics where you can expect trouble. Not only may you cause distress for yourself, but you may affect your relations with other people and cause them pain, too. You should always be conscious of what you're doing and consider the risks and the benefits.

That said, for good or ill, having to think consciously about your life and formulate your thoughts in a deliberate way is likely provide some surprising insights. On a whole I think they'll be for the best.

However, to repeat a point made elsewhere: in this area I'm an amateur and don't know what I'm talking about.

University

I was going to become a teacher. It was the only job I could imagine: the only one whose entry route was reasonably clear because I saw teachers every day and could imagine their life. I'd no idea how to become a lawyer, a doctor or a businessman. It was difficult for me even to conceive what it was they actually did. As for Nellie and Hughie, it no more crossed their minds that I'd become a professional man than that I'd become a Martian.

My classmates went to teacher training college. So did my girlfriend, Kathy Redfern. I didn't realize I was bright enough to go to university until my teachers said I should try. Indeed they even suggested I should apply to Oxford.

The decision to go to university freed my imagination and I began to consider other things. The idea of studying law grew on me though it's hard to understand why, except that I think I was vain enough to fancy myself as an advocate. At all events, when I turned up at Oxford for an interview, it was as a law student.

I was quite unprepared. I knew nothing of law or of interview technique. I wasn't aware that people *did* prepare for interviews or what happened at them, and, unsurprisingly, I made a poor fist of the affair, though I think I would have been offered a place to study languages if I hadn't by now set my mind on being a barrister.

It seems bizarre now, but at the same time as I was trying for law at Oxford, I was also applying for an Army-sponsored scholarship which would have committed me to the forces after graduation. I was invited to a camp in Wiltshire and put through my paces for several days with the other hopefuls. And at the end I was offered a place at

Staff College to train as an officer, but not the scholarship. The Army suspected that, if I once went to university, I'd lose interest in a military career. And they were right.

These two incidents – the interviews for Oxford and the Army – represent other points at which my life might have taken a radically different turn had I succeeded at either. However, when I failed at both, I wasn't particularly disappointed. I hadn't any expectations of Oxford, and the Army was just a brief enthusiasm

I went to Durham by coach. It was winter. When I came out of the bus station, the city was covered in snow. It was still falling, and through the veil I could see the Castle and the Cathedral lowering on the Peninsula. I had nothing to compare them with except Christmas cards and Dickens. Carrying a change of clothes in a cheap suitcase, I trudged up a footpath that led by the river and through an alleyway onto Palace Green. It was night-time and quiet, and the snow, extending across the Green between the two ancient buildings, was patchily lit by lamps.

I fell in love with the city instantly, and that love has never left me.

Fortunately I was offered a place at Durham (and also at Leeds and Liverpool) and in my exams that year (1966) I received the highest marks of any student in Oldham. So it was official. I actually *was* smart.

The academic year began in September and I duly appeared. It was a revelation. Durham was an old-fashioned university, founded by the Prince-Bishops in the 1830's to educate clergymen. It sat uneasily in a class of its own. It wasn't old or prestigious enough to rank with Oxbridge but neither did it fit with the more science-based universities of the late Victorians or the brand new fashionable places such as Essex.

I was a member of University College (always known as 'Castle'). We occupied the Castle itself and several half-ruined and verminous Queen Anne buildings around the Green and the Bailey. Also, for unfathomable reasons, there was an annex several miles away at Chester-le-Street: a second castle, Lumley, which belonged to the Earls of Scarborough and was reputedly ghost-infested. First year students were posted to Lumley and given a bus pass to get into the city.

It was a way of doing things that was dying and I don't think it long survived my generation of students. The colleges were single-sex. Each evening dinner was a formal event with the students in gowns and a Latin grace. We ate in the Great Hall. It was lined either side by the retired battle flags of various county regiments. They hung in tatters, held together by a sort of netting, which was decorated with stray pieces of cutlery thrown by the students on the livelier occasions. The dress code demanded an academic gown and a tie, but was unspecific on other matters. So students wore polo neck sweaters, R.A.F. greatcoats and whatever else took their fancy, and on one occasion a wit turned up in nothing more than his underpants – with tie and gown, naturally.

We were waited on at all meals, even breakfast, by a shoal of college servants in crimson cotton jackets. Of these the most famous was John the Maid, who had a dangerous sense of humour, a prodigious memory for names, and was enormously popular – which was as well, because his habit was to pour soup over students he didn't like. In the same vein of impoverished gentility, our rooms were cleaned and beds made by a team of bedders. I had two run-ins with my bedder: once when someone peed in my waste bin and I didn't notice because I'd lost my sense of smell; and once when Chris Hulbert and I shot up our room with an air gun.

In later years I'd now and again run into John the Maid doing his shopping in the city. By then he'd served hundreds of students since I was at Castle; yet he still knew who I was though I'd never been a big name. Seeing me, he'd stop, put his fingers to his lips, and say excitedly,

'Ee, it's Jimmy Williams, isn't it?'

John's ambition was to own a little shop selling china and knick-knacks.

I moved in an unassuming circle of people who, like me, had been educated in state schools, studied seriously and looked forward to modest professional careers. There was another circle of public schoolboys and svelte young women. The two were on good terms but didn't really mix.

I found university glamorous. The setting and the girls were beautiful and the horizons were unimaginable. Black-tie dances and parties were still customary and I bought a dinner suit in my first term. I could have hugged myself with delight.

In contrast, vacations were a let-down. I didn't in the least look forward to them after the excitement of Durham. For one thing I was obliged to take a job, and at various times was a postman, a dustman and a hospital porter. I enjoyed being a dustman. It came with a strange freedom, like being a cowboy on the open range, with nothing but my trusty dustcart and a bacon sandwich.

Nellie has an interesting take on my vacation jobs.

She says proudly, 'When you worked during your holidays, Daddy and me let you keep your money. We didn't take owt off you for your keep.'

She's making a serious point. For her generation and class, teenage children were an economic asset, who contributed to the housekeeping. My sister Anne did so from the age of fifteen when she started work at a handbag factory; and so did Denis from his wages at the colliery.

I paid nothing. Nellie sees her gesture as a sacrifice on her part.

One vacation, my father used his contacts to get me a job labouring for two brothers who dealt in scrap metal and waste paper. Their father was semi-retired, a veteran of the First World War, who used to sit in the yard peeling armatures with a knife to recover the copper. He was known as Owd 'Egginbottom to distinguish him from his sons, the younger Hegginbottoms.

One day Owd 'Egginbottom said, 'They taught us French in the Army, doesn't tha know?' He cleared his throat and exclaimed, '*Haltylakwivee*! That's French, sithee.'

'Oh.'

'Ay. *Haltylakwivee*. Tha'd say that, and, if they didn't give the reet answer, tha could *shoot* 'em. Ay!' He shook his head. '*Haltylakwivee*. I still remember after all these years, sithee.'

Haltylakwivee? I'd studied French but struggled to make any sense of it until the context gave me a clue.

Haltylakwivee!

Halt! Who goes there? Halt, who goes there!!!

Haltez là! Qui vive!

If I'm right, it seems events go like this:

SCENE: *World War I. A guard post somewhere in France. Night-time. A rustling noise is heard.*
PRIVATE 'EGGINBOTTOM: Haltylakwivee!
STRANGER: Quoi?
PRIVATE 'EGGINBOTTOM: [*threateningly*] Ey up, I'm talking to thee, lad. Haltylakwivee!
STRANGER: Comment? Qu'est-ce-que-vous dîtes, espèce de cochon? Vous parlez comme une vache espagnole.
PRIVATE 'EGGINBOTTOM: Reet! Tha can't say tha's not been towd!
[*He fires. BANG!*]
STRANGER: [*faintly*] Merde!

It's no wonder that French casualties were so high.

I did a joint honours degree, studying sociology as well as law. I found law to be neither an inspiration nor a burden. I enjoyed sociology.

During my first year I decided to become a barrister and I joined the Inner Temple, one of the Inns of Court located in London between the Strand and the Embankment.

The Inns had started life in mediaeval times as quasi-monastic foundations but had largely lost their religious and teaching functions. In fact it was quite difficult to see what function they did serve except as an occasional dining room for barristers practising in the main Law Courts and as a thorough inconvenience for students.

The English bar in the late sixties was a curiosity. Its academic demands were quite low and there was almost no formal provision for teaching: in fact most students took a correspondence course. The only thing it did insist on was that one 'keep' twelve terms at one's Inn. To 'keep' a term meant turning up on three evenings for a bad dinner of soup, roast beef and junket, with sherry, wine, port and snuff. Accordingly the process was known as 'eating dinners' and it took some three years to complete.

Traditional barristers held that 'eating dinners' conferred a mystical benefit from associating with one's peers and with experienced men who would bestow wisdom. In reality the students stuck together and drank as much as they could get away with. Conversation was limited by the fact that one's fellow diners were strangers and, as like as not, came from India or Nigeria and had only a moderate grasp of English. On my first visit I fell in with a young Sri Lankan, Feisal Musafer, and we are still friends nearly forty years later.

I spent a deal of money on this nonsense and gained nothing from it. Because it took three years to complete, it was advisable to start early. So, from the end of my first year at Durham, I began taking the coach to London several times a year for the sole purpose of a bad and boring meal. The cost was kept down because the parents of a friend, Ian Lucraft, generously gave me a bed for the night.

In my time I've pursued a number of fields of study, the main ones being history, languages, sociology, law and writing. In each case, what has particularly stayed with me is not information, the bare facts of the matter (though, of course, much of it has). Rather it seems to me that each subject has a characteristic mind-set, a paradigm for looking at the world, a set of analytical techniques. It's this aspect that I've valued most because I've retained it when the raw information has become out of date or forgotten.

Studying law armed me with the tools to deconstruct and reconstruct arguments and evidence with a degree of logical rigour. Sociology led me to see issues in the context of systems of social and personal relations and in terms of observed behaviour rather than theory. The other subjects have similarly contributed to my intellectual foundation and all of them have influenced the way I've come at these autobiographical essays.

To give an instance, my portrait of Nellie is heavily influenced by an effort to see her behaviour as a response to her time and social class. I don't think it would be as it is without the insights provided by history and sociology. Similarly I've made a point of emphasizing my lack of experience in dealing with the world: my limited imagination in understanding its opportunities: my tendency to accept and live with circumstances as they are. The causes of this mind-set are no doubt complex and it may be that stupidity and laziness play a part. However, I hope I've also made sense of it as an outcome of my background and upbringing. If I have, it's again due to the insights provided by my education.

If my writing is sometimes leaden, it's because I'm a lawyer. I don't claim education is all to the good.

University gave me some friends who have so far lasted a

lifetime. They haven't made any great splash in the world and their names are unlikely to mean anything outside a limited circle. But in that respect I'm like most people.

It was also at University that I met my wife. She was studying Social Theory and Administration and we had some lectures in common. I noticed her because she was (and still is) strikingly beautiful.

There was a moment in our first year when we might have gone out together after meeting and being attracted at some event or other on Palace Green. Had it happened then, two years before we actually fell in love, it's quite likely matters would have turned out completely differently.

In the event, in the last term of my last year, I was at a loose end for a date to attend Castle Day, an annual fete and garden party for the college. As I was coming down the steps of the sociology department, I saw Shirley and asked her on the off-chance that she might accept.

She did – and provided the subject for another essay.

Notes on "University"

Nellie is eighty-seven. As I write these notes on 22 October 2004 she's in hospital for tests after coughing up a lot of blood. The suspicion is she has lung cancer. But whatever the case, she's on the final stretch of her race. My Dad went fifteen years ago and Nellie has soldiered on, loving and missing him. Still she's happy enough because she has a talent for happiness despite her guilt about the business of Hughie's first family.

Now her possessions are reduced to little more than two dresses, a couple of nighties, a packet of catheters, a hearing aid and some paper hankies. She doesn't mind. Her money, such as it is, goes towards her care, but again she doesn't resent it because she feels under no obligation to leave money even to me, her most loved child. It would be bad for me. I don't mind either.

When I visit her, her face lights up. She doesn't complain about anything.

'They're all very nice to me,' she says. 'I think there were someone here before you – a girl – I don't know who she was. Carol came. I can't remember if it were today or yesterday.'

The girl was from the care home. The staff are very considerate. They're poorly paid women who smoke and drink tea when they get the chance but they're genuinely fond of the old ladies. Carol is Nellie's friend, an excellent woman.

Nellie knows she'll die soon. It doesn't bother her. She's frightened of pain, but death is a matter of indifference and she's tired of living. Her only interest in life is me and my family.

'Are you happy?' she asks.

131

'Yes,' I say.

'Ooh, I *am* glad!' she says. 'That's all that matters.'

She isn't on drugs, but she seems to be floating through what remains to her. Her lack of interest in material things and focus on the experience of happiness are more pronounced, but they've always been there.

Biography is different from fiction. The people really suffer. They really die. And they do both in their own time for their own reasons.

Autobiography is different from historical biography because the process continues even during the writing of the book.

Since I began these essays, the following people have died:

(1) Lionel Trippett – friend, editor and writer of elegant pornography. Shirley and I knew him at University. He was a great wit and raconteur.

(2) Uncle Joe Williams – Hughie's brother. In my essay "Gents and Gypsies" he was the archetypal gypsy.

(3) Auntie Doll Williams – Joe's wife. Ex-Jehovah's Witness and harmonium player by some accounts. A lovely woman by universal agreement.

(4) John Davison – Shirley's brother. John was something of a spiv who matured with age and became a decent person. My boy Tom bought his car.

(5) James Hale – friend, editor and agent. A man of great skill, charm and tenderness towards his authors.

(6) Norman Gannon – husband of Shirley's sister Jean. An unassuming and good-natured man, liked by everyone and adored by his family.

It isn't to be expected that I'll get to the end of this book without someone else dying. But I don't know whom or when, no more than you do.

Three of my closest friends have cancer.

In biography, unlike fiction, death has no artistic meaning. It may have a moral, but that's largely a matter of chance. Because death can happen during the actual writing of an autobiography, the act itself has a sinister, dangerous quality. It's especially real.

I mention this because, once appreciated, death lends an urgency and – let's admit it – a thrill to autobiography. It's also poignant.

In autobiography the good guys may not win.

The story may just stop and remain forever unresolved.

The hero may not survive to the end.

THE KINDNESS OF STRANGERS

Olive Brown was a relic of the Raj. She was born in India and spoke Hindi until she was taken from her *ayah* to begin her training as an English lady.

She told me, 'My parents said, "You won't need an education. You'll never have to work."'

But she did. Her husband was killed in a tank in the Western Desert and she was left with two little girls and had to supplement any inherited money with clerical jobs and letting spare rooms. Her problems were then compounded by a serious stroke that left her paralysed down one side.

Olive was a committed liberal. She campaigned to abolish the death penalty and nuclear weapons. She kept an open house that was occupied at various times by Parsee engineers, Kurdish exiles and a clerk from the Woolwich Arsenal.

She lived in Glenluce Road, Blackheath, in a pleasant, untidy house with a panelled dining room full of newspapers in tied bundles and a garden tangled with loganberries which Shirley and I picked one summer. It was here that I turned up in the autumn of 1969 like Dick Whittington, with my future packed in a rucksack. I was twenty-two.

The connection with Olive came through Lionel Trippett, who was a close friend of Shirley, though I scarcely knew him. He'd been a 'character' at university because he was a mature student, a witty, cultured man with a languid and worldly manner. In a previous life – before Durham – he'd worked in publishing and edited Dennis Wheatley and for a time lodged with Olive. In later life he became an odd job man for various publishers and wrote Victorian pornography on demand.

After graduation, I went off to Italy for a month with my friends Mike Runge and Mike Shinn. On my return I had to decide what to do.

I was studying to be a barrister, but because of the slackness of the legal education system there was no requirement to study anywhere in particular and the practice was to take a correspondence course. If I'd wanted to, I might have stayed at home in Oldham. But that would have ended my relationship with Shirley.

Shirley was starting a diploma in social work at the London School of Economics. I decided to join her and so found myself on a coach with my possessions in a rucksack and my bankbook in my pocket with a few hundred pounds to get by.

I had no friends in London, no job to go to, no clear plan of study, no bed for the night. I'm not an adventurous person and it astonishes me that I had the courage to take my future in my hands and go forward so blindly, but I was driven by my love of Shirley and the certain knowledge that, if I stayed in Oldham, I'd never break free of its constraints.

We arrived at Victoria Coach Station. Shirley was going on to Watford where she was staying with her friend Madeleine Blakeley. I had only a bare hope of finding somewhere to stay and little idea how to set about it. Shirley gave me Olive's telephone number and I tried it.

It should be remembered that Olive didn't know me, didn't expect me and was up to her neck in Parsees, Kurds and clerks. She didn't have a spare room but something in her recognised that I was just a naïve kid and, from the goodness of her heart, she offered me the couch in her sitting room for a few days until I could find a place.

When I stepped through the door at Glenluce Road, an elfin figure, hobbling with aid of stick, greeted me with a sweet smile and offered me tea in a breathless old-fashioned voice.

I have two souvenirs of Olive. The first is a set of three sketches I drew for a portrait of her that I painted. The portrait is with her daughters but I have the framed sketches in my study. The second is a memory.

She had an odd interest in collective nouns: expressions such as 'a flock of birds' or 'a pride of lions'.

She liked to make up new ones.

She asked me, 'What's the collective term for prostitutes?'

'I don't know,' I said.

'An *anthology* of pros!'

To be truthful I'm not sure this one originated with her, but the second undoubtedly did.

She asked, 'What's the collective term for volunteers?'

'I don't know.'

'A *reluctancy*!'

However, when it came to volunteering for any good or liberal cause, Olive wasn't in the least reluctant.

Frank Rodriguez always claimed his full name was *Francis* Frank Rodriguez.

He said in his Canadian drawl, 'The priest told my dad that Frank wasn't a *Christian* name and I had to be called Francis, but my dad wouldn't have it. So they compromised and called me both.'

Frank was an oddity, a white West Indian from Antigua, the youngest of twenty children by the same mother. Six of his brothers had been killed in the First World War. At some point he'd emigrated to Canada and it was as a Canadian that he came to Britain to fight Hitler. When Shirley and I got to know him, he was a pudgy little fellow in his mid-sixties with white hair and a voice somewhere between a purr and a growl; but in the nineteen forties he was a dapper young man with Latin American good looks.

Joan Rodriguez was a tall, spare bluestocking: a highly cultivated woman who wrote poetry and worked as a librarian. She'd graduated from the London School of Economics in 1928, and a photograph of her shows a long-headed beauty. At the age of sixty she chain-smoked and dressed with a shabby air of former gentility like an Agatha Christie character – an author she liked.

Frank and Joan together reminded me of Roman and Minnie Castavets in *Rosemary's Baby*. They were an exotic mismatch. Joan was restrained and naturally elegant: someone who, in other circumstances, might have been an intellectual. Frank was simian and earthy: not particularly bright but intense with energy and emotion. I imagine that in his youth he radiated sexual magnetism and it was this that had captured Joan. In former years their marriage had been rocky but in retirement they settled into a stable if strange life. Joan spent her days reading while Frank played solitaire.

After a few weeks, Olive told me of a flat going at a house in Mycenae Road. Shirley and I strolled round and found Frank in the street doing some painting. He was ebullient and from the start treated us as if we were his children come home to visit. He had no daughter and always called Shirley 'my little girl'.

Frank had a great heart and is the most unprejudiced person I've ever met. He and Joan already shared home and kitchen with a pleasant Pakistani couple called Abdul and Ishrat Khan. Frank explained to me how this came about.

'When Abdul came to see me, one of the neighbours said, "If you take those Pakistanis in, I'll never speak to you again!" – so I did.'

I think he saw something in Shirley and me, a couple of children just starting out in life and we appealed to his warm nature. He and Joan were the best of landlords and most generous friends to people to whom they owed nothing.

137

In that first year Shirley attended her course at the LSE. I got work teaching sociology to visiting American students and French to old ladies. At the same time I studied for my Bar exams.

We had no money. I went through my savings and didn't want to ask my parents for help, though I'm sure they would have provided it. My correspondence course cost forty pounds (which in 1970 was a month's rent on a very nice furnished flat – though I think Frank's rate was low). It was Frank and Joan who stumped up the cash as a free loan out of the simple goodness of their hearts.

Shirley and I married in August that year. I studied on the honeymoon and passed my Bar exams in September. Shirley also got her diploma and found work as a probation officer in Lewisham.

Although I was now a barrister, I wasn't entitled to practice. The regulations required me to find a more senior barrister and attach myself as a pupil for twelve months. It was also necessary to get a place in an established set of chambers ('chambers' is what barristers call their offices). To become a pupil I had to pay a fee of a hundred pounds. I also had to keep myself for at least six months.

To save that hundred pounds I took a job as a clerk and receptionist at the Social Security office in Greenwich at an annual salary of nine hundred pounds, and I worked for a year.

I got to know Lionel better. He found himself a flat in Swiss Cottage and Shirley and I used to visit him on Sundays to play *Diplomacy*. His flat-mates were a Jewish cantor named Richard and a doctor and jazz musician called Max.

We also entertained ourselves on Saturday evenings playing coarse bridge with Frank and Joan. Frank's style was idiosyncratic. He had no notion of any bidding systems and relied instead on magic. If a hand troubled him, he'd stand up and make a circuit of the table, casting spells.

We took a small part in local politics. Jim Spencer was a dockworker and trade unionist and a very decent honest man with an amiable wife, Teresa, and two small boys. He canvassed us and we joined the Labour Party and attended the ward meetings. It was fun. We witnessed the results of the 1970 general election from a privileged position in Lewisham Town Hall, where the victorious Tories were full of grog and buying drinks for everyone. We got to meet Richard Marsh (later Lord Marsh) who was our Member of Parliament and a cabinet minister.

After the lost election, Richard Marsh threw a party to commiserate for the defeat. It was there that I ran into Conrad Ascher, who'd stood in Norwich and failed dismally. Understandably, he was fairly plastered when we talked and I discovered he was a barrister with chambers at 4 King's Bench Walk in the Temple.

I told him I needed pupilage.

'Oh, dear boy, come and see me when you're ready.'

So I did.

It was unsporting to take advantage of a drunken remark at a party, but I had no contacts in the legal world and had to do what I could. I think it was a shock to Conrad when a total stranger reminded him of a forgotten promise, but he never doubted he'd made it and he was prepared to stand by his word. Again I got the benefit of someone else's favour. It was all quite undeserved.

Conrad practised in only a small way, and he put me on to Leonard Sieve in the same chambers. It was a Jewish set headed by Leonard Lewis QC, but no one minded my presence as a *goy*. Frank, as you might expect, had a very positive opinion of Jews, and this particular incident was the first of many kindnesses Shirley and I have received from Jewish friends.

Leonard Sieve was a middle-aged barrister with a busy but undistinguished practice, mainly defending petty criminals in the various London courts. During the War he'd worked as a 'Bevan boy' in the coalmines and this had left him with socialist leanings. I liked him.

I traipsed behind Leonard carrying his papers around the shabby corridors of the court system, which still had a Dickensian air. On one occasion a *hasid* in black hat, beard and side curls tried to convert me to the fellowship of the Lubavitcher Rebbe. When I explained that I lacked an essential qualification, he said without batting an eyelid, 'You'll make sure to give this leaflet to Mr Sieve, won't you?'

He was a pious man – and was convicted of tax fraud.

We did divorce cases. It was still an occasional requirement that the petitioner make a full disclosure to the court of any adultery he or she might have committed.

I witnessed the following incident. Leonard and I were in court waiting for our case to come on. A jolly West Indian lady was giving evidence of her indiscretions. In accordance with the usual practice she was handed a list.

'And have you committed any adultery that is not mentioned in this list?' asked her barrister.

'No,' said his client, before adding brightly, 'But I'd *like* to!'

In contrast our own case lacked obvious humour unless one knew a little secret. Leonard stood up and obtained a divorce for a dark-skinned Mr Khan, who swore to tell the truth by Allah on the copy of the Holy Koran handed to him by the court usher.

The secret was that Mr Khan was a Roman Catholic from British Guyana.

I was later to get a divorce for a woman who seemed to think the idea that her husband should maintain his children was the most indecent proposition she had ever heard.

Divorce introduces you to the bizarre heart of other people's marriages.

I was a pupil with Leonard for six months, but my heart was set on returning to Durham. Through the university law department I gained an introduction to the chambers of Wilfred Steer QC in Westgate Road, Newcastle and James Chadwin accepted me as his pupil for six months, though there was no commitment to give me a place afterwards. Still, on the strength of my hopes, Shirley and I moved to Durham and bought a house. It marked the start of my career as a barrister.

During that transition period, from leaving university in the summer of 1969, to our return to Durham in the spring of 1972, Shirley and I were very vulnerable. We had little in the way of money, experience or contacts: in fact few resources except our raw intelligence, a good education and a willingness to work. We could have been felled easily by misfortune or led in a wrong direction. The help given by people who owed us nothing at all was invaluable.

If our attitudes are conditioned by experience, my encounters with Olive, Frank and the rest have given be a positive view of other people. Strangers don't frighten me. I'm not suspicious of them. I like to think the best of people not the worst.

And by and large, these opinions – though they may seem naïve – have served me well. I dislike very few people. And, if I have any enemies, I'm too stupid to recognise them.

On the other hand, I am aware that some people don't especially care for me, but I try not to mind. I don't think the worse of them for that reason. Whether or not someone likes me seems a very poor measure of a person's worth.

NOTES ON "THE KINDNESS OF STRANGERS"

The basic structure of this essay is simple. It's a straightforward narrative of the main events of the period between my leaving university and becoming a practising barrister, told in the order in which they happened. Looked at more closely, you'll see that this framework is filled out with a series of short anecdotes or scenes, which don't advance the story but provide colour and detail: for example the tale of the *hasid* tax evader and the incidents in the divorce court. All of the material is adapted to develop a theme: in this case the great kindness shown to me by people who owed me nothing.

If you return to the Notes on *My School*, you'll see that in the present case I've followed the threefold division of storyline, detail and theme that I examined there in more depth. In making a plan for an essay, I also suggested you might want to list the available source materials. Now I propose in addition that you make notes of the characters you intend to introduce.

The present essay features a number of people you haven't met before. They include Olive Brown, Frank and Joan Rodriguez, Jim and Teresa Spencer, Conrad Asher and Leonard Sieve. I've given a thumbnail sketch of each of them at varying lengths. Schematically they can be shown like this, taking Frank Rodriguez as an example.

Frank Rodriguez

Frank Rodriguez				
Appearance	**History**	**Character**	**Idiosyncracies**	**Stories**
White Pudgy 65 + white hair purring voice once dapper Latin American Simian	Antigua Youngest of 20 6 dead brothers Canadian Soldier Marries Joan	Earthy not bright energetic emotional sexual magnetism ebullient unprejudiced	White West Indian Like the Castavets Plays solitaire Calls Shirley "my little girl" Casts spells	Becomes my landlord Takes in the Khans Lends me £40 Playing bridge

The order in which I've described Frank roughly follows that given in the table – i.e. beginning with a description of the person – and I think it has a common-sense logic.

However, none of this is a rigid rule. Use it only if it suits. You can argue for more or fewer categories than the ones I've given and make a case as to which category a detail best fits. It doesn't particularly matter. My suggestions are no more than an outline scheme to help you develop and organise your thoughts. If you see an empty column, it should give you pause to wonder whether your portrait is balanced. But there's no absolute requirement to deal with all aspects of a person if the context doesn't require it.

Two elements in particular will bring your efforts to life, namely the subject's idiosyncrasies and any particularly telling stories. In the case of details of appearance, think carefully about those parts (either the details themselves or the language you use to describe them) which also convey something of the person's character or in other ways make him or her vivid (which elsewhere I've referred to as 'loaded' language). As a quick exercise, review my description of Frank to see how consistent it is with the rest of the picture. Does the description of him help you understand the man? How much of it is useful? Can you see him?

It should be evident that I'm very grateful to the people who helped me during the critical period 1969-1972. I've suggested that it was their behaviour that contributed to my own attitude to others. I've no great regard for Mankind in the mass or the abstract, and I expect nothing but evil of mobs or armies. But my experience at the hands of individuals has been almost uniformly good and persuaded me of the great fund of goodwill that most people possess.

I accept the risk that I'm completely mistaken about this. Indeed I strongly suspect I am: leastwise when I hear people talk about each other, especially when speaking in generalities. On the other hand, on these occasions, I sometimes wonder if the speakers are simply mouthing commonplaces ('It's a dog eat dog world') or whether they've actually taken stock of the extent to which others have helped and continue to help them. Surely my experience of day-to-day human goodness can't be unique? This is a topic about which I feel genuinely ignorant. I'm not out to convert anyone to my point of view.

One of the things your autobiography is likely to bring out is your basic orientation towards other people. I've used the present essay deliberately to reflect on and explain my own position, but whether you make it the theme of an essay or not, it's likely to appear in the general tone of your writing. You may want to think about this. If you accept that your attitudes are bound to come out, you should perhaps consider in more depth what they actually are. Do they really reflect your own thoughts and experiences or are they just prejudices picked up here and there from other people? What are their origins? Are they rooted in incidents of your own life?

In selecting material for my essays, I haven't set down stuff just because it happened. I want to know what it all means.

THE ROAD TO THE TIBERIUS CLUB

The lackadaisical legal education system of thirty-five years ago had an odd effect on the English Bar. Its leaders were men – mostly men – of terrifying analytical intelligence who could tear an argument or a witness into shreds without raising a sweat. But it was also the occupation of a gentleman, where well-bred families could place their idiots (often lonely bachelors with strange habits) without alarming the public. These poor souls got by on their inherited income, supplemented by bits and pieces of divorce work and the defence of petty criminals. It was one of these types that I came across in Newcastle County Court in 1976.

He was a lumbering, red-faced, beefy man in his late twenties but he looked a generation older with his unfashionable haircut and brown brogue shoes made for country walks. I'd seen him lurking in various robing rooms, doing nothing much, and picked up snippets of his history. He came from a county family with a manor house carved from an ancient peel tower somewhere in the wilds of the Borders.

A few years before, a retired general had decided the Reds were about to overthrow civilisation, and set about forming a militia to rush to the aid of the government in its hour of need. There wasn't any Red menace and the government didn't require any help; and the enterprise, which never amount to more than a handful of fantasists, fell apart in mutual recriminations as these things often do.

My opponent had been an officer in this barmy army.

Shirley and I left London for Durham in the spring of 1972, when I was twenty-four years old and thought myself a splendid chap with long hair, a tremendous set of side-whiskers and a suit with flared trousers. For five thousand pounds we bought a small semi-detached house on the strength of my prospects, using a thousand pounds lent us by Nellie, and Shirley obtained work at a school for disturbed children at Newton Aycliffe. We also took our dog, Annie, a golden Labrador bitch with a dodgy temper that we bought on our first anniversary. Frank and Joan Rodriguez had allowed us to keep her at our flat.

I became a member of Wilfred Steer's chambers. They were located on the upper floors of some shops at the corner of Grainger Street and Westgate Road, Newcastle. Behind the block ran an alleyway that was sometimes used as a shortcut. And it was here that the Tiberius Club was located.

From what followed I gather it was a casino; but I never went inside. I recall a door and a small glass-fronted cabinet fixed to the wall: the sort that would have held a menu if the place had been a restaurant. It showed a photograph of some thickset men, who looked as though they'd be handy in a fight, though they wore dinner jackets. The photograph never changed. But from time to time the staff did – in which case new heads were glued onto the bodies, creating the impression that the original owners had been bumped off and hastily buried in an unmarked grave.

For the first six months I followed my pupil master, Jim Chadwin. He was a stocky, bustling Scot, who practised mostly as a criminal defence lawyer. He was a fine advocate, and, if I'd had the wit to study him closely, I might have learned a lot. In later years he defended the Yorkshire Ripper for his dozen or so murders.

After this probationary period I began to practise for myself. One of the staples was undefended divorce. It involved taking some poor bedraggled woman through a standard account of her husband's brutality and desertion, and took about fifteen minutes and little preparation.

147

Indeed it was so simple that on one occasion, when I forgot to bring my file with me, I wrapped a copy of the *Daily Express* in a sheet of paper, pretended it was my brief; then took my client through her paces on the assumption that her husband had behaved precisely like the rest of them – and she agreed that he had.

A well-connected moron could make a very decent living if he armed himself with half a dozen of these divorce cases on two or three days a week.

The other staple was making speeches in defence of petty crooks who were pleading guilty but hoped not to go to jail. By and large these speeches had no effect whatsoever, since the judges were a hard-bitten lot, unimpressed by young counsel, and sentenced according to a tariff.

Occasionally, however, one could make something out of the court's idiosyncrasies.

Judge Sharp, who sat at Durham, had had his brains addled by an addiction to boxing when he was a boy at Fettes School. He held to the peculiar view that it was a part of the Common Law of England that two men could agree to knock each other senseless in settlement of their differences, provided no weapons or boots were used. In such a case, not only would the accused not go to jail, but the judge would instruct the jury to acquit him. I had a couple of small successes by persuading Judge Sharp that a piece of bloodthirsty mayhem, in a stinking alley behind a pub, was in fact a duel between two English gentlemen in exercise of their God-given right.

Two other pleas in mitigation could also cut ice with some judges and I offer them for the insight they provide.

'Your Honour,' quoth I more times than I can recall, 'if my client is allowed to go free today, he has a job which starts on Monday.'

In the North East where jobs were scarce, judges were fairly sympathetic to the unemployed and took the loss of a prospective job seriously. For this plea to succeed it was usually necessary to produce a letter from the employer in question. It's worth noting that, faced with a stretch in jail for burglary, a man who's been unemployed for five years will frequently find he has a job that starts on Monday. A miracle, I suppose.

The second useful plea goes something like this:

'Your Honour, if my client is allowed to go free today, he intends to move – *to Hull.*'

Two elements in this otherwise bizarre statement appeal to judges. The first is that it offers the prospect that the accused will be moved off His Honour's patch, and – since judges don't expect criminals to reform – this is an acceptable alternative to actual honesty. The second is that Hull is viewed as the outer chamber of Hell (except in Hull, perhaps), and to be banished there is retribution enough.

I ran this plea successfully substituting Belfast and Cape Town. But I fancy Bath or Oxford wouldn't do.

The case that brought me to Newcastle County Court in 1976 and my encounter with my red-faced opponent in the brown brogues involved the sum of a hundred and twenty pounds – an amount that was fairly trivial even in those days. I acted for the Defendant.

My client was a sharp looking character of thirty or so, with the evasive eyes and sly smile of someone who thinks he knows a trick or two. He'd hired a small firm of landscape gardeners to do some work for him and then refused to pay them. His story was that they'd left him with a lawn full of weeds and had failed to supply an unspecified number of bedding plants. As disputes go, this one was tedious and no one would have supposed it contained a trap for the unwary.

I had an expert witness who was going to support my case and I anticipated making mincemeat out of my opponent.

149

What happened in the gardening case is just an instance of the insanity that appears daily in the courts.

I was once called on to defend a man who'd stolen a vehicle in order to get home after a night on the beer. It's a common occurrence and I wouldn't ordinarily mention it. In this case however, the vehicle in question was a car ferry. The accused had found it unattended and sailed it across the River Tyne.

Another time my client pleaded not guilty to passing a dud cheque at a shop in Darlington. He insisted he had a rock solid defence despite the fact he'd freely admitted the offence and signed a written confession.

'But I didn't do it and you're going to get me off,' he said.

'I am? And what's the defence?'

'*Alibi*! I was nowhere near Darlington when they said I done it.'

'I see – and I suppose you've got a reliable witness who'll swear to this?' I said sceptically, thinking his witness would be a fellow crook who'd claim they were drinking in a pub together.

'Oh aye, man, my witness is a belter! You see, when they say I was passing that cheque in Darlington, I was in Middlesbrough – in the Crown Court – with *you*!'

Meantime, in the gardening case, my client took the stand and my opponent cross-examined him. His solicitors had done some research and uncovered a stack of debts and unsatisfied judgments. In short, as I suspected, he was someone who made a habit of bilking his creditors.

None of this strictly mattered. It didn't answer the question: was the lawn full of weeds? Had the Plaintiffs failed to provide the agreed bedding plants? The answers didn't turn on my client's evidence but on that of the independent gardening expert. And it was him I called next.

So there he was. He spoke well. He seemed to know his

stuff. He said the things he was expected to say. I sat down.

There's a convention in cross-examining experts. Because they're independent, it's rare to call them outright liars – which is an argument reserved for attacking policemen as a last resort after your client is alleged to have confessed.

To digress: in the days before taped interviews were required the accused frequently claimed he'd been 'verballed' by the arresting officer. As one judge noted, 'It's surprising how an accused man – faced with a total lack of evidence against him and the awful prospect of acquittal – will experience an overwhelming desire to confess to a policeman in the absence of any other witnesses.'

As for experts, you question them as to their qualifications, tactfully suggesting your own expert is made of altogether better stuff. Then you go into the technical details of the subject. In the present case my opponent might have suggested that, surely, the witness would agree that, as a matter of common practice attested, perhaps, by the United Nations Convention on Weeds in Lawns, a ratio of ten perennial weeds to every square metre of lawn was acceptable. And so forth.

Instead my opponent began a hostile interrogation of my witness as if he were a crook of the deepest dye. Or possibly a policeman.

This confirmed my opinion that the man was an idiot.

I came to the Bar in a period of expansion and for four years made a good living. However, in that year I reached a plateau, which was quickly followed by a sharp fall so that I was left many days twiddling my thumbs in chambers.

Part of this decline was caused by external factors. The prosecuting authorities in Teesside changed their practice and stopped pushing work out to the local solicitors who were my clients. And one of the latter, who'd given me a deal of work, threw in the towel and ran off to Kendal with his secretary.

There's no legislating for that sort of event, but it wouldn't have mattered if my practice had had a broader base.

The truth is I was never comfortable at the Bar. I was a frivolous, vulgar lad from a poor home, trying to get by with his raw wit and an exaggerated opinion of his natural charm. But don't mistake me – I was treated kindly and given a fair chance to succeed. If I'd had more gravitas and ambition, I don't doubt that I should have succeeded.

A legal practice requires that clients be cultivated. It demands considerable social skills and an instinct for building networks of contacts. I had neither – I still have neither. Although I've got a cheerful nature and – so I understand – a witty way of speaking, most of the time I'm content with my own company. My best friends by far are Shirley and the children. As for networking, I'm simply hopeless at it.

The truth is I breezed along for five and a half years, not taking the care to develop my skills as a lawyer and advocate, and relying on chance to bring work my way. In the end the latitude allowed to a young man was exhausted and it became obvious that I'd failed.

Nemesis was waiting for me in Newcastle County Court.

So there my expert was – in the witness box, being harassed by The Idiot. I'll call my witness 'John Smith' because I've long forgotten his real name.

In the circumstances he stood up well. He held to his opinion about the shoddy state of the lawn and wasn't going to be shaken out of it by The Idiot's offensive tactics. I thought I was fairly on my way to a victory.

At this point my opponent produced a bill.

He asked, 'Is this your invoice for your services, Mr

Smith? Twenty pounds plus one pound and sixty pence Value Added Tax?'

'Yes…' agreed the witness cautiously.

He wondered where this was going.

I wondered where it was going, too.

The Idiot grinned. He asked in a voice that sounded as if he'd a lollipop in his mouth, 'What is your Value Added Tax registration number?'

A pause

WITNESS: (*in a squeak*) I'm not registered for V.A.T.

THE IDIOT: Then, pray, how comes it that you have charged Value Added Tax in your bill when you are not lawfully entitled to do so?

WITNESS: Clerical error.

THE IDIOT: What kind of clerical error is that? Would you care to elucidate for the benefit of the court?

WITNESS: (*looking around desperately*) Clerical error.

THE IDIOT: (*indignantly*) So you say. But how does an amount of Value Added Tax include itself accidentally in your bill? By what species of error?

And so forth. My expert witness is a liar and a tax fraudster and that's an end of it.

Yet none of this has anything to do with the state of that damned lawn.

Surely things can't get any worse?

It was in our first house in Durham that our eldest child, Tom, was born in 1974. That afternoon I was in Stockton County Court with a fist of undefended divorce cases in front of His Honour Judge Forrester Paton, when the clerk brought him the message and he read it out. I took my clients through the usual beatings and adultery and quickly got out.

Tom was born at home. It was something Shirley wanted for all the children. After Tom she also gave up painkillers because they only made her tired and prolonged the business. I was ecstatic. I was twenty-six years old and a father.

That evening, after a beer at the Colpitts Hotel, I stood in the darkness in the alleyway behind the Hulberts' house and sang *All Things Bright And Beautiful* at the top of my voice. It was one of the happiest days of my life.

Next year we moved to Oak Tree House, a converted pub in High Shincliffe, a village a couple of miles outside Durham. With the house we acquired a surrogate grandmother, Monty, who clung to us for nigh thirty years and whose affairs we managed at her death aged ninety-three.

Monty was interesting in that she'd been deserted by her father, Louis Levinson, as an infant in arms. Though she knew next to nothing of him, she idolized him. The scar of this early separation remained with her for the whole of her life.

But, to continue…

Two years after Tom, my son Alex was born. He had enormous shoulders and Shirley gave a yelp as he came out. I was present on the occasion of all our children's births, and when Hannah came in 1982, the place was a circus: two midwives, both boys, Shirley's sister Jean and her brother-in-law Norman were all there. While Shirley was giving birth, I was in the kitchen stuffing a chicken for lunch. I made occasional sorties and helped her since she spent the whole labour walking in circles round the room and finally delivered our daughter in a birthing chair.

But I'm getting ahead of my story.

Alex was born, and my law practice was collapsing. I began searching for a way out and the following year I finally found one. It was a job in industry as an in-house lawyer, but it required us to move to Wiltshire and to abandon Durham where I'd hoped to live and die.

I can't disguise that this was a blow. My previous disappointments – not obtaining places at Manchester Grammar School or Oxford – had the nature of accidents, but my failure at the Bar was all my own work. I failed because I deserved to fail. And, after the passage of near thirty years in which I've acquired a deal more experience and – I hope – more self-knowledge, I think I should still fail if I were to return to the Bar today. The fact is that my character and judgment were and still are unsuited to being a barrister.

However none of this was a disaster. When Shirley and I put our defeat behind us, packed our traps and moved south with the kids, we may not have been heading for fame and riches. But we were talking a road that would lead to happiness and satisfaction.

Meantime my expert witness and VAT fraudster was wriggling on the end of questions about the state of his bills, and I was telling myself that it couldn't get any worse.

But, of course, it could – and in ways too bizarre to foresee.

By now my witness was in a state of nervous exhaustion after being ponderously worked over in cross-examination by The Idiot. The latter, however, seemed to be winding down – after all there are only so many ways of making your point – and I was trying to figure out a riposte.

An old joke goes: 'Well, apart from that, Mrs Lincoln, what did you think of the play?' I realized I was going to have to get on my feet and make a pitch along the line: 'Well, apart from that, your Honour, what do you make of the lawn?'

But before I could get round to this, my opponent

rounded on the witness again.

Red-faced, sweating and eyes bulging, he fixed him with a glare and declaimed in a fruity voice filled with indignation: 'I put it to you that you are *not* Mr John Smith, the expert landscape gardener.'

The witness stood as if afflicted by rigor. The judge leaned forward. My solicitor and I looked at each other.

'You *are* indeed Mr John Smith –' said The Idiot accusingly and thundered '– the crooked croupier from the Tiberius Club, *who is currently under a six month suspended prison sentence for theft*!'

At this point my hapless witness croaked, 'Yes!'

And fainted.

But apart from *that*, your Honour…?

The judge reduced the bill by ten pounds on account of the poor condition of the lawn.

NOTES ON "THE ROAD TO THE TIBERIUS CLUB"

I've often recounted the Affair of the Tiberius Club as a story against me. It was so outrageous and unlikely, that it was funny even at the time. I had such a high opinion of myself in comparison with The Idiot that my comeuppance was well deserved.

Although I failed in my career as a barrister, the present essay isn't about failure with all its negative connotations. In fact the sequel was a career which was altogether more congenial, so that, in a way, 'failure' was to be the foundation of my happiness. Rather my subject is a portrait of the brashness of youth, and my first conscious encounter with the limitations that life imposes.

In this instance the limitation was in my professional career. In your life it may be something different. Perhaps you've been denied marriage or children or in some fashion or another you have a handicap. Whatever the case, I can't imagine you've found the experience easy. Whether or not you choose to meditate on it in your autobiography is a matter for you.

As far as my failure at the Bar is concerned, I've passed through it and survived (though I didn't like it). I don't blame external circumstances or anyone other than myself. However, this analysis applies only to my situation and doesn't bind you. There's no compulsion to be generous or philosophical. Maybe in your case it really was the fault of God or the other guy – I can't say.

I'm stepping again into the area where I try to exercise caution: namely in giving advice or suggesting that a moral benefit will come to you from writing your autobiography. My inclination is to believe that thinking consciously about the limitations of life – the causes and effects – will be beneficial and that an essay specifically on this topic is a good idea. However there are dangers. An essay which allows you to formulate your existing feelings more clearly is the most likely result and it may do no more than confirm your prejudices. But there is also the possibility that you may shock yourself. Whatever the outcome, you should be prepared, in particular if your conclusions drive you in the direction of blaming others. On balance I think it's more likely that it will lead you to forgive them.

This essay employs my favourite technique of framing the theme in an anecdote. The Affair of the Tiberius Club serves as a neat metaphor for what happened to me and it binds all the other elements tightly since it figures not only at the beginning and end but in three places in the body of the text.

In addition there are two other elements. There's a fairly straightforward chronological account of my career in my twenties. And there are also a number of anecdotes and asides; and, because anecdotes are often the most vivid and interesting parts of a story, it's worth studying how they're worked into the narrative

In this essay they appear mainly in two places. After mentioning my pupilage with Jim Chadwin, I begin an account of my own career and set out a series of general comments and anecdotes before switching back to the tale of the Tiberius Club. The second section begins with the story of the villain who nicked the Tyne Ferry and ends with the dud cheque incident. The transitions are marked by a short sentence or phrase – none of them terribly clever and nothing that should be beyond your own ability. My reason for breaking this material into two sections was to prevent the reader from losing track of the historical narrative or the larger theme. In addition the Affair of the Tiberius Club requires telling at length if its ridiculousness is to be savoured; but to set it down all of one piece would

158

unbalance the essay.

In essence this essay contains three parts: (1) the Tiberius story; (2) the historical narrative; and (3) the minor anecdotes and asides. I've broken up each of these parts and interleaved them to prevent any one of them from dominating the essay.

SO THIS IS MY LIFE?

In 1996, during the holiday of *Eid al Fitr*, I began writing a novel in a bar in Bombay.

So this is my life?

It isn't what I expected.

After a Bonfire Night party for the friends at the Bar whom I'd soon lose, I started my new career as an in-house lawyer with the Burmah Oil Company based in Swindon. It was the autumn of 1977 and I was thirty years old.

Shirley and I moved to a thatched cottage with the curious address of The Sawmills, The Bottom, Urchfont. It was picturesque – and thoroughly inconvenient. By one of the bizarre but meaningless coincidences that dog life, a year or so before our move we bought a jar of 'Urchfont Mustard' at a delicatessen in Durham – the only time I ever saw this brand. We now discovered the mustard had been made in the very house we'd just bought.

Ambition is an odd thing. I was later to meet a colleague who qualified as a barrister but never practised. He suffered from an unsatisfied desire for a career he'd never have. Many people have a longing to live in the country, one they'll never fulfil. I tried both, and failed at one and didn't take to the other; but I've never regretted either. The attempts cured me of ambitions that might otherwise have survived to frustrate me.

The Burmah Oil Company was a conglomerate that had been brought to its knees a couple of years before by the combination of a whizz-kid chief executive, a shady Greek and a gang of corrupt Indonesian generals. It was in the process of restructuring itself after the disaster, and part of my job was to negotiate new loans and dispose of a large fleet of rusting oil tankers.

The tankers had been acquired by the Greek to service oil shipment contracts negotiated with the generals, but the Indonesian state oil company had defaulted, leaving Burmah with a large debt on the ships and no income to pay it off. The whole affair was surrounded in a thicket of shell companies registered in Panama, who fronted for the army. Their names hinted at their purpose. One was called *Hocus Pocus*.

This was fine, but Shirley and I are northerners by instinct and upbringing. We never particularly cared for Wiltshire and Shirley felt desperately isolated and depressed, raising two small children with few friends and no family around her. Burmah owned a small contracting company in the Manchester area, and when a vacancy for a commercial lawyer presented itself, I grasped it eagerly. We upped stumps once more in the spring of 1981.

My new employer was in the business of designing and supplying plants for processing various gases and chemicals. Much of its business was in the old Soviet bloc and I found myself traveling to Poland, Czechoslovakia, Hungary, Bulgaria, East Germany and Russia itself.

The following exchange occurred in a Prague taxi in October 1981.

ME:	I notice there are flags flying on all the lampposts. Is there some sort of international visit going on?
TAXI DRIVER:	Yes, the Russians are visiting us
ME:	Oh? I hadn't heard. When did they come?
TAXI DRIVER:	Thirteen years ago.

The dying decade of the Soviet Empire was a world of shabbiness, empty shops, dimly lit streets where one might spot (as I did) a policeman beating up a local down an alleyway, and nightclubs full of tarts. It had a strange, melancholy charm as if one were in a black and white film.

It wasn't in the least threatening to foreign businessmen if they were in a respectable line.

Poland was one of the most liberal regimes in the period before martial law was imposed. Currency touts loitered in the doorways of the international hotels. Taxi drivers and waiters offered to swap zlotys for sterling at three times the official rate. As I was walking with Bob Boland in Łazienki Park a red squirrel bounded up to me with its paws cupped and held out.

'See?' I said. 'Even the bloody squirrels want to change money.'

At the Victoria I ate the rare European bison for dinner. But they couldn't supply mushrooms even though they were listed on the menu and being sold from barrows in the street. The place claimed five stars.

The Europaiski was an hotel dating from the *belle époque* that had grown seedy under communist neglect. But it had a good restaurant and kept up a certain old-fashioned style with a cabaret featuring an illusionist. Bob and I wandered in there with a *Castrol* salesman. He was a frequent visitor to Warsaw where he slouched around the public areas of the Victoria in bedroom slippers. On this occasion he carried a manila envelope full of company key rings and stickers.

'Watch this,' he said.

He pulled out a fistful of key rings and immediately the waiters swarmed round like seagulls on a rubbish dump, scavenging for these western trifles.

'They do that every time,' he said. 'I dunno why.'

He gave Bob and me some of his stock and two weeks

later we were back at the Europaiski. Feeling like dopes, we took out the keys rings and the effect was exactly as before. Waiters in their dozens flocked round us clamouring for gifts.

Another two weeks saw us back there yet again, but this time without key rings. Still the waiters remembered us and came for their gifts. We had to refuse and they duly vanished except for one.

'You want to change money?' he asked hopefully.

The collapse of that world found me in East Berlin with David Faux. Reunion was still a little way off but the border restrictions had effectively ended. One evening we wandered along the Wall in the sector by the Brandenburg gate. Turkish immigrants had set up tables where they were selling lumps of concrete covered in graffiti which had been hacked off the Wall by the *Mauerspechte*. The proud insignia of the dying regime had found their way here. It was possible to buy a certificate of commendation as a People's Rabbit Breeder and any number of buttons and badges. The army of the DDR was effectively demobilizing itself, popping over the border to sell its uniforms for Deutschmarks. I had a vision of these new capitalists skipping home joyfully in their underwear. But if they did, I never saw them.

I bought a medal rewarding its owner for twenty-five years loyal service as a police informer.

As the decade turned into the nineties, a new problem came my way; an arbitration that stretched out for seven years on and off.

The source of the problem was a pipeline that was to be laid from a refinery on the west coast of India several miles out to sea, where tankers could moor at a buoy and pump product ashore. There was some confusion over the necessary permits to lay the pipe at right angles to a dredged shipping channel, and the project was aborted.

First, however, we laid a pipe which started on a river estuary and finished on a beach – and which did precisely nothing. The mooring buoy languished in a yard in Bombay. Millions of pounds were wasted and I was kept in business.

The days spent in the hearings were tedious, but sometimes bizarre. Though we liked the Indians and got on very well with them, we could make no claim to understanding what was going on.

I was sitting in court one day, when the senior counsel sitting next to me lifted a buttock and delivered an audible fart that resonated round the room. No one said anything, but a few minutes later, like the mating call of an elephant, equally senior counsel on the other side delivered an answering fart. To which my leader replied…and so forth.

What was it all about?

I hadn't a clue.

What was I supposed to do? Ignore them? Applaud? Join in?

Was it an insult, a challenge or an accident?

Did I have farting rights?

As the years passed by the process of the arbitration took on a life of its own. We settled into it like trench warfare, with no confidence it would ever come to an end.

We began to take our families there on holiday.

For the first four years the hearings were held in Delhi. Our base was the Maurya Sheraton hotel. In December 1993 I brought Shirley out for ten days. She lounged by the pool or shopped while I sat through the hearings, and afterwards we went to restaurants and clubs and danced. We spent a magical evening watching Indian classical dancing in the ruins of an ancient cistern, sitting in the open by a charcoal brazier surrounded by night and stars. That weekend we went to the Taj Mahal and Shirley got to ride an elephant and see a dancing bear. In the Red Fort we met a woman whose job was to strike a match – nothing more. By it we saw the light reflected off a myriad fragments of glass by which Great Mughal's *nautch* girls had once applied kohl to their eyes.

Subsequently the affair became peripatetic and we sat, as the mood took us, in Bombay or Bangalore. Then the Indians, who had little time for leisure, proposed we help them out and start to hold the hearings in holiday resorts. So we went to Kodaikanal, a hill station in the Western Ghats: seven thousand feet up by a lake surrounded by eucalyptus forest. Jolly Indian ladies and their offspring joined their husbands, and, while the men laboured at the arbitration, their families took donkey rides round the lake and in the evenings played bingo. Later we went to Ooty, another hill station with an Anglican church, which was high in the Nilgris hills among tea plantations. We also went to Goa.

It was too absurd for words.

After four years, the first two arbitrators couldn't agree on a decision. Since the parties had appointed one arbitrator each it was an inevitable outcome and the time and money had been squandered. After a lapse of a year, we began the second phase before a single neutral umpire.

This time round we changed our leading counsel. As crooked lawyers go, our new man was the biggest villain unhanged, but we engaged him because he had enormous prestige and political connections. He was also old and decrepit after suffering several strokes.

He was hired in my absence and I first came across him at a hearing in Bangalore. He arrived late and was carried in, supported under the arms by two of his servants. For the occasion he wore sandals, shorts and a dirty T-shirt. And he went promptly to sleep.

With his assistance we brought the matter to a close in 1998. Technically the arbitration was a victory with an award in our favour. However, since the award corresponded almost exactly with the amount of money we had spent getting it, the process had proved completely pointless.

In short, the seven years I spent on this matter were enormously entertaining, but in all other respects a waste of time.

However, since I don't expect life to be particularly purposeful, this was all fine by me.

During that decade I seemed to be cursed by arbitrations. Part way through the Indian affair a dispute blew up in Abu Dhabi, when we were sued by a pair of tough Glaswegians in the matter of some scaffolding and insulating.

I ran the defence jointly with my great friend Fabulous Fred Day. We camped in the Al Ain Palace and powered ourselves on Heineken, gin and cigarettes through two years of intermittent but grinding hearings before a tribunal composed of a Croat businessman, an Egyptian lawyer and an English chairman. The last was a colourful character in his seventies with a plummy voice, white hair and a superb handlebar moustache.

The chairman may have looked a gentleman, but in fact Fred and I were on a hiding to nothing because the Glaswegians had bribed him. This sort of arbitration is a rough old game and I rather admired them for pulling off such a successful stunt. We reciprocated when our local lawyer had our opponents thrown in jail for passing dud cheques. Ah yes, business is wonderful!

The Brothers Grimm dressed like football players in the seventies, with long hair in ringlets and gold jewellery. They had many fans. Alec (as I'll call him) wandered late into one of the hearings and announced without too much concern, 'Some bastard's just heaved a brick through my windscreen.' We nodded sympathetically and continued.

So they bribed the chairman and won the arbitration handsomely. However, I know my business and got the award overturned by the courts on a technicality. As I write today [2004] the dispute has been tied up in the courts for ten years. We're likely to win another victory, but, frankly, it would have been cheaper to give Alec and Angus what they were asking for.

Sometimes I think that very little of what I do makes any sense. Not the least of its oddities is that, after beating each other up for so many years, Angus and I are on very good terms. It was just business – nothing personal. The Mafia point of view.

It was in Abu Dhabi that Fabulous Freddie introduced me to poetry and that Billy Brooks told me his story about Ben Ley and the 'carafe' once worn at a wedding. It was also during this arbitration that, in a slack moment, I fetched up in a bar in Bombay and began writing a novel.

The night that we won the appeal overturning the arbitration award, Fred and I shared a bedroom for mutual safety. Alec had a reputation for killing people for which he'd done a spell in prison. The following day we thanked God for being alive and got out of town.

So – to repeat – this is my life. Frankly, it seems bizarre.

In Paris I stood drinks for a Flemish Nazi tropical fish dealer, a former member of the Waffen SS, and a Luxembourgeois tractor salesman who spoke English with a Glaswegian accent.

In Qatar, I found myself offering comforting words to a secret policeman whose son had been murdered.

There seems no rhyme or reason to any of it.

Of course much of my time is spent doing mundane stuff: writing and reviewing contracts, negotiating disputes and giving commercial advice. I've been doing it for twenty-three years. I haven't changed employers and I haven't been promoted, and these facts don't bother me in the least. I found something I enjoyed and which seemed to be suited to my character. My life wasn't broken and so I did nothing to fix it.

However none of it was what I expected or could have foreseen. Nor was it what I wanted.

There's a saying that life is what happens while you're planning to do something else.

I was planning to be a successful writer.

NOTES TO "SO THIS IS MY LIFE?"

On its face this is a straightforward essay: a series of anecdotes in roughly chronological order. However, once one realizes that it covers events over a period of twenty-seven years [1977 – 2004], the shortness and simplicity require an explanation.

Two matters in particular contribute to these features. The first is that the essay is almost entirely limited to my working life and mentions little else that might have been going on at the same time. The second is that I've made no attempt to grind through day-to-day detail. Instead I've confined myself to a number of more or less amusing tales; and, even then, you should understand that individually they are none of them essential to the sense of the essay: I might have chosen others and, if they were good enough, achieved the same general effect. This is because their purpose is essentially illustrative.

As far as the first point goes, it was possible to limit my subject matter because I've dealt with other topics elsewhere and so one doesn't have a strong sense of their omission. For example, throughout this period I was taking regular holidays, which are the subject of a specific essay. I was also making my way as a father, loving my wife, composing bad poetry, having religious doubts, and doing a bunch of other stuff.

If I'd wanted to chart the progress of all these simultaneously, I couldn't do it in an essay of the present form or length. Most likely I'd have divided the overall period into parts, each of them bounded by events that would in some fashion give them their character, rather as I've divided university from school. However I ask myself: would it have been revealing to discuss in the same breath the battles Fabulous Fred Day and I had with the Brothers Grimm in Abu Dhabi in 1995 with the holiday we took as a family in France that year?

As a subject, holidays are a good instance of my point. Individually they're largely meaningless, but, viewed over decades, they show patterns and provide insights – or they should do if my essay *My Holidays* is any good. In a chronological history of my life, holidays would be overlooked or lost among other apparently trivial details.

From this discussion I hope you get an idea of the technical problems posed by the rigid chronological approach, and the different result you'd come to by following it. Of course that doesn't mean it's excluded, but you need to decide how far it's appropriate in any given case.

I'm not a public figure. My doings are not of such great interest that you'd want to investigate every particular of them. These essays are fundamentally an exploration of my character combined with an impressionistic picture of the world in which I live. These things are what your grandchildren will want to know about you.

If I were a public figure or a doer of Great Deeds the position might well be different. The details of my actions would be necessary to understand my impact on more general history. It would be necessary to have the facts accurately told and with close attention to their order and dates. Amusing stories of the kind told by after-dinner speakers would have their place, but it would be very secondary. I am not writing that book.

This distinction should be borne in mind when you're writing your own essays. My anecdotes have been selected above all for their colour. They don't describe everyday incidents at the office – on the contrary the incidents are exceptional. What makes them relevant is not that they're typical but that they're *characteristic* – by which I mean that, while working in an office is a common experience, the things that happened to me in India and Abu Dhabi tell what it is that makes my job and that part of my life uniquely mine. You should look for the same in your own career.

In the course of three decades the technology and organization of work have changed. I've seen telex machines disappear and fax machines seem set to join them. Drawing boards have been replaced by computers; electronic typewriters have gone, and much else. These changes have affected the social experience of work. The typing pool has ended. Secretaries are becoming rare. In my company fat men with beards and sandals used to make plastic models of chemical plants to help in their design. But the models are now collectors' pieces and the fat men have retired.

The smell and feel of offices have changed. The coated papers used in early photocopiers and fax machines are gone and their scent has departed with them. Where now is correction fluid?

I haven't written about these matters in the present essay, but – to repeat a point made earlier – history isn't just a recitation of events. It's a succession of sensual and social experiences. Instead of following my line, perhaps you'd like to concentrate on this aspect.

In the last summer of his life, my Dad – unusually – opened up on the subject of his work in the pits when he was a lad of fourteen, and told me, among other things, the names of the ponies he'd tended. I didn't note any of it and I've regretted the fact ever since.

Significant parts of manufacturing industry have collapsed in the last thirty years and, with them, whole worlds of language, sights, sounds and smells. Those four subjects could form headings under which you could try to recreate the feeling of how the past was.

Three years ago I was approached by Peter Goodwill, a friend from my Burmah days in the late seventies. He was working on a memoir of his father's career in the army during the Second World War. He'd done a considerable amount of research and written up most of it, and he wanted some advice on the result. Obviously I was happy to give it.

Much of my advice dealt with matters of detail such as style and punctuation. However there was one major difficulty, which Peter was never able to overcome in a completely satisfactory way. It was this: the memoir read at times like a regimental history – the voice of his father and sense of his presence were missing.

The source of the problem was easy enough to identify but almost impossible to remedy. It lay in the available sources. Peter had found a lot of material – some of it in obscure archives – dealing with his father's unit. From it he knew where his dad has been posted and, in some detail, the events that had happened at the level of the unit – for example, he knew it had been active as an anti-aircraft battery at the time of the heavy German air raids on Glasgow in 1940.

What Peter didn't know was how his father had reacted. Was he heroic? Was he frightened? Maybe he slept through most of the raids or had a weekend pass at the crucial dates. It was impossible to tell. Mr Goodwill was a taciturn man who didn't care to talk about his experiences, didn't write many letters and didn't keep a diary. None of this is unusual but the outcome is that, for all Peter's efforts, his father's voice is largely absent.

The fact that Peter wanted to write his memoir and went to such trouble to do so shows the degree of interest your descendants and other relatives (and possibly friends) have or will have in your life.

This story should encourage you to help them.

THE TRAINEE MILLIONAIRE

Writers of popular fiction hope to hit the bestseller lists. Mostly they fail – in fact they'd be better off cleaning cars. That's the stark reality of the business and there's no point complaining about it.

Dr Johnson once said that no one but a fool ever wrote except for money – which shows that like other writers he was happy to sacrifice truth for a witty remark. It would be more accurate to say that no one but a fool ever got into writing in the expectation of making serious money.

I expected to make serious money. I was a trainee millionaire.

Little Jimmy always wrote stories from the days when he trotted off to school in clogs and balaclava. He got 'well done' and a gold star in his exercise book and in his last year at junior school won a French dictionary, the J. M. Ross Prize for General Excellence.

In my teens at Greenhill Grammar School I applied myself to more serious literary efforts. I translated the first act of Racine's *Andromache* into iambic pentameters, and wrote two acts of a play, *Edward VI*, in verse. Judging from my later, less ambitious productions, I imagine they were terrible, but I'm sorry I didn't keep them. However, like Nellie I'm unsentimental about that sort of thing and probably threw them out.

At university I came across D.H. Lawrence. Nowadays I find him unreadable, but his phallocentric high emotion bowled me over when I was twenty. I began a novel about a boy from a northern manufacturing town and his relations with his mother.

But I wasn't Lawrence.

I couldn't bring myself to write about dicks.

My first serious effort at a commercial book came in 1970, during the first year that Shirley and I were in London, living with Frank and Joan Rodriguez. I had some bits and pieces of teaching and was studying for Bar exams, but I still had free time and applied it to writing a thriller. It was called *The Peking Delegation* and I wrote it in eleven weeks. Lionel gave me the names of some literary agents and I sent the manuscript off, only to have it returned with the kindly lie that the market for thrillers had collapsed. Again I threw the manuscript away, but, as I now recall, it was unpublishable and quite beyond remedy.

Subsequently in my twenties I wrote some science fiction short stories that were never intended for publication. Their interesting feature was that I began experimenting with pastiche, a technique I returned to more than twenty years later, when I began writing *Scherzo* in a bar in Bombay.

Turning thirty is a time when people often take a pause to think about their lives: a point at which we expect to have established the foundations and likely shape of life. It was the prospect of becoming thirty that in part made me quit the Bar and embark on another career; and, in the same vein, I decided that, if I were to regard myself as a writer, I'd better get down to the business of producing my first publishable novel.

That novel was *The Hitler Diaries*. It was to be a straightforward commercial thriller with no pretensions either to originality or fine writing. I began it in 1978 and finished the first draft two years later, shortly before the move from Wiltshire to the Manchester area.

In outline, it's about an attempt to publish a set of diaries from an unknown source, but purportedly written by Hitler. The hero is a controversial historian, very loosely modelled on David Irving (not himself a hero), who is tasked with verifying the authenticity of the text.

Does this sound familiar? It should. The novel was published in hardback nine months before the famous forgery was perpetrated and there was a remarkable similarity between the fictional and factual scenarios so that there was an interest from the press and I got a double page spread and photograph in the *Daily Mail*.

I wasn't wholly surprised by this. It seemed to me, even as I was writing the book, that the basic idea was an obvious one and I was surprised it hadn't been done before or, indeed, that no one had tried to fabricate a set of diaries. Forgery was in the air. There were doubts over Khruschev's memoirs. Alan Williams had written a decent thriller about Beria's diaries. Clifford Irvine had faked those of Howard Hughes.

My instinct was correct. Frederick Nolan was a thriller writer with a fair reputation and the Second World War was his ground. Shortly after Sphere published the paperback of my book, he wrote to one of the publishing periodicals accusing Sphere of taking an idea he'd originated and putting me up to write it.

According to Nolan – and I've no reason not to believe him – he'd been in negotiation for a book whose theme was precisely mine: the publication of Hitler's diaries. He gave some details, including the means by which the diaries were whisked out of Berlin in 1945 (which was one of the methods I actually considered, though I rejected it). He said the negotiations had been abandoned after he'd submitted some preparatory work to the very people who now published my novel. The coincidence was bizarre – but that's all it was: a coincidence. Other than denying Nolan's main allegation, my publishers and I did nothing. I've always been sympathetic to his point of view. The situation was so strange that his suspicions – even though mistaken – were entirely reasonable on the facts as he knew them.

The affair of the forgery and the intervention by Frederick Nolan were not the end of the coincidences that dogged this first book. My publisher took an interest in *The Hitler Diaries* because he he'd just been offered *The Goering Diaries*. He also happened to have published David Irving and recognised my 'hero'. His first conclusion was that Irving himself had written the book and inserted a flattering self-portrait.

On a trip to Zurich at about this time, I was explaining the business to a Swiss lawyer and had just got to the point in the story where I mentioned Clifford Irvine and the Howard Hughes affair when he smiled and revealed that he was Irvine's attorney, and proved it by producing a book signed by his client. Unsurprisingly the book was about forgery.

With all this in mind, I thought I was about to hit the big time and leap from trainee to actual millionaire in short order. My publishers sold the American, the Japanese, the Dutch and the Portuguese rights and I saw the words 'International Bestseller' on the (purely imaginary) cover.

It's no surprise then that I was feeling elated when I passed through a branch of John Menzies in Euston station, where the staff were reorganising a boxed display of bestsellers. The manager was standing over the girl, commenting as she placed each title; and I stood close by, leafing through a copy of Monty Python's *The Meaning of Life*, and ear-wigged the conversation.

The girl picked up a copy of *The Hitler Diaries* and looked to her boss for a cue. And all the while I waited for some words of praise – an anticipation of glory.

Well? Come on. *Say it!*

He shook his head.

'That one's been a disappointment.'

No, I'm sorry – repeat that – I didn't hear you – you meant...

'A disappointment.'

Oh...ah...yes...how true.

In fact *The Hitler Diaries* did well enough. The *Times*

Literary Supplement described it as '...an accomplished first novel. Richard Hugo writes with keen wit and sharp social observation and steadily builds up an impressive atmosphere of menace.' In the light of this and the foreign sales, my career as Richard Hugo, writer of thrillers seemed fairly begun. Macmillans, who'd brought out the hardback, bought my next effort, *Last Judgment*.

This second book was also a thriller, this time around the themes of a missing painting, lost in the War, and said to be by Da Vinci, and a German plan to launch a biological weapon in the final days of the Third Reich. It was conventional, but marked an advance on the first novel in being tautly plotted and faster paced. I got more decent reviews and international sales, but still nothing in the nature of a breakthrough that would establish my reputation.

My friend Alan Fox had been encouraged by my efforts to make an attempt of his own. He was an engineer and had some background in nuclear work. He came up with the notion of an incident at a Soviet nuclear reactor in which plutonium was dumped in a cooling water lake feeding the Volga with potentially catastrophic effects. He worked at his research on and off for a couple of years but couldn't bring himself to the actual writing of the book – not an unusual experience, I suspect. At all events, he gave me his notes and I worked them up into my third novel.

By comparison with the earlier novels, *Farewell to Russia* was naturalistic. The main characters weren't stereotypes and the action was fairly plausible. Stylistically it was influenced by Le Carré, though – I'm the first to admit – nowhere near as good. Still I think it was a decent book and Ted Allbeury gave it a very kind notice. He wrote, 'There are going to be very few novels of any kind this year that are as well written as *Farewell to Russia*. Totally authentic. Totally readable. Richard Hugo is one of the half dozen best writers on espionage that we have. Far too good to miss.' One of the strengths was that the story was based on the international contracting business and Eastern Europe, both of which subjects I knew first hand.

Four months after I delivered the manuscript, the disaster at Chernobyl happened. Though the details of that incident were different from the one in my book, it was still a chilling coincidence that my fictional nuclear catastrophe was followed by a real one. It revived memories of the diary business five years before and attracted some publicity. Nevertheless it wasn't a breakthrough book. I sold some international rights and made a little money, but this one like the others soon dropped out of sight and I didn't give up my day job.

In the real world the Cold War was coming to an end. It had been a staple for espionage writers and there were real issues over what would replace it as a subject. In the world of writers, Tom Clancy was pushing thrillers in a very heavily researched, high-tech direction, which I had no inclination to follow.

Conspiracy of Mirrors (which was published in the USA as *The Gorbachev Version*) was in the way of a swan song for the old Soviet Union. It was set in the transition time and one of its themes was the effort of a KGB agent to transform himself into a new kind of policemen suited to the changed conditions. It also contained one of my more complex plots based on the idea of 'The Great Jewish Antibiotics Ring'. This was a notional conspiracy that had continued for forty years. I say 'notional' because the whole point was that the conspiracy had no reality: it was merely a title to which successive generations of Soviet secret policemen fitted whatever supposed crimes they chose: it was in a sense a metaphor for the system of secrecy and paranoia.

Macmillans were at first very enthusiastic about the book, but they seemed to be the only ones. The critics ignored it and the sales were poor. Publishers will carry underperforming writers for only so long, and after four novels that had delivered only moderately, Macmillans were reaching the point of losing interest. And I can't say I blame them.

However I'm slightly in advance of the story. My editor at the date of *Conspiracy of Mirrors* was James Hale – one of the best in the business and a charming and sympathetic man. In the summer of 1988 we met for lunch at The George, opposite the Law Courts in the Strand, and had a general conversation about the state of the world.

A couple of years before, publishing had been shaken when someone had the idea of commissioning a sequel to *Gone With The Wind*, by a writer other than the original author. The book was lambasted by the critics but did well and set off a move to ransack popular classics for other money-spinners.

'I've got a suggestion of my own,' James said. 'Somebody should do a sequel to *Doctor Zhivago*.'

I agreed that someone should, and on the spot I came up with the notion of a novel based upon the subsequent life of Lara's daughter, Katya. But because the subject was a historical romance – a genre I hadn't worked in – and probably because I'm stupid at times, it didn't occur to me that James was intending I should write it. He had to tell me directly, 'You can do it. You have a wonderful sense of place and a feel for Russia.'

Me...? Oh, hell, why not.

That same day I bought a copy of the original novel and, before the week was out had produced a short outline and a first chapter. James and I convened a meeting with my agent.

Publishers prefer to deal with agents because the latter understand the business. My first editor, Alan Samson, had put me in touch with Vivienne Schuster, an excellent woman who handled my first four novels successfully and whom I liked. The meeting, however, wasn't a success.

Vivienne was concerned with the copyright issues surrounding *Doctor Zhivago* and, since our lunch at The George, James had become involved in one of the power struggles that seem to be endemic in publishers: he was distracted and left Macmillans soon afterwards, so that the book lost its sponsor.

Although my original motive had been coldly professional and frankly mercenary, I became attached to *Lara's Child* for its own sake. I pressed on unsupported and after twelve months I'd produced a third of the book, which I offered to Vivienne. She remained sceptical, but she tried one or two publishers and found no takers.

This was a blow. Because of the size of the task, I didn't feel I could continue unless there was some sign of interest, and so, reluctantly, I put the manuscript aside and reverted to writing thrillers. I spent 1990 writing *Charlie Ho and Kathleen Turner*. It bombed. Macmillans had lost interest with James's departure and no one else cared, so it was never published.

The end of that year marked a crisis. The market in thrillers was moving away from me with the end of the Cold War and the development of high-tech, high-action novels. *Lara's Child*, was incomplete and dormant. Vivienne had no suggestions and I felt she wasn't especially sympathetic to the direction that writing was taking me, though this comment shouldn't be taken as a criticism of her.

After leaving Macmillans, James Hale had set up as an agent on his own account. I phoned him one evening for a general chat. When I told him the situation concerning the Zhivago sequel – which he regarded as his baby – he volunteered to take me on if I'd explain to Vivienne that he hadn't made the first approach. I did as he asked, and from 1991 until his death in 2003, James was my agent and friend.

'You're going to be a multi-millionaire,' I was told quite

casually by one of the junior editors at Transworld. And so I was, apparently.

James quickly found a buyer for *Lara's Child* at a hefty sum for the UK and German rights. With the ever-kind Rosie Buckman, who handled foreign sales, he found takers for most of the overseas markets. One day we did a quick count and reckoned my share of the sales as a million before disposal of the American book and film rights. Oh, I was definitely going to be a multi-millionaire!

The problem was copyright. The protected period after Pasternak's death hadn't expired, but it wasn't clear who owned the rights to *Doctor Zhivago*, or whether my novel infringed those rights, or, indeed, whether the original was protected at all. Although I'm a lawyer, I couldn't make head or tale of the subject. Pasternak had certainly sold some of the rights to the Italian publisher, Feltrinelli, but the scope of the grant was unclear. There were also issues surrounding the circumstances of publication, which had been without permission of the Soviet Government and which Pasternak repudiated (though probably under pressure). Throw into this mix the application of various international copyright conventions and debates over how far I was really using Pasternak's material, and you'll see how confused everyone became.

Transworld took legal advice and obtained an opinion that *Lara's Child* was sufficiently distant from the original in terms of material that it didn't infringe any copyright that might exist. I seemed to be the only person who noticed that the lawyer expressing this opinion hadn't actually read the book and was therefore in a poor position to have any views on the subject. However, on the strength of that advice Transworld published in England and their parent, Bertelsmann, published in Germany. The other foreign editions were held pending any move by Feltrinelli after their threats to sue.

Feltrinelli sued.

Both Transworld and I were surprised that the Italians

didn't come to an accommodation to exploit the possibilities of a sequel to *Doctor Zhivago*, but they didn't. They may have had high-minded artistic motives or it may be simply a matter of wounded pride – I can only speculate. Whatever the case I've never held any feelings against Feltrinelli. They acted in good faith defence of what they saw as their rights, and their behaviour was entirely proper. I'm hardly in a position to complain even though their action was against my interests.

The suit was brought in Germany and Bertelsmann won in the lower court on the ground that *Lara's Child* was a loose adaptation, not close enough to the original to constitute an infringement. Feltrinelli appealed and won in the higher court. Bertelsmann's board then approved an appeal to the Supreme Court, but I never heard that it came off and I have to suppose it never happened. Events had overtaken it.

Perhaps naively I'd never doubted that *Lara's Child* would be a run-away best seller. I had no illusions that it was a work of great literary merit, though I'd written it seriously and competently and a number of critics had liked it well enough. *Scarlett*, the sequel to *Gone With The Wind*, had been generally rubbished but made money for all concerned. I'd no reason to suppose my case would be different.

With this background I appeared on television, sharing space with Minette Walters (whom I'd never heard of and who I thought was very small beer compared with the successful author I was about to become), and I was also a guest at the Cheltenham Literary Festival in the autumn of 1993. Everything seemed set fair and I waited for the public to buy the book.

They didn't.

Actually they did after a fashion – technically it was a bestseller for a nanosecond in both Britain and Germany – but the sales were way below expectations and I'm sure Bertelsmann made a loss on the advance. Why the book failed remains a mystery to me and the very fact that I don't understand is probably indicative of my limitations.

The failure of a book isn't an identifiable event: more a gradual fading, a silence where one expects applause. One day towards the end of 1994 I looked around at the world and it was much the same as it always had been – and, contrary to my expectations, I wasn't a millionaire at all.

I'm proud of *Lara's Child* and glad I wrote it despite the fact that the episode raised my hopes only to dash them. One of the benefits was a surprising insight into my own character.

During 1992 and 1993, when the affair was going well and I was being assured on all sides that I was going to be rich, I found the experience disconcerting and not entirely pleasurable. There were two reasons for this.

The first was moral – I was, after all, Nellie's boy, who'd been taught that money never did anybody any good: I was Hughie's boy, who'd learned that riches were not the reward of success but the spoils of chicanery. Of course I didn't think that writing *Lara's Child* was disreputable (quite the opposite: I think it's a moral book), but to be paid millions for doing it seemed to me wholly disproportionate to the effort. Still I have to be truthful: I imagine I'd have buried my qualms and kept the money – but I'm not so arrogant as to think I'd have deserved it.

My second reason was existential. A universe in which I was a millionaire simply wasn't believable. I passed the two years of my 'success' as if in a dream, not really crediting the solidity of the world that was being described to me. When the prospect of wealth vanished, it wasn't the real world that collapsed. On the contrary it was a fantasy that ended and reality reasserted itself. And I thought, 'Yes, of course. *This* is what life is really like.' And I continued my work as usual,

Don't mistake me. I'd have liked the money, though not for the high lifestyle but only the security so I could apply myself to writing full time. Even more than the money I'd have valued the recognition of my books (which confirms, I suspect, that I'm more than a little vain).

However I didn't become a millionaire and – for part of me at least – it was a great relief. I went back to the business of loving my family and being happy.

NOTES ON "THE TRAINEE MILLIONAIRE"

At first sight this essay deals specifically with my career as a writer and may have no obvious connection with your own life. However an alternative title might have been "WHAT I MOST WANTED TO DO", because its underlying theme is ambition. Although I don't think I'm generally an ambitious person, I really did want to become a successful writer – and for that matter I still do, though I recognise it's unlikely to happen at this stage of my life.

If you take ambition as your theme and forget the rest, there's enough in that subject for an essay, though it may be a painful one and I don't suggest it as a topic for a beginner. In organizing such an essay you may want to cover the following points:

(1) **What are my ambitions?** I don't consider the answer to this to be self-evident. It's very easy to think of conventional ambitions such as money or a successful career. In my case, however, my behaviour (as distinct from what I thought) shows that family and a desire for a quiet life figured more highly than I suspected.

(2) **What are the sources of my ambitions?** One reason for dealing with ambition as a late essay is that a reflection on other aspects of your life is necessary before a realistic answer to this question and some of the others can be attempted.

(3) **How did I set about realizing my ambitions? Who helped? Who hindered?**

(4) **Have I succeeded or failed in my ambitions?**

(5) **Why have I succeeded or failed in my ambitions? Am I the author of my own success or failure?** This question and the two preceding

ones contain something of a trap. They force you to examine the extent to which you accept responsibility for your life or blame others. Because it's the expected thing to do, almost everyone will *verbally* accept responsibility for their life before proceeding to attack the reputations of other people whom they really blame. A similar trap arises when someone is asked, 'Where do you think you've made mistakes and been at fault?' and replies, 'I'm too kind for my own good. I trust other people too much.' Properly examined, this isn't exactly a self-critical statement, but a fancy way of shifting blame. It's a sort of psychological game that may fool you, but it's unlikely to fool your readers. If you come up with these answers, it's time to think again.

(6) **How do I feel about my success or failure?** It's counter-intuitive to greet defeat with relief, but in the final section of this essay I suggest that my reaction to the failure of *Lara's Child* contained a substantial element of relief. I acknowledge that I may be merely rewarding myself with a moral consolation prize, but I don't think so. At all events you should test your own sincerity before coming to a conclusion.

Speaking generally I consider ambition to be a difficult subject to write about truthfully. In many societies (in America for example) ambition is regarded as an important positive cultural value, and this limits what we feel we can say and indeed distorts our ability to think about the subject in case we come up with answers that are heretical. We have a great deal of psychological investment in our ambitions, which drives us towards claiming the credit for their success and disclaiming real (as distinct from verbal) responsibility for their failure. After all, if my success has been principally due to dumb luck, what right do I have to keep the money? Maybe I should give it to the poor?

In brief what bedevils an honest treatment of this subject is self-interested, conventional thinking. Can you be detached enough to overcome it? Can you face answers that may be unpleasant? Before you respond, consider that the reply 'Yes, I can face up to unpleasant truths' may be no more than another piece of psychological trickery: a purely verbal concession made only because it's the expected thing.

I want to turn now to editing: specifically to moving material so that it finally appears in the appropriate place and to minimizing repetition. My friend and agent, James Hale, appears in another essay, *James Hale and Oscar the Cat*, which is included later in this collection though in fact it was written first. When I wrote it I didn't have the present essay in mind or any firm plan for organizing this book. It followed that, at the time, I had to include in the essay all the information necessary to make it intelligible even though such information might not be relevant to the main theme. In the particular instance, the subject is largely James's character and it contains a number of letters I wrote to him as he was dying. Yet, clearly, it's necessary for the reader to understand who James is and my connection with him. This follows from the principle, announced at the outset, that essays should be self-contained enough that they can be read satisfactorily as stand-alone pieces.

In the original version of *James Hale and Oscar the Cat*, I included a section on the subject of *Lara's Child* in order to explain our connection. That material is now covered in the present essay as part of a larger discussion of my writing career. To avoid repetition, I've therefore cut the passage in the later essay and, when you read it, you should have no difficulty spotting the patch inserted by me to bridge the gap caused by the cut.

This piece of editing stems specifically from the decision to collect my essays and arrange them in a particular order and it could only be made relatively late in the day. Once that decision had been taken, it was no longer necessary to stick to the principle that the essays be self-contained. It was possible to recognise that the other essays existed and to reorganize my material to insert it in more appropriate places and reduce duplication.

A more radical piece of editing has involved the elimination of an entire essay. It was one of the first I wrote and its subject was the effect of our backgrounds and education (mine, Nellie's and Hughie's) on our ability to interpret the world. The same theme is touched on here and there among a number of the early essays. The deleted essay (which was called *The Filing Cabinet In The Corner*) was fine as an item in isolation, but when I placed it among the others it seemed to have no identity of its own and simply intrude in the development of the story of my family and my early history. Accordingly, I took out of it a couple of passages and placed them elsewhere. And the rest has gone.

To follow this point you should turn back to two of the earlier essays. In *Nellie* I recount her conversation about the mysterious 'Old King', and in *The Last Cowboy in Wrexham* I tell of my father's prejudice against Churchill because of 'Tonypandy'. Both of these stories have been taken from the deleted essay and weren't in the first drafts of the essays where you now find them. Because they represent a late change, if you look carefully you should be able to see the joints to the passages either side.

If you remember the discussion in the notes to my first essay, when I mentioned *pericopes* – short loosely connected pieces – this ability to move material around should be understandable. In the case of the 'Old King' and 'Churchill' stories, it really doesn't matter when, where or how they happened. Their only significance is as an illustration of my parents' characters and backgrounds, and their final location has been decided with that object in mind.

This discussion of editing is limited to organizing your material and reducing duplication (though I've kept more duplication than I would do in a novel, so the character of my pieces as essays should still be obvious). You can also edit for grammar and style, but that's outside the subject of this book.

BIZARRE AND DANGEROUS

Before Feltrinelli engineered my downfall and I was still
in millionaire mode, I began work on *Irina's Story*. It was
to be another panoramic historical romance set in Russia,
though it had no other connection with *Lara's Child.*
James Hale had a grand scheme for my future, which
involved turning historical potboilers out at a couple of
hundred thousand pounds a time to top up my millions.

We joked about it. I was to be The Greatest Living
Nineteen Century Russian Novelist Writing In English.
My pen name was Alexander Mollin.

Transworld gave me a small advance prior to delivery
of the manuscript of the new book, but by the time it was
completed in 1995 the indifferent performance of *Lara's
Child* and the litigation in Germany had caused my stock
to plummet. Personal relations remained good, but they
wanted nothing more of me. *Irina's Story* was not at that
date published. It represented two and a half years work.

For the better part of twelve months I was bereft of
ideas. I'd attempted two genres of fiction and after a little
early success had failed at both. Now I had neither a
publisher nor an idea for a book.

One morning I was listening to the radio at breakfast
when I picked up an item about *castrato* opera singers.
Castrati were male sopranos, created, as the name
suggests, by the emasculation of young boys. They were
particularly characteristic of Italy in the eighteenth
century, when some, like Farinelli, had the status of pop
stars. All of this is bye the bye: what struck me was that a
castrato opera singer would make a good detective in a
murder mystery.

God alone knows why I thought so.

The three years from 1996 to 1999 have been the most enjoyable and most productive of my writing career – a surprising outcome from a dismal beginning. During that time I wrote three technically difficult and original murder mysteries and, if I didn't succeed in reinventing the genre (which was my ambition), I had great fun. At the end I fell flat on my face again, but I'm so used to it that it scarcely matters.

In the beginning my aim was more modest. I wanted to write a fairly light-hearted murder mystery with a novelty detective. The character of my hero, Ludovico Il Tedesco, a twenty-one year old *castrato*, pimp, liar and coward, impressed itself so strongly on me that I started with little more than that and a vague notion of a setting in eighteenth century Venice.

This is the origin of *Scherzo*, which I began in the poolside bar of an hotel in Bombay during a break after the battle with the Brothers Grimm.

The plot can be explained briefly. Ludovico is a poor singer who gives concerts for the nobility. His patron is Signor Morosini. Another nobleman, Signor Alessandro Mollin, is murdered one night in circumstances suggesting a ritual slaying. Ludovico becomes involved in the investigation through an association with a visiting Frenchman, Monsieur Arouet, who may or may not be Voltaire. The route to an eventual solution takes him through encounters with a beautiful widow, a vengeful son, a mad Jesuit, sundry Freemasons and Casanova, and the conclusion is a dramatic fire.

The narrative is in the first person and is in a pastiche of eighteenth century style. It uses the form of the 'epistolary novel', a kind common at the time in which the action is told through letters and diaries. The tone is comic and there's a motif of forgery and impersonation, which are subjects that interest me

The style and form were adventurous in themselves, but

in addition the novel has two other unusual features, which I was to employ on the others in this series.

The first is a shift in the focus of interest. In the conventional murder mystery the identity of the murderer is central. *Scherzo* retains this element, but adds to it a further one, namely a mystery as to the identity of the detective. Ludovico isn't the detective. He's the Watson figure reporting the doings of his master, Monsieur Arouet. But who is Arouet? Is he the philosopher Voltaire, traveling *incognito*, or is he a charlatan trading on Voltaire's name? The reader can never be absolutely certain.

The second distinctive feature is a residual doubt as to the solution to the mystery. Monsieur Arouet presents one, which is accepted by the other characters, but, as Ludovico points out, there are two alternatives, both of which account for the evidence. The official solution *may* be true, but it's accepted largely because it's convenient. In this respect *Scherzo* differs from most whodunits, which claim to know what 'really' happened.

It took James Hale several attempts before he could find a publisher who was receptive to a book as strange as *Scherzo*, but the one who was – Nick Webb of Simon & Schuster – fell for it completely. He simply loved it.

I knew Nick slightly through my friendship with Lionel Trippett, who'd worked with him before Lionel took up pornography and a job with the Campaign for Nuclear Disarmament. In fact Nick had published *Last Judgment* in paperback almost a dozen years before, but the contact was very slight.

Nick's enthusiasm struck even me as excessive and resulted in an odd difference of opinion. I was firmly of the view that all I'd written was an amusing murder mystery. Nick, on the other hand, insisted it was a literary novel of great merit. And he backed his judgment by submitting *Scherzo* for the Booker Prize.

'It doesn't cost anything,' said Lionel with a hint of

1

malice when I broke the news. 'And it means he doesn't expect it to sell. Literary novels don't sell – unless they win the Booker, of course.'

Scherzo didn't win the Booker – didn't even make the shortlist. And neither did it sell.

Instead it received a very handsome notice from Frances Fyfield in the *Mail on Sunday*. She described it as a 'sparkling and utterly charming novel' with a 'devilishly clever plot and deceitful finale'.

Writing *Scherzo* and Nick's fulsome tribute increased my confidence. For the next novel I decided to try something outrageous.

I'd been interested in Proust since Fanny Kuler, my French teacher, introduced me to him at school, though I'd never got beyond reading *Swann's Way*. One of the technical ideas that now began to interest me was that of using other styles of writing than that usual for murder mysteries: Proust or Shakespeare for example.

'It's a literary conceit,' Lionel sniffed, adding, 'Nobody much does it these days.'

Taking my line from Proust, I wrote *Recherché*. Its principal themes are the reliability of memory and the function of stories.

The Narrator, John Harper, is a middle-aged lawyer who has abandoned his wife to run off to the south of France with his secretary, Lucy, who's twenty years his junior. There they fall into the company of an elderly neighbour, the exotic Harry Haze, a central European émigré who's spent a lot of time in the United States. He begins to tell the lovers his life story – beginning with the statement that he's a vampire.

Lucy disappears but no body is found. The police suspect Harper of killing her but have insufficient evidence to arrest him. Meantime Harry continues to tell his tales, which become increasingly strange and comic. Clearly they're fantastic – but in that case why is he telling them? The Narrator suspects they possess a moral which he, Harper, is meant to understand, or possibly they have a hidden meaning that disguises an incident Harry can't bear to talk about openly. Then Harper catches a glimpse of Lucy under circumstances that suggest she has perhaps become a vampire.

In *Recherché* I developed further the technique of pastiche. In *Scherzo* I'd limited myself to taking off an eighteenth century style, but now I had Harry tell his stories as Proust, Oscar Wilde, Damon Runyan, Vladimir Nabokov and others. In addition I used what the Germans call *Rahmentechnik*, a method in which one story is enclosed inside another: in this case Harry's stories are included in the broader account given by the Narrator.

Again I re-focused the nature of the mystery. The reader is drawn to expect the central murder to occur in Harper's story of the events surrounding Lucy and her disappearance. The reason is simple: the Narrator's account seems 'real' because it resembles ordinary life more closely than Harry's tales which are obviously silly. However, whatever other significance Harry's tales may have, they also hint at a night of sheer horror and bloodshed that occurred one autumn fifty years before in a small American town – *if Harry can be believed*. In short the murder is located in Harry's fantasy world where the reader does not expect it.

In the end the book offers solutions both to the mysterious disappearance of Lucy and also to the meaning of Harry's stories. However we can accept these solutions only if we can believe the Narrator. But can we? Harry's stories remind us we can't always rely on others to speak the truth, and Harper himself is deeply implicated in the events he describes and may have motives for lying. He claims to have seen Lucy alive after her disappearance – but we only have his word for this.

Nick Webb was enthusiastic about *Recherché* as he had been for its predecessor. *The Guardian* described it as 'a skilful exercise, bizarre and dangerous, in a lineage that includes Fowles' *The Magus*'. Neither opinion did me any good and the book sold poorly.

Of all my creations, Harry Haze – vampire, war criminal, stand-up Jewish comic, possible murderer, and teller of fantastic stories – is the one of which I am most pleased. I too am a storyteller and there's something of the snake oil salesman in me. Sometimes I feel a vocation to bring spiritual comfort to the very rich. I think what holds me back is the fundamental decency of my parents and the lessons learned at Methodist Sunday School. Also Shirley would laugh at me.

The third of my literary murder mysteries was *The Strange Death of a Romantic*.

The hero, Guy Parrot, is a doctor who at the end of the War finds himself commissioned to establish a small army hospital in a villa near La Spezia in Italy. To his horror the villa is the same one in which he stayed with a group of rich friends in the summer of 1930, during which something happened that caused him to have a nervous breakdown. La Spezia is also the place where the poet Shelley was living when he met his death in a sailing accident in 1822.

During the holiday in 1930, Guy and his friends spend their evenings telling stories to each other. Their subject is the death of Shelley, which they decide to treat as a murder mystery. As the stories are told, they come closer to establishing that Shelley was in fact murdered and the identity of the murderer. At the same time, the stories have a subtext reflecting tensions within the group of friends which will end in a death and a disappearance.

In the course of renovating the villa in 1945, Guy uncovers a skeleton in a water cistern that supplies the house. He connects it with the events of 1930 though he has no idea of who the person is. The solution to this mystery will provide Guy with the key to understanding the events of 1930 that had almost destroyed him.

In *Strange Death* I pushed parody and pastiche to their extreme. Each of the stories told by the party of friends is in a different style, and so we have the murder of Shelley in versions resembling *Rebecca*, a Noël Coward drawing room comedy, *Just William*, a Barbara Cartland romance, an American crime novel of the thirties, and Byron's *Don Juan*. I also developed my use of *Rahmentechnik*. The book runs three storylines simultaneously: the events of 1945, 1930 and 1822. This may sound complicated but in fact the book is funny.

As with the earlier novels I tried to change the nature of the central mystery. Previously I'd turned it into the mystery of the identity of the detective and then relocated the murder so that it happened in the 'wrong' place. In *The Strange Death of a Romantic* I devised a murder without a victim. The reader is presented with a 'solution' to the 'murder' of Shelley and the murderer is named. Yet everyone – including the characters in the book – knows that Shelley died in an accident and wasn't murdered by my suggested murderer, or, indeed, by anyone.

'Good God!' said Nick when he saw the manuscript.

T. J. Binyon, in the *Evening Standard* called it 'the most interesting crime novel of the year', and added generously, 'Williams writes with great wit, subtlety and assurance – any book which contains in its opening pages the sentence, "The moon was up, the sky a limpid violet, and the Americans were romantically bombing Bologna" immediately captures the attention.'

This time there was no talk of the Booker, but I was told that one of the judges suggested the novel be put up for the Golden Dagger. I don't know if that was done. I heard no more of it.

Again, despite the high opinion of Nick Webb and the good review, the book sold poorly. Recently [December 2004] I saw it remaindered at a bookshop in Bath.

Shortly after buying *The Strange Death of a Romantic*, Nick went down in a management fight and left Simon & Schuster. I owe him an enormous debt because he kept faith with me despite poor sales and allowed me to write three books of which I'm proud and which I very much enjoyed doing. After his departure, it wasn't to be expected that his successor would pick up Nick's pet project and when I delivered my next manuscript it was rejected.

And that's pretty much how things stand, with my writing stalled, though I keep my hand in with various projects, including these essays. I can't say if I'll be published again or not.

My career as a writer has last twenty-five or so years [1978 – 2004] and I've had eight novels published. During that time seven years have been wasted on five books that so far have come to nothing. On each occasion I've had to take my knocks and start all over again. This may explain my emphasis on the psychological aspect of writing: the necessity of driving oneself to a task that's often thankless.

James Hale told me that I was in the top twenty per cent of earners, and I imagine this to be true. However, as with all the arts, earnings are steeply skewed in favour of a tiny number at the very top and the majority have to get by with a day job.

The fact that I've received little recognition as a writer doesn't detract from the joy and satisfaction I've had from my efforts. I'm also very sympathetic towards those people who aspire to be published but will never realize their dream. The truth is there is prestige attached to being a published author, even in a small way. And it's been fun.

I've also met some wonderful people.

I arranged to meet Helen Simpson outside the British Museum – which turned out to be convenient for her favourite boozer. A short, cuddly, bubbly woman with earrings like Christmas tree baubles and a mass of ethnic rings erupted in my direction, waving a *Gitane*. She escorted me to The Plough, where we consumed pints of bitter.

Helen is a copy editor. Nick Webb pushed her in my direction to work with me on the three books we did together. Her dedication and talents are enormous. To be a good copy editor requires great powers of concentration and thoroughness to correct errors and clumsiness in the author's text. Copy editors are also fact checkers who save writers from their own ignorance. Helen attacked my books with a passion and forced me to write as well as I can. And in the process she became a close friend.

It was Helen who introduced me to Adrian Dowson, a talented artist forced to turn his hand to anything to make a living: book jackets, tarot cards – whatever pays.

Chatting with her on one occasion at The Plough I asked, 'How's Adrian? What's he doing at the moment?'

'Adrian?' Helen said breathily through a fug of cigarette smoke. 'Oh, I think he's designing a website for a lesbian. She runs a sado-masochistic brothel in the Czech Republic.'

Perhaps it isn't my work that's bizarre and dangerous after all.

NOTES TO "BIZARRE AND DANGEROUS"

In my 'bizarre and dangerous' novel *Recherché*, Lucy, speaking about Harry Haze, says to the Narrator, 'Your problem, John, is that you look for explanations in the wrong place. Do you remember when we heard the first of Harry's stories? We wondered why Harry was telling them, what they meant – as if there were an explanation outside them. There isn't. Harry told his stories the only way he knew. If he had understood more or differently, the stories would have been different. Do you follow me? The stories can't be explained – at least not by Harry. They *are* the explanation.'

Critics make a distinction between texts that are 'open' or 'closed' according to how susceptible they are to different readings. An almost perfect example of a closed text is a telephone directory. It has only one function and one interpretation.

Works of art are more open and, speaking generally, the more open they are, the greater the reward from studying them: though the corollary is that they're more demanding. Conflict can come about when there's disagreement over this fundamental aspect of a text. Religious persecution has arisen because, for dogmatic reasons, churches have regarded the Bible as closed and claimed to know its 'real' meaning, when the truth is that it's a very open text – the proof being the number of different Christian sects.

Of all my books, *Recherché* is the most open to interpretation. Indeed – odd though it may seem given that I wrote it – I'm not at all sure what it means. To paraphrase from the passage just quoted: the book isn't a thing to be explained: it *is* the explanation as best as I can give it.

By analogy, human lives are open texts. If it weren't so, it would be unnecessary for each generation to re-write the biographies of the past, and whether Napoleon was primarily a military dictator or an enlightened statesman would have been definitely settled.

The extent to which your autobiography is an open or closed text will depend on the degree to which you apply specific interpretations: the extent to which you claim to know your own character, the causes of the things that have happened to you and the meaning of your life. It isn't my intention to discourage you from trying to make sense of everything: one of the benefits of writing an autobiography is precisely that it gives us a chance to think about these things. Some interpretation is in any case inevitable: it's implicit in the selection and organisation of our material and the way we tell our story. What you mustn't expect is that others will inevitably accept your reading of your life.

My own autobiography is written light-heartedly, but nothing in the contents says it has to be. Nothing in the bare facts of being born into relative poverty and following a mediocre career as a lawyer and writer leads necessarily to feeling happy about the whole business. I just am.

Why?

I don't know. This book really *is* the explanation.

James Hale and Oscar the Cat

I got to know James in 1981 when Macmillans were publishing my first novel *The Hitler Diaries* and he was working as a senior editor. When Alan Samson, the editorial director, left we did a couple of books together. By common consent he was one of the finest editors of his generation. I found his contribution to my books invaluable because he loved them and was deeply committed to getting his authors to make the best of themselves.

It was James who proposed one day in 1988 in a boozer opposite the Law Courts, that I write a sequel to *Doctor Zhivago*. It was a mischievous suggestion and caused no end of trouble, but like a pair of giggling kids we thought it was a wonderful idea and I set about it.

For unconnected reasons nothing came of the book at that date. James was involved in one of the mysterious blood-lettings that go on from time to time in publishing firms, like the last act in a revenge tragedy with bodies all over the stage. He left and set himself up as an agent and I had no further contact with him for the better part of three years. He became my agent only after I parted company with Vivienne Schuster (about whom I have no word of complaint).

Together James and I did *Lara's Child* and the three 'bizarre' novels. At the time of his death, there were two novels in manuscript, which he was trying unsuccessfully to sell. This failure must have disappointed him, but it was in no way his fault. In fact I remain astonished and humbled by the dedication with which he worked to the end.

My family acquired two cats. Puzzle was a sleek, tiny, pretty, nervous queen. My soft-hearted daughter, Hannah, picked Oscar: the unwanted end of a litter who turned into a ragged, disreputable-looking character with a lop-sided ear, bad teeth, a droopy belly and a smelly collection of bum tags. But he had charisma.

James was a cat person. I was an occasional visitor to his house in Peckham and was pestered by a pair of handsome felines as he busied to cook one of his special omelettes for the two of us. Outside the sun shone on his neatly tended walled garden. Inside, he smiled sunnily, smoked a cigarette and sipped at a glass of white wine while regaling me with gently humorous stories about publishing.

It was early 2001 when I discovered he had cancer. He had a long spell in hospital and, once he came out, admitted he had only a couple of years to go.

'What are you going to do?' I asked.

'Carry on as before,' he said. And he did.

During what was left to him, we spoke at least once a week on the phone. He was always his blithe, charming self: alert, alive, interested in others and deeply sympathetic. Though long expected, his death came almost as a shock because he never hinted at any regret or concern for himself. It was an inspiring performance.

James lived in London and I lived in the north; so, although we often spoke, we met infrequently. Accordingly, during that first illness, all I could do was drop him a few lines of e-mail. It was difficult to think of a suitable subject or a suitable tone. After a few words concerning his situation, which would probably come over as platitudes, what was there to say? In the end, knowing his love of cats, I hit on the happy idea of writing about the doings of Oscar, and afterwards, among other things, we chatted about my hero moggie.

At the beginning of August 2003, James went into hospital for a second and final time. I wrote to him, proposing a visit. Hilary replied, saying he was too ill to receive many visitors but inviting me to write to him again about Oscar because he had so much enjoyed reading about the old fellow.

So I did, and what follows is my account of Oscar as told to James in his last days.

7th August 2003

PROFOUND THOUGHTS FROM OSCAR THE CAT

James,

I told my old tom, Oscar, that you were in hospital again. "Who the fuck's he?" he mumbled before telling me to get out of his light. That cat! What an ironist!

I've just got back from India. "Wotcha bring me?" asked Oscar, but his attention span is poor and he stuck his nose into the cattochunks before I could answer. I brought him my own cheery self, I wanted to say, but I don't know that he cares. Buddha had something to say about letting everything go, but I think that was in favour of serenity rather than cattochunks. Still, my cat is a Buddhist after his own fashion.

The window of the office where I was working in Delhi overlooked a main highway. A poor woman with a cart had set up a food stall there. It was heaped with maize cobs, which she roasted on a charcoal fire kept going with a small straw fan. Workers and the general crowd of scroungers one finds in India stopped there for lunch. Then, in a wonderful display of ecology, two cows turned up and began dining on the outer leaves of the maize cobs, which were thrown onto the ground. So, when the woman finally leaves, there are two satisfied cows and nary a sign of waste. Good innit?

Read and laugh. My thoughts and hopes go with you.
Love
Jim

8th August 2003

MORE OF OSCAR'S WISDOM

Dear James,

In this hot weather Oscar lies about, fermenting like the contents of a restaurant skip. He is attending to the Tao *of his cushion: exploring its essential cushionness.*

Some years ago we were on holiday in France and walking down a country lane flanked by a hedge. Everything seemed so peaceful and harmless in the sunshine, but, when I came to glance at the hedge, I saw that it was set with spider webs along the whole of its length, and in the centre of each web was a colourful spider so that the whole row was a gigantic trap for flies. So it seemed that my first take on the scene – true enough as far as it went – ignored another more sinister meaning, though that too was beautiful in its way (the webs milky with dew and the spiders large and bright).

I was reminded of this image in the hotel in Delhi, where the first floor comprises nothing but shops: jeweller – carpet vendor – shawls – jeweller – carpet vendor – shawls etc. circling a large atrium. And lounging out the front of each shop is the owner or one of his lads: bored, hungry, predatory: waiting to catch a passing tourist, spin him in a shawl and bleed him of cash. Well, they got me, didn't they?

Next week (14 August to be precise) is our 33rd anniversary and at the beginning of September Shirley and I are going back to the village where we spent our honeymoon. In Delhi I had a ring made up for the occasion: a peridot set in six small diamonds, rather art deco *in feeling.*

"Whaddaya think?" I asked Oscar.

"Hghrrumph!" he said, and hawked up a porridge of cattochunks wrapped in a hairball. His humour runs to the satirical and the style owes something to German

Expressionism.

There we have it really. I am a shallow soul, sentimental in nature and attaching importance to trinkets. Oscar is aloof, sardonic, minimalist. Exploring the Tao *of his cushion is his life's work, and who's to say he's wrong?*

"Speak some words of wisdom to me, O Sage One!" I ask him.

He gives me the glassy look.

"Jeez! I love it when you scratch my arse!" he says, and his mad yellow eyes roll over.

Am I ever going to figure that cat out?

Love

Jim

James replied the same day.

Dear Jim,

First forgive writing, spelling and grammar; for some reason these faculties have deserted me (you will understand that Hilary has now taken over at the keyboard).

I have the greatest admiration for Oscar; he clearly knows a diamond when he sees one.

I'm going to write to you again when my brain has come back. Meanwhile, hang in there and thanks for all your warm and affectionate messages.

All the best

James

P.S. Love to see you; but I'm not quite ready yet.

In the event, James never did write again and I never saw him. All I could do was keep telling him about Oscar.

11 August 2003

I HOPE YOU PASSED A COMFORTABLE WEEKEND

Dear James,

The wild strawberries tickle Oscar's belly as he toddles down the terrace steps to the lawn about his mysterious purposes. There he goes: fat, floppy-eared, weepy-eyed; his fur gathering twigs, rubble and bum tags. He doesn't care. He has spiritual gifts, and apart from his cushion and cattochunks, cares nothing for material things. He is a Franciscan.

I mentioned that Shirley and I were returning this year to Slapton in Devon, where we passed our honeymoon. It was there that, walking in the pitch night with the sea to my right and the freshwater lee to my left, I first saw the Milky Way. I was twenty-two. In the village is a ramshackle Georgian manor house with the owl-haunted ruin of a chantry tower. We rented a flat there and, being too poor to have a car, pottered about the beach or took the bus to Plymouth. The tower was in the remains of a walled monastic garden, and there Shirley and I stripped to the buff and capered about giggling.

We returned next year and this time I found an old novel by Arnold Bennet, a charming thing about a man who takes up writing while sick and becomes a successful popular novelist. It was printed on a thick cartridge, bound in blue board, damp, faded, foxed – and smelling wonderful so that I remember it thirty-two years on. I love the smell of books and always sniff them when I read. In 1992 in a store in Princes Street Edinburgh, I was tempted to buy some aftershave because it reminded me of old damp books. When I go on holiday I always want to visit second hand bookshops. Their scents seem to bind together all the holidays I have ever had (including one in Paignton when I was fifteen and bought H Trevor Roper's

The Origins of the Second World War*) in one continuous thread of experience. We returned to Slapton a dozen years ago (a nice edition of* Earthly Powers *seen in Totnes where there is a marvellous tea shop – but I had the book already – still I remember this copy) and went on a guided tour of the flora in the woods and margins of the lee and along the shore. What I want, however, is to be twenty-two again and doing rude things with Shirley in the ivy shadows of a sunlit garden.*

Meantime my furry pilgrim, Brother Oscar, trundles about the garden ferreting in the bushes.

"Do you like the smell of old books?" I ask speculatively (knowing so little of the life of cats – it may be possible).

A cautious eye, all scabbed with grunge, glares at me. "Naw – cattochunks," he answers at length.

"You like the smell of cattochunks?" I ask.

"And my bum," he says and gives the article a lick.

Books and bums? – the principle could be the same in both cases, I suppose.

He remains distracted. What are *cats up to in my garden?*

Somewhat morose, he says, "I don't suppose you've seen my testicles, have you? I could swear I used to have a pair. I must have put the bloody things down somewhere and forgot."

I don't have the heart to tell him.

Love
Jim

Hilary wrote next.

12 August 2003

Dear Jim,
I really can't tell you how much James appreciates the activities of Oscar.

207

He's very weak now, Jim, but when I read them to him there is that wonderfully familiar smile on his face. Keep them coming, if you can.

Bless you
Hilary

So I carried on.

12 August 2003

OSCAR AND UNCLE JOE

Dear James,
Oscar may be of a religious and philosophical temperament, but I receive hints that he is not wholly above the issues that trouble the rest of us. When I arrive home, I often find him lurking furtively by the garage. I had occasion to look down the side where the garage abuts the hedge, and what did I find but a massive heap of spent cigarettes ("dimps", my father called them, who would search for and smoke them when he was broke). Now, I admit to being addicted to the weed until a couple of years ago, but surely my contribution to the pile would have rotted by now? I have to face it, my cat may be a smoker.

My mother's brother, my bachelor Uncle Joe, used to lounge in bed of an evening smoking Park Drive *and listening on an ancient wireless set labelled with exotic stations like Hilversum. His fingers were nicotine stained and he had a long, horny thumbnail he used for trimming wallpaper (he was a decorator). He kept a seven foot high, homemade, luminous Frankenstein in his kitchen.*

When he moved in with my parents, it was like having a character from Pinter come to stay. He was tall and gaunt and walked with a loping stride; his manner was cheekily lugubrious and his conversation laconic, never stretching much beyond "How do, lad?" Imagine Max Wall and you won't be far from Uncle Joe.

Now what is the connection with Oscar? It is the sense of being in the presence of an intelligence which is self-contained and deeply obscure. With Joe it was always like having an oversized cat in the house: someone who did not engage in conversation, who demanded little beyond his food and fags, and who wandered off in the evenings, stalking the streets like a revenant, *occasionally dropping into a pub for a pint. It was disconcerting to think that this was one way that a human life could be lived and still be apparently happy.*

"What did you make of Uncle Joe?" I ask Oscar.

"You talkin' to me, white boy?" he replies.

"Sorry – forgot – Uncle Joe was before your time."

Oscar says nothing. He fixes me with his glittering weepy eyes for a moment, then sticks his snout into his bowl of cattochunks. But in that moment I have an uncanny sensation. I mean: one hears about reincarnation, eh? I make no claims, but one has to wonder…

"I'll be outside by the garage if you need me," says Oscar.

"OK."

"I don't suppose you've got any…?" He shifts from one foot to the other. "No, don't bother. I'll see to myself."

Did he mean Park Drive *cigarettes?*

"Oscar, did you mean…?"

I must stop talking to cats. The buggers don't respect you.

Keep safe, James
Love
Jim

It was obvious that the end was close. In my next letter I tried to say something of how fond of James I was and how grateful for his friendship. I discussed this writing thing that we were engaged in.

13 August 2003

OSCAR FOR THE BOOKER!

Dear James,

"I fancy taking a crack at the writing game," said Oscar. "It can't be all that difficult if you do it." (He's always full of himself when I've got rid of his fleas.)

"You have to be able to write well," I told him.

"Look who's talking! Shakespeare already!"

I was watching TV when he came to sit on my face.

"You're upset," I told him. We have foxes in the garden, and when they're around he can't slip out for a smoke.

He stared at me balefully.

"I'm twelve years old, fer chrissakes!" he said. "My best years are behind me!"

I know what he means. At my age I no longer expect success, not that I mind overmuch: a bit of disappointment keeps me on my moral toes. The truth is that for much of my life I've behaved like a prick, and that's a defect rarely improved by lashings of fame and money – not that I wouldn't be prepared to take my chances if they came my way. Failure seems to have brought out my warmer sympathies for the human condition.

"There's no money in writing," I said. But Brother Oscar is a true Franciscan.

"All I need is a few bob for my cattochunks. Speaking of which..." he flopped off my lap to have a speculative rummage in his bowl. "Look at me! Look at me! I'm eating! Look at me!"

As always Oscar goes to the heart of matters. Writers will do it for cat food as long as there's someone watching.

Why did we do all that stuff, James? What a pair of wankers we were if it was only for fame and money. No, I think there was a vision in the books, even though we

210

struggled to get it out. Aldous Huxley said that the agonies of mediocre writers are as heartfelt as those of their betters – just not as well expressed ("Who the fuck is Aldous Whatshisface?" asks Oscar. "You being literary again?"). The process is always more important than the ostensible goal, which amounts to nothing once the game pieces go back in the box. The joy and reward of writing, as of every other activity, come from human interaction. I'm glad I did the books with you, James, and no one else. How otherwise could I have experienced the glamour and excitement of Lara's Child*? How should I have had the confidence to attempt the exotic crime novels? The journey really was more fulfilling than the destination, and I owe that to you.*

Oscar so far hasn't produced anything. I asked why not.

He opened one eye. "So much to do and so little time. Writing – cattochunks – cushion. Two out of three ain't bad."

There's no distracting a Spiritual Giant like Oscar. For him the Way of the Cushion is everything. Still, he has insights into the world of us lesser hylics.

"I've been reading the literary press," he said.

"I'm impressed," I admitted.

"Would I make it as a writer if my tits were bigger?"

Love

Jim

It's legitimate to ask to whom I was really writing at this stage. Though nothing was said, I knew it was unlikely that James was any longer in a position to follow my ramblings – or, indeed, Oscar's. But throughout his illness he'd insisted with courage and cheerfulness on being the same old James that everyone loved. Unable to imagine any other, I continued writing to that one, and the subject was something I knew would interest him. In the event it's probable he died even before my letter arrived.

211

Here it is anyway.

14 August 2004

OSCAR THE METAPHYSICIAN

Dear James,
Today is our thirty-third anniversary and we have never been happier in each other. I gave Shirley the peridot ring. Oscar looked at it sceptically. "So what would you have given?" I asked him.

"Cattochunks?" he offered. "A cushion?" His eyes glazed over dreamily. Sometimes his limitations show.

We met at University and, on graduation, went down to London together, two impossibly naïve working class kids from the North. I didn't even have a bed for the night, but found a sofa at the home of Olive Brown, a widow of the Raj and the former landlady of Lionel the Pornographer.

James, do you remember Lionel? We talked about him for almost twenty years but you never met him. He was in the literature racket, too, and his conversation over more than thirty years was a roman fleuve *in which, like Nicholas Jenkins, we revisited the same cast of characters as they got older and, after such a length of time, I could never recall with certainty which ones I knew in the flesh and which ones were creatures of Lionel's narration.*

As a writer, I find something deeply appealing and a little poignant in the notion that we have parallel existences populating other people's stories: that, indeed, for some whom we have never met, our fictive characters have more reality (and are definitely more vivid) than the dull originals.

Somewhere there is a crowd of Jameses, Hilarys, Jims and Shirleys, quite likely more amusing and debonair than we are, and the thought is charming and rather comforting. They step into stories like guests at a cocktail party, staying only as long as we like them and then leaving in a whiff of glamour to be met again at another party.

There is a natural biography quite different in structure from the chronology-driven formal biographies. It comprises a disconnected collection of pericopes, each beginning, "I remember the time when…" And with those words we are off on a delicious ramble that has no particular connection with the ordinary run of Time, in which story calls up story until we are sated. Mmmm! Yes!

Oscar wanders in from the garden, where he has been having a quiet drag and searching for his lost testicles. He flops onto my lap and stares into my eyes.

He says, "I've got this scab right in the middle of my back where I can't reach it. I was wondering…?"

He nuzzles me until I stroke him and meanwhile glances at this letter.

"Wossa 'pericope'?" he asks

"I don't know. It's a posh word and I thought I'd use it – try it out and see if it suits me."

"There – there – scratch me there! Ooooh Aaaah!" Already it seems he's forgotten the train of thought, but then he snorts, "The things you write. You'll be saying next that you're a figment of my imagination."

Am I a figment of my cat's imagination?

Love

Jim

So James died. Hilary informed me in a very kind letter. Part of it reads: "*James died at noon today. He was very peaceful and he was ready to go, so it was the right time. He was doped up for the last 36 hours, but I read him Oscar's thoughts on the Booker and hope he heard them.*"

I wasn't James's closest friend, or his most important author. But one of his special qualities was an almost fatherly tenderness towards his writers: the ability to convey a sense that we were always foremost in his thoughts. This was abundantly evident in his focus on our affairs and his sustained cheerfulness to the very end. Most authors will achieve only modest success, yet James was able to convince us that our work was important. I suspect some of us wouldn't have been able to carry on, and I'm certain we should all have been less productive without his encouragement.

After a private family funeral, Hilary organised a memorial service for the end of October. It was held in the lovely St. James's church in Piccadilly. Iain Banks read Woodhouse's *Printer's Error* and Greg Snow gave the address. There was an anthem by Tallis and a choir, soprano and trumpeter. Two hundred people attended – perhaps more? Certainly enough to make clear how loved and admired James was. In a moment of inspiration, Hilary asked us to wear flowers and that the women wear their gayest hats.

And that was that. We were all left to carry on as best we could.

After the service Shirley and I sloped off to Brussels on Eurostar for the James Hale Memorial Dirty Weekend. James would have approved.

Having lost one friend, I renewed an acquaintance with another, Tarja Koivula, whom I hadn't seen in seventeen years since I was in Helsinki researching for *Farewell to Russia*. Now she was living in Brussels. And so the world moves on.

Notes on "James Hale and Oscar the Cat"

I began my essays before James died, but I don't recall that we ever talked about them: certainly I didn't have a book in mind. The Oscar letters, too, were written without any view to publishing them. If they seem studied or artificial, that's because James and I were both in the writing game; and, too, they were written under very particular circumstances. I was writing for him and for me – but definitely not for you. You must take them as they come.

Despite these comments, it strikes me that the letters reflect some of the methods I've used in composing my essays: for example, the figure of Oscar is used to frame anecdotes or discourses about other matters. Also some of the material covered in the essays is treated briefly in these letters: such as the account of Uncle Joe Wright (he of the Frankenstein in the kitchen). I note that the word 'pericope' crops up in the last of them. I recall coming across it in a book of biblical criticism and thinking it would be a nice word to take out for a walk. Now it'll have an additional association: that I first used it in my final letter to James. Much of my technique involves weaving such patterns of association from different materials.

An autobiography is a form of testament: the fullest opportunity (if you choose to take it) to say who you are and what you did and why. It also allows you to say how you *feel*, whether about people, places, paintings or the politics of your neighbour. If you want to spill venom over the page, go ahead – I shan't stop you.

Human beings are social animals and much of the meaning we find in life derives from the responses of other people. Some years ago, on a business trip, I found myself

215

at a loose end in Cairo and visited the Pyramids. They were impressive in a way, but the truth is they meant little to me because I wanted to see them with Shirley and not with a suave Egyptian middleman known as 'The Hood'. As one of my letters to James suggests, my whole experience as a writer is heavily coloured by the fact that I worked in collaboration with him.

A description of our friends is in part a description of ourselves. I enjoy life and I like people. These aren't the rewards of any special cleverness but simply because I've been fortunate and have received little but good from the hands of others – which is a confession that will seem foolish if you're of a cynical turn of mind, but there it is. I'm conscious that I owe my friends and others a great deal and that my love and gratitude are only imperfectly expressed. This failure is partly explained by the distractions of everyday life: the belief that things can always be put off to tomorrow, the difficulty of finding the right opportunity and the problem of the right words. And, too, like anyone else I can be just plain embarrassed to show my emotions.

Whatever your views of humanity in general and individuals in particular, your autobiography provides a space to set them down and an opportunity to reflect at length on your relationships. The dead often die untimely before the things are said that ought to be said, and the living, whether close to us or estranged, are often beyond us for the reasons I've suggested. Essays such as the one I've written are an imperfect way of paying debts that ought preferably to be paid in the face-to-face exchanges of life. But they're better than nothing.

Meantime I kiss Shirley as often and as ardently as I can. Eloquence can go hang itself.

FABULOUS FREDDIE TEACHES POETRY

We're in Freddie's Bar, an informal shebeen set up in Fred Day's hotel room – it being Ramadan in Abu Dhabi in 1996 – and the place smells of socks, cigarettes and gin. He and I are in town to run an arbitration against two Glaswegians, one of whom has served time for killing another man. We call them the Brothers Grimm.

Our base is the Al Ain Palace. Nowadays it's famous for a bar full of East European and Filipino tarts, but once – until the Greek manager ran off with the money – it was a quiet hotel financed by the best illegal liquor store in the city.

All of which is only approximately true – like Fred's stories.

This is by way of background. Fred is in mid-flight, telling one of his tales while serving drinks.

'Anyone want another glass of The General?' he asks convivially – 'The General' is General Booth or General Gordon.

Fred is from Shepherds Bush and talks like a barrow boy. He's plump, pink-faced and white-haired where he isn't bald, and he peers at the world through thick glasses while offering it a snifter. Suitably primed, he's a fount of tales in which he figures as the hero who saved the day. For which reason they're known as 'Fabulous Freddie Stories'.

I half-believe them because he tells them with such panache.

So he goes on.

'No?'

Fred pauses dramatically. With a wave of the gin glass he mesmerises his audience of construction crew passing

217

through on their way to Das Island, which is a womanless, sulphur-reeking hellhole in the middle of the Gulf.

'No? – then I shall continue. This girl says to my eldest – Young Fred – she says: "Your dad is *drunk*!" – "Wot?" says Young Fred. – "*Drunk!*" says the girl, and she points at me: "He's lyin' on the carpet in the middle of the floor." Which I am. "Ah!"" says Young Fred: "But is he recitin' Rudyard Kipling?" – "No," says the girl: "He is *not* recitin' Rudyard-bloody-Kipling." – "Then he ain't drunk," says Young Fred.'

Young Fred is right about his old man. When Fred is drunk, he recites Rudyard Kipling's poetry from memory. His natural voice is that of Kipling's soldier, Tommy Atkins. He declaims verses like a 'turn' in an Edwardian music hall. You expect him, the next moment, to put on a kilt and sing Scottish comic songs.

In my teens I wrote some doggerel. At university I attended one or two meetings of the Poetry Society but couldn't make head or tail of them. I once met a poet on a train. I was travelling to London to the Court of Appeal and dressed in black jacket and pin stripes so she thought I was going to a wedding. But these incidents were only brushes with poetry.

My real interest originates with Fabulous Freddie reciting Kipling when drunk.

As well as occasionally reading poetry, I've taken to writing it, though very rarely. I don't rate my efforts highly. The only thing to be said in their favour is that they aren't serious. Bad humorous poetry may be dreary, but bad serious poetry must be truly awful.

For a long time I've been suspicious of the pretensions of artists – my own included, if I can be said to be an artist. I doubt if our railing at the world accomplishes much, and whenever I see a media star protesting for the underprivileged my gorge rises – though I may be being ungenerous. The first poem reflects my doubts.

A VOTE OF THANKS TO THE POET WHO ABOLISHED WAR

The next item on the agenda is a vote of thanks to
[rustle of papers],
The poet who abolished war;
Who said...he said...[more rustle of papers]
I don't have his exact words to hand and do not
myself claim to have read them,
But my wife and I intend to when we next go on
holiday.
(To Tenerife, if you must know.)
[Clears throat] He said
That war is a Bad Thing.
That is the gist of the thing.
People get killed.
Children are orphaned.
Plague and pestilence stalk the land.
Council tax increases and governments borrow
money.

It was a revelation!
We had never guessed,
Though some members of the party opposite claim to
have known all along yet done
Nothing about it.

Be that as it may,
Mister...the name'll come to me shortly...
After what he said, the world's governments
abolished war,
And the causes of war:
Tyranny,
Injustice,
Poverty,
Intolerance,

High taxes,
And lazy beggars who sponge on the likes of us
instead of working.
And now we have
Harmony,
Singing,
Smiles,
Discussion,
Incense,
Street theatre,
And more black faces than we ever used to see,
Because even Peace has its price.

And, between you and I, Universal Peace is what we
do have,
Or, at any rate, will have
As soon as our last remaining enemies
Are forced to read poetry.

And so we express this vote of thanks to...
(Miss Arkwright, please take a note to get the name
right for the plaque.)
The Poet Who Abolished War.
Don't you wish we were all so eloquent, eh?
[Cries of, 'It's the way you tell 'em!']
Including members of the party opposite [laughter
and banging on tables].
Seriously though
We have to fight for Peace,
Which brings me to the next item on the agenda:
The report of the Highways Department:
Dog shit on the pavements,
And dictators hanging from the street lighting.
The Borough Solicitor has received complaints.

The dates of the next two poems (early 2002) indicate I
wrote them at about the time my agent and friend, James

Hale first went into hospital with the cancer that would ultimately kill him. The themes reflect a concern with illness and mortality, but I deal with them in a comic way, which – perhaps unfortunately – seems to be in my character.

WELCOMING OLD FRIENDS

Now comes with age the army of its ills
Like glum conscripts in a bad cause,
Stepping from the bus in ones, with raincoats and packed lunches,
Fleeing poor homes, hoping for better;
And sly in the eye.

Now comes the chorus of my complaints,
As predictable as *The Messiah* at Christmas.
Adam, framed for Original Sin,
Is cursed with Original Bad Back
From all that gardening in Eden –
And all that sex,
I hope.
Oh, Lord, take away the Bad Backs of the World,
But leave us the sex!

Now comes the day-in day-out boredom of Misery
Sharing my creaking couch like a relative
Or an old black dog who farts
But is loved out of familiarity.
He hangs about the wings with dreary humour:
The last of the Music Hall comedians,
A cheeky chappie, boyish but long in the tooth.
He likes the rain and waiting for buses,
Queues, and the fact that things are not as they used to be.
He is probably Welsh.

221

The second poem was written a few days later and reflects similar concerns.

IN PRAISE OF MORTALITY

On Day One of Eternity the angels praised the Lord.
Great was their joy.
On Day Two of Eternity the angels praised the Lord.
It was very ecstasy.
On Day Three of Eternity the angels praised the Lord.
Bliss it was to know this would go on for ever.

On Day Four of Eternity one of the angels sent a note
Asking to be excused from praising because he had a
headache.
God replied that there were no headaches in Heaven
But he would forgive him
On this occasion.

On Day Five of Eternity there were murmurs of
complaint
That the joy of praising the Almighty was not being
distributed fairly.
Some angels were not getting their share of bliss
And the others were insistent they should have it.
They did not want to hog all the praising and the bliss
to themselves.

On Day Six of Eternity there was a general feeling
that a mistake had been made.
Many angels confessed that they had been sinners all
their lives
And had no business being in Heaven at all.
The Almighty told them that He had forgiven them all
the same, and that was that.
They should get back to work.

On Day Seven of Eternity a barrack room lawyer
pointed out
That, on the occasion of Creation, the Lord had rested
on this day.
The Lord said that the story of Creation was a metaphor
And that, truthfully, there were no days in Eternity.
'Roll on Monday,' said the wits.

Shortly before his own death James was forced to have an
old cat put down. The incident was full of intimations of
mortality. I wrote the following poem.

TO MY DEAD CAT

My cat has died.
I loved him, but
He didn't give a fuck for me.
He was greater than I, because
He was above the world and its strange affections.
I am greater than he, because
I loved him, and
Shared the richness of his strange life.

Since James's death I've written only one poem, but I
attach no particular significance to this fact. My poetic
muse is slow and halting – as well as possibly cloth-eared.
Like the others, this piece is straightforward in its
meaning.

MAPS

You won't find me easily on a map.
I live in the place where the pages join,
The exact spot lost somewhere
With half of the name that names it.
  You had better look for ordinary places:
  Leicester, Cleethorpes and Kathmandu,

Towns in plain view with roads to get you there
To Runcorn, Widnes and Samarkand.

Yet no one lives in Leicester.
The *muezzins* are silent in the minarets of Derby and
Dar es Salaam.
The people have left for the crack where the pages
join
And half of their name is visible
And half is hidden.

NOTES ON "FABULOUS FREDDIE TEACHES POETRY"

This essay forms a group with others that also incorporate material taken from elsewhere. They are *My Holidays* (scrapbook) and *James Hale And Oscar The Cat* (letters). One or two more, such as *Shiny Jim and Adolf Hitler*, rely in part on photographs, if only for inspiration or to fix an image. In writing an essay based on my poems, my aim is to indicate the range of material you can use, some of which may require no more than a little shaping.

Be creative from the stuff you have around you. For example, I can imagine that extracts from projects written at school or university may come in handy – and diaries naturally. A common feature of all this material is that it throws a more spontaneous or contemporary light on the matters it covers and so varies the retrospective tone of the rest.

As for poems, most people have written verse at some time and most of it is bad – in fact it's terrible. However you shouldn't be too critical or embarrassed by your efforts if you remember your limited purpose, namely to tell your life story for the benefit of your family, rather than entertain the public with wit, wisdom or fine use of language. Even bad poetry sometimes shines with sincerity, and that can redeem it.

PARLEZ VOUS WILLIAMS?

Many families have words or expressions they use among themselves. Here are a few of ours.

aggrieve/agreeve   *verb* – To agree to do something while reserving the right to complain that the decision has absolutely nothing to do with you.

Cattochunks   *noun* – Cat food (usually dried)
This word came from Lionel Trippett, who kept a series of disreputable black cats. They included Big Mog, Whinge-Fart, Scooter, and the grisly and sinister Harass, who used to go bald in summer. Harass got his name from a remark made by Lionel to an annoying child (Nick Webb's daughter) that she should 'go to harass the cat'.

Caustive   *adjective* – (1) constipated; (2) tending to cause constipation.
I've only ever heard Nellie use this word. She has the preoccupation with bowel movements, which was

226

common to the working class fifty years ago. It was as important to be 'regular' as it was to be honest and she was forever dosing herself with laxatives. Typical remarks include, 'I'm feeling a bit caustive', or 'Eggs are a bit caustive'. Nellie considers constipation to be a fit subject for polite conversation and, given half a chance, would discuss the state of her bowels with the Queen.

Cheesehound

noun – A small mongrel dog, usually short-haired and greasy.

When we were sixteen, Mick Mills and I went hiking in the Yorkshire Dales. As we passed a farm, a small dog joined us for a couple of miles and couldn't be shaken off. This was the first of many cheesehounds. My son Tom also uses the word.

coproëme

noun – The smallest unit of bullshit.

This one is for the specialist. If linguists ever get round to the semantics of bullshit, they will need technical terms appropriate to the subject. I offer them

227

'coproëme'. Words such as 'synergy', which are not used by human beings of sound mind and balanced judgment, are coproëmes. As far as I know there isn't another word that fits the case, so I have hopes of this one making the dictionary.[*]

dog milk

noun – soya milk
Shirley loves it, but the rest of us can't stand the stuff.

(the) dog shit question

noun – The question that concerns ordinary people in their daily life.
The Prime Minister was addressing a constituency meeting. He explained the international terrorist threat, global warming and the state of the world economy. At the end he asked the assembled audience, 'Do any of you have any questions you'd like to ask me?'
'Aye,' said an old man, 'Ah've got one. When are you going to shift the dog shit from the pavement outside my house?'
Shirley often finds herself chairing meetings of staff or

[*] Nick Webb adopted the word for his book *The Dictionary of Bullshit*.

social service users. If she throws the meeting open to contributions from the attendees, someone will inevitably raise his or her version of 'the dog shit question'.

Downalator

noun – an escalator moving in the downward direction. Conversely: "upalator".

The word "escalator" suffers in practical use from not indicating in which direction the thing is moving. Given that the up and down escalators are often at some distance from each other, this may lead to confusion. We often use escalators as a meeting point in stores and similar places and came up with 'upalators' and 'downalators' to avoid ambiguity. This pair of words has real benefit and is still employed by all of us.

Dreckfest

noun – An evening spent watching trash television with my son Tom. Also *Drecknight*.

Foliomancy

noun – casting spells with paper.

This is something that bureaucrats and other paper-

229

pushers do when they want
to cause trouble or mystify.

juju stick

noun – umbrella
Tom and I invented this term
from the observation that if
we go to the trouble and
inconvenience of carrying an
umbrella, the weather will
stay dry. Conversely, if we
fail to carry an umbrella it
rains. The effect seems to be
magical and has nothing to
do with whether or not we
put the umbrella up. If the
sky threatens rain, Tom and I
can be observed shaking the
juju stick at the clouds and
muttering primitive spells.
The sight can be
disconcerting for the
uninitiated.

Lily

(1) *noun*: my wife Shirley;
(2) *verb*: to disappear
unexpectedly into a shoe
shop located in a parallel
universe.
Some explanation is
required. It had been noted
that we were, perhaps, a bit
strange (see 'juju stick') and
we began to refer to
ourselves as 'The Munsters'
and allocate nicknames
accordingly. Of these, only
'Lily' stuck and the children

230

and I always refer to Shirley
as Lily. The second meaning
stems from Shirley's
disconcerting habit of
vanishing when we are
walking anywhere. When her
absence is noticed, someone
will remark, 'Oh, she's
lilying somewhere.' The
somewhere remains a
mystery, but the most
popular theory is that Shirley
has access to a parallel
universe consisting largely of
shoe shops.

Lionel food

noun – Alleged eatables
which (a) contain enough
cholesterol to stop a clock;
and (b) are considered
unclean by most religions.
Our friend Lionel had a taste
for the adventurous end of
delicatessen and a relaxed
view about the hygiene of his
fridge, the inside of which
looked like a skip found
behind an abattoir. In
addition to conventional
dabbling in cheeses and
pâtés, he liked to tuck in to
confections of brains, snouts,
tails, trotters and other
unnameable body parts.
In the 1980's he produced
the English edition of *Real
Men Don't Cook Quiche*. His

231

recipe for 'Wessel Wellington' began: 'Take one bull's penis – trimmed'.

Lionel used to go on tours, descending on his many friends. When one of these was imminent, we had to buy in a stock of 'stuff' to satisfy him (he was an inveterate nibbler). It was in this context that the term 'Lionel food' came into the family. It has stuck to describe anything in the *delicatessen* line, though our diet is not as heroic as Lionel's.

metafood

noun – various sauces, pickles and condiments that ought to go well with real food – but don't.

Tom devised this one. It came from our many expeditions to Sainsbury's, where I would stare in awe at bottles of piri piri sauce and wonder what one did with it. Metafood generally comes in bottles and jars. The labels frequently hint at colonial origins: that the inventor may have been a jolly Australian Blackfellow who boiled down a crocodile with the inspired idea that it would go well on ciabatta. Jars of metafood lurk at the back of cupboards until past their best-by date and are then given to charity. This is perfectly safe because no one will ever eat them. Metafood is often bought by men when not properly supervised by their wives.

Polysynonymoglossalalia *noun* – letting one's tongue run away with a series of words all meaning the same thing.

I made this up for fun and used it in my novel *Recherché*. The world can probably do without it.

spending *verb/gerund* – a frivolous waste of money

This is purest Nellie. When she says it, she adds her particular emphasis and spits the word out – and the rest of us have caught it from her. The meaning is best captured by contrasting 'buy' with 'spend'. One always buys *something*, which means some sort of return for one's cash. But when one spends, one merely spends money, and there is no necessary implication of getting anything of value in return.

In general Nellie disapproves of *spending*. 'She likes to go

233

out *spending*,' she says of
some lost soul, meaning that
she smokes, bleaches her hair
and went out with Americans
during the War, or would
have if she were old enough.
Quite likely she doesn't stone
her steps, the hussy!

On the other hand, Nellie can
be indulgent and in this
mood *spending,* in
moderation, is an innocent
though naughty leisure
activity. She smiles
mischievously. She says,
'Sometimes I like to go on
the Tommy Field and have a
good *spend.*' The Tommy
Field is a market, and Nellie
means she can be reckless
and blow a tenner on a
stuffed toy and a sponge
cake.

Nellie struggles to come to
terms with the relative
affluence Shirley and I have
achieved. She's glad but
suspects no good will come
of it and I shall end up in old
age selling matches in the
street unless I put something
by. She looks around my
house and says, 'I see you've
been *spending*,' then adds,
'Still, I suppose you can
afford it, having two wages
coming in.' She'd probably

say the same to Bill Gates.

spoon!!   *noun and exclamation* – Response to an offer that really ought to be refused.

In my garage is a cast iron ladle with a long handle, used for clearing the sump of a garden drain. Painted on it by a previous owner are the words 'The Devil's Spoon'.

There's a proverb which runs, 'When you sup with the Devil, use a long spoon'

My sons and I often play games together. When one of us makes the other a dodgy offer of co-operation, the response is to click one's fingers as if calling a waiter, and to ask for a spoon.

stragedy   *noun* – rather like 'strategy' except everyone dies in the last Act.

Organisations devise 'stragedies' in the deluded belief that they're making things better.

taurocoprolingual discourse   *noun* – bullshit (see also *coproëme*)

This is another expression I made up just for fun.

winding up the wizzle   *verb* – to engage in unknowable activity (c.f.

235

Lily)

I do most of the cooking and the whole family eats together on Sundays. At the point when I get the food to the table and ring the bell, Shirley vanishes. Toilet? Telephone? Shoe shop? No one knows. Hence the following exchange:

DAD (*bad-temperedly*):
Damn it, the food's going cold! Where's Lily?
TOM: She's probably winding up the wizzle.

NOTES ON "PARLEZ VOUS WILLIAMS?"

To some degree, everything we do reflects our identity and history. A biography of sorts could be constructed from our Council Tax bills. They would show the places where we lived and our relative prosperity over time, and, though not very revealing in themselves, could serve as an anchor point for a fuller narrative.

Many people could write an entertaining story under the title '*Great Cars and Old Bangers*'. Begin by listing all the cars you've owned, the dates when you bought and sold them, their appearance and driving characteristics. From there you can go in a number of directions, none of which are exclusive. You could set out why you bought or sold a particular car; or describe the person you bought it from; or the journeys you made in it; or the times it broke down; or its sentimental associations.

I have no strong feelings about cars, but thirty years ago I bought a blue grey Saab from a dealer in Witton le Wear, County Durham, at a time when Shirley and I had only one child, Tom, who was a screaming babe as we drove up and down between Durham and Oldham to visit Nellie and Hughie. I associate this car with the best beer I ever drank. It was Cameron's bitter and Chris Hulbert and I sank a pint in a pub called *The Australian,* on a sunny day in 1975.

We took this car with us when we moved to Wiltshire in 1977 and kept it until 1979 when I was given my first company car. I recall a couple of ferocious skids that wouldn't happen with a modern car, and a very dodgy choke that was prone to freezing in the open position and flooding the carburettor.

Nowadays a white Saab of the same vintage parks in

the street where Tom lives. I'm struck by how unfinished and unsophisticated it appears; yet its sleek, elegant line is still beautiful and reminds me of when I was a young man of twenty-five.

So there you have an outline of an essay I don't propose to write, but this brief treatment may give you an idea of what it might look like and tempt you if you're a fan of cars. My present subject is words and expressions invented and used in my family – but it needn't be. The reason for introducing the matter of cars is to make a point that the ostensible subject of the essay isn't particularly material. I've chosen the subject of words because I'm a 'word person'. I'd have chosen cars, or fish I've caught, or cardigans I've knitted, or any of a hundred other things if any of those subjects interested me. An activity carried on over a lifetime will have stories clinging to it like barnacles.

The particular quality of invented words is that they reflect our interests, our education, our sense of humour and no doubt other things. The structure of the essay isn't so different from the one I would have used for the topic of cars. I began with a bare list of the words I consider as our family property. To this I added the definitions. And, in a final stage, I threw in a few details of how we came by them and some anecdotes about their origins or use.

Bearing these points in mind, you may like to take up a similar *indirect* subject to see what you can make of it. The important thing is to pick something you're comfortable with: something typical of your interests or in other ways characteristic. You should think what you can make out of your hobbies, or, perhaps, the houses you've lived in.

Why not list all the weddings you've been to and say something about them: the bride, the groom, the gruesome guests? Or funerals – the ones I've been to have mostly been enjoyable and good tempered.

The Scrapbook Approach

The following pages contain photographs and sketches with notes to give you some idea how you might tackle all or part of your autobiography using what I have called 'the scrapbook approach'. The basic idea is straightforward enough. Select a theme or a passage in your life and assemble the key photographs that best illustrate it. Write a paragraph about each one. You may choose to focus narrowly upon the circumstances under which the picture was taken. But, equally, it may call up associations: memories of other people or occasions. I would give in to the impulse to follow the trail of memory wherever it takes you.

Shiny Jim and Adolf Hitler

There's an urban legend that, in the 1920's, Hitler worked in Liverpool as a house painter – and, if so, why shouldn't he have been in the Wrexham St. John's Ambulance Brigade with my granddad, Shiny Jim? Granddad, with the moustache, is in the back row, left. His smart turnout gave him the nickname that was remembered even fifty years after his death, when Millie, the abandoned child he took in, tried to trace her 'family'. In his last years he was invalided and a wheelchair user. He died in about 1934 and was given a military funeral.

Hughie and Nellie – 1950's

When cameras were rare and expensive it was common to have a portrait taken at the seaside against a painted backdrop – often comic. This one was most likely taken at Blackpool, where we made several trips in the early fifties. In the past people weren't used to having their photographs taken and this probably accounts for the stiffness and slightly startled expressions on my parents' faces.

Little Jimmy and Anne circa 1952

Hughie took this with his little Brownie. We were living at 5 Warwick Street, Werneth, part of a small terrace. It was overrun by mice; there was only a single cold water tap; baths were taken in a galvanised tub that hung on a nail in the yard; and the toilet was an outside 'tippler', shared with the neighbours. The cat once fell into the toilet and had to be fished out by Hughie and my brother Denis. Despite the poor amenities, my memories of the house are good and I was sorry to leave it. Nellie sold it to my Auntie Anna for less than the market value because she thought that was all it was worth – and threw in an interest-free loan.

Hughie and Little Jimmy – early 1950's

We stayed at Mrs Povey's guesthouse at Blackpool. This picture was taken on the South Pier, where I saw the comedienne Hilda Baker in a show. My days were spent on the beach, burying my Dad in sand. At intervals we bought tea at one of the many cafés along the promenade. The serviceable white crockery was posher than anything we used at home. In her eighty-seven years, Nellie has never owned a teapot. Invariably she tells me, 'Sugar and just a *little* milk.' I can never get it right. 'There's too much milk,' she says and shakes her head.

Nellie and Hughie at Goodrington circa 1957

Between the ages of eight and fifteen or sixteen, I holidayed with my parents, my Uncle Fred and Auntie Winnie and my cousins at Paignton. During the day we made a base on the beach at Goodrington, where we hired a hut. These were the dying days of the beach photographers who would take snaps on the fly. On the promenade was a stuffed horse they used as a prop. Hughie, The Last Cowboy in Wrexham, couldn't resist it.

At Denis's wedding 1962

Denis and I have always been close and I look up to him still. He was the breadwinner for a time, when Hughie suffered a mining accident. Nellie and he had many arguments, but Denis would never abandon her, even though she wasn't his mother. Nellie admits that Margie 'settled him down' and that he has many fine qualities. My brother Jack should have been best man but, typically, he turned up late and Denis allowed me to step in.

Olive Brown 1969

Olive was a relic of the Raj and a war widow who kept open house in London and was a contributor to every liberal cause. When, after leaving university to seek my fortune, I arrived without a bed for the night, she allowed me to sleep on her couch until Shirley and I found a flat with Frank and Joan Rodriguez. In return for her kindness, I painted her portrait, for which this is a preliminary sketch.

Salford Registry Office – 14 August 1970

Our wedding cost forty pounds. Shirley wore a pale green dress. Our 'bridesmaids' were Mike Runge (left) and Mick Mills (right). For a moment it seemed the whole affair would be called off for lack of witnesses, because we had let the guests get at the booze before the ceremony and they were reluctant to leave off. We couldn't afford a photographer, but one turned up and we refused to hire him. He can be seen sulking in the doorway. My brother Denis ate a whole French loaf for a bet, and Nellie declined to come to the door to bid us farewell on our honeymoon. 'I think I'm too drunk to stand,' she said with a beatific smile.

Hannah 1983

I made this sketch of my daughter during a holiday near Laval. We went to the lake at Port Brillet, where Shirley first saw an otter and we ate the most memorable meal of our lives in a simple workman's restaurant. Hannah was playing on the bank of the lake as I drew her. The sketch is from the scrapbook we kept that year.

Lionel Trippett

Lionel was a mature student when we got to know him at Durham University in the mid 1960's. He was witty, intelligent and cultured. Most of his career was in publishing, but he worked for the Campaign for Nuclear Disarmament in his later years. He is remembered for his delightful pastiches of Victorian pornographic novels, and for his recipe for Wessle Wellington, which begins: 'Take one bull's penis – trimmed.'

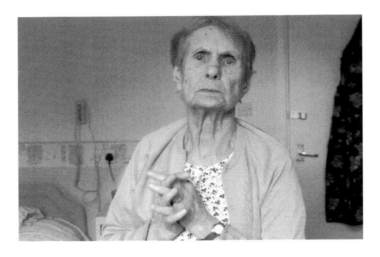

Helen – 2004

'I didn't know my name until I were eleven,' she says. Everyone called her Nellie, but she had a secret longing to be known as Helen. Now in a care home, she is called nothing else. She loves Hannah to take her photograph. She cries with delight, 'What a silly old grandma you've got!' When I was younger she liked the novelty of hearing her voice on my tape recorder as she sang *Edelweiss*. 'Ee, don't I sound *common*!' she says, and laughs at herself.

Shirley

This is my favourite photograph. It catches everything about her that is open and lovely. The frank smile is the one she gives just before she tells me I'm 'a silly bugger'.

THE CLOCK

The old man at the North Pole said, 'I lent ten bob to Guy Burgess the night before he defected to the Soviet Union.'

He was a very old man. Burgess had defected some forty years before, after a long career as a Russian spy.

'He never paid me back.'

'No, I don't suppose he could,' I said.

The North Pole was a large pub on Finchley Road, where Lionel and I sometimes drank when I stayed overnight on business at his flat in Swiss Cottage. It was convenient for Lee Ho Fuk's restaurant where we often ate. The restaurant has since disappeared but it used to have a small mosaic strip of a Classical character in the doorway, remnant of an earlier incarnation, probably Italian. In this respect it reminds me of Casanova's Chinese Restaurant, so named by Anthony Powell for much the same reason.

I stayed at Lionel's on and off for three decades, bunking two or three times a year on his comfortable couch. We usually had a pint or two in a local pub, sometimes the North Pole but more often the Washington, a glittering palace of glass and mirrors, haunted by actors I knew but couldn't put a name to. We didn't visit the Mortimer or the Hero of Acre because they were only Powell's inventions, but there was a connection between the two sets of pubs. They both reflected the rootless, Bohemian side of London life.

One evening Lionel and I were discussing the *filioque* clause in the Roman Catholic creed when a stranger chimed in with a comment on the Greek Orthodox version. I can't imagine anywhere else this would happen. Indeed it's odd that Lionel and I were discussing the subject at all, but Lionel had an amateur interest in strange religious beliefs. At university he'd remarked that theology students could not only fail their exams but lapse into heresy while they were at it.

The Clock was a pub in Charing Cross Road, on the ground floor of a charmless modern building housing the Y.M.C.A. We met there because Lionel was working for a publisher in Bedford Square and it was convenient

A large part of our evenings together was spent bringing each other up to date with the doings of friends and acquaintances. Lionel never married and had a large circle of contacts dating back to the mid-sixties. His habit was to make a tour out of London once or twice a year to pick up gossip. He'd announce, 'I'm thinking of making a "progress",' as if he were Queen Elizabeth the First descending on her favourites – which wasn't far from the truth since his visits meant having to abandon the kids to wait on him and keep him supplied with his diet of offal and strong cheese.

This evening at The Clock wasn't different in principle from any other. Lionel was in sparkling form, delivering stories in his usual breathless upper-class tenor. He told me about Bill and Brenda (educationalists, formerly of Somerset but recently settled in the Greek isles), Bridget (converted from Methodism to Lesbianism and living in a commune in Leeds), Jonathan (much divorced lawyer who succeeded in California). I'd seen none of them in almost twenty years, but they remained vivid because of Lionel's tales.

And that's the point. After nearly twenty years I wasn't sure which of these characters I'd actually met and which existed merely as figures in Lionel's stories. I'm fairly certain about Bill, Brenda, Bridget and Jonathan. But did I ever meet Tim's girlfriend, the one with a whiff of Irish tinker about her like Shirley's Auntie Molly who died of drink? And in any case, did Bill and Brenda really exist for

253

me, when I'd met them only once and for the rest relied on Lionel?

The slow rhythm of Time makes even Reality a doubtful bit of goods.

That same long rhythm brought a group of us together in the summer of that same year, 1987: former students of Durham university on the threshold of middle age but still with fairly young children (I think even Bridget had acquired a child somewhere on the voyage to Lesbos). Annie Hulbert organised a reunion of those who'd gone up in 1966 and we gathered on the playing fields of Maiden Castle and it was sunny.

I've a good memory for faces and had no problems recognising everybody. Ten years later I'd have been cautious of the haunted look of the over-fifties and heard Death sharpening his scythe; but at forty optimism wasn't entirely dead and we were all pretty jolly in the sunshine.

I particularly remember Geoff Lello, who was an accountant with right wing views. It was odd therefore that he had a beard and looked like Lenin. His wife, Georgie, was unchanged. She'd been a loud-voiced gossipy girl and had become a loud-voiced gossipy woman, and I wondered why Geoff hadn't murdered her – not for the usual motives but simply for peace and quiet.

Chris Barrow Williams was unmistakable and unforgettable because I'd met him in Freshers' Week when we both pursued a girl named Sally. He had small features and a high forehead in a similar mould to William Hague, the Tory leader, and spoke with a nasal drawl and a note of irony. Like most of us, he married a girl he met at university, an etiolated creature with hay fever so pronounced that I recalled it even after so many years. I remembered – though God knows why – that he was an Arabist and had gone to work for Massey Ferguson.

I said, 'Hullo, Chris,' and held out my hand.

He said, 'Hullo,' and held out his. It was limp with

uncertainty, which should have told me what was going to come next.

'I'm sorry…' he said.

'Yes?'

'…but I don't know who you are.'

'Ah.'

He doesn't know who I am.

Of course.

Twenty years have gone by. I've vanished. I'm no longer even a character in the stories he tells.

I want to shout out that he's mistaken and that things are precisely the other way round, because I am and always was witty, intelligent, debonair and eminently memorable, whereas he…frankly he was one of those grey characters in sports jackets and flannels who hung around unfashionable student societies and he ought to be bloody grateful that I give him the time of day.

'Jim Williams?' I offered hopefully.

'Jim Williams?' he repeated. He seemed to remember the name, but nothing came with it. He smiled benignly then passed away into the sunshine. I remained, holding a glass of wine and shimmering like an apparition.

The following year a party of old school chums, from my days at Greenhill Grammar School, gathered for dinner before pushing on to a night club called Henry Afrika's. We ate at the Café Monaco in Union Street, a Berni Inn that had once been considered the height of sophistication because it served steaks.

Tosser Thompson, our popular Latin master, used to hold court there. He wore dove grey suits sprinkled with cigarette burns and smelled of aftershave. He lived with his mother next door to my Auntie Winnie in Hathershaw and was known to be 'one of those', which, in the sixties, was as explicit as most people could be in polite company. In Oldham, the Café Monaco was as louche a haunt as any that Oscar Wilde knew. It required an explanation if one went there for any other reason than a wedding anniversary.

Peter Winterbottom had moved to Hull. Christine Taylor had taken up Christianity but looked well on it. Vera, who'd once been merely frumpy, now had the sly air of Dorothy Parker. Sandra had been sun-bleached to near invisibility and longed to return to South Africa. My former bridesmaid, Mick Mills, on a brief return from exile, was slowly turning French. Isabel was unchanged.

We talked a lot, but I remember only a remark made by Barbara Dyson – Barbara whom I'd have known anywhere for a handsome if slightly mannish face with bones that would preserve her good looks to the grave. She gave me a friendly smile and, meaning it kindly, said, 'I recognised everyone else, but I wouldn't have recognised you.'

I'd vanished again.

Time and history have interested me since childhood, but a greater sensitivity to Life's temporal rhythms came on with middle age. I'm sure this happens to many people as we put the bulk of life behind us and try to make sense of it. But, in my case, it was shaped by two literary sources. Anthony Powell's *A Dance To The Music Of Time* was one, and Proust was the other. Since I write books, this isn't particularly surprising.

My French teacher, Fanny Kuler, gave me the briefest introduction to Proust. To an eleven year old Fanny was a Holy Terror. To a seventeen year old she was charismatic and vivacious. She was locked up from time to time for madness or nervous breakdowns – or so it was said. I kept in touch with her and with my old German teacher, Harry Martin, until they died in their eighties. Indeed Harry came along that night at the Café Monaco, but shuffled off into the gloom after the meal instead of being treated to the drag queen who compered at Henry Afrika's.

I think that Tosser would have come along to the night club too, if only to loiter in the interesting gents toilets, but he'd died years before from his sixty a day smoking habit.

'You ought to know something about Proust,' Fanny said with a note of distaste.

She handed out the French text of *Swanns Way*. We looked at the first page, which we couldn't make head or tale of. Then she told us about Proust's cup of tea and his *madeleine* biscuit and how these and similar sensations, stimulating earlier ones, start us on the path into the realms of memory (a task accomplished in the present essay by a remembered story about ten bob lent to Guy Burgess).

The tale of tea and biscuits is as much as most people get of Proust (assuming they get anything at all). It's, so to speak, 'what Proust is all about' and it can serve to immunize us against the rest of him. After all, what's the point of going on once you've 'got it'?

'I don't propose we do any more,' said Fanny after that first page, taking back the books like screwing the cap back on the medicine bottle.

It would be more than twenty five years later that I picked up the first of a three-volume Penguin edition and finally read *Swann's Way*. Only in 2001 did I have a sudden feeling that I could go the whole hog and polish off the lot.

Proust's book falls into the class that can't be read at just any old time but has to be met when the stars are right. Pleasure, in the ordinary sense, doesn't play a part. There may indeed be pleasures (Proust turns out to be a comic), but the experience overall is one of endurance and satisfaction, much as mountaineering must be.

In the end, like everyone else, I remember the tea and biscuits. A second reading may cause more detail to stick, but the thought of facing the book again induces a dizzy sensation. It's enough to say that I've 'done' Proust and have indeed 'got it'.

When I met Lionel at The Clock, I'd read only two or three of the dozen short volumes of Powell. I'd enjoyed them well enough but didn't find him funny (as the critics promised I should) and didn't grasp the point at all. Where was the plot? The books began and ended for no obvious reason and characters such as Templer and Stringham, who were important in the first volume, got scarcely a mention in the next. The incidents seemed to be random stuff and the people spent most of their time just gossiping about each other.

'I'm thinking of making a progress,' Lionel said vaguely.

He went on to mention the latest news concerning Bill, Brenda, Bridget, Jonathan, Steffie (who used to be married to Jonathan but was now one or two divorces removed), Nick Webb and others.

Concerning Jonathan, he'd never been more than a nodding acquaintance at university. Later he took off to America to become a Hollywood lawyer, shedding wives in the course of his career, which was glamorous but had little to do with the spotty tick I once knew. In fact there wasn't any connection at all except the one Lionel made; and he might easily have attached the later history to a wholly different person for all it resembled or could have been predicted from the Jonathan I knew.

I might have said I didn't believe it, but after twenty years of stories I couldn't discriminate between truth and fiction. The super-reality of Lionel's tales was far more convincing than my pale and uninteresting memories.

'Eureka!' I said.

'What?' said Lionel.

'Eureka. I suddenly understand Anthony Powell and about Time and the Dance and the rhythms of Life!'

'Really?' Lionel drawled.

'Yes! For the last twenty years you and I have been doing exactly what Jenkins does in the course of the book. We talk about people as they form new patterns like the figures of a dance.'

I went on to point out the name of the pub – The Clock!

– and that it couldn't be more appropriate.

Lionel, however, who could speak amusingly about weird subjects like the *filioque* clause, was rarely interested in topics he hadn't raised himself. So now all he said was another faint 'Really' before telling me about a barge holiday in France with Nick Webb and his wife Sue.

For my part, after this meeting I finished reading *A Dance To The Music Of Time* and it made sense and it turned out that the critics were right and it was very funny.

Lionel died in two thousand and two. When I got the news it occurred to me that after an acquaintance of thirty years, I'd never visit his flat again. The feeling was uncanny. The place was so tangible and distinctive that it seemed to have a personality. I knew it so well that I could place each book in its space on the shelves. Yet it was now about to vanish into the realm of non-existence. How could something so concrete cease to exist?

At this time I was in the middle of *Time Regained*, the last volume of Proust. Some form of conclusion was in the air, both in literature and life. I sensed it without knowing what I sensed.

It isn't a literary affectation to say I've travelled Swann's Way. For the last sixteen years and throughout my reading of Proust and Powell I've cycled most days along it.

It comprises two suburban streets in Cheadle Hulme, called Swann Grove and Swann Lane.

Note the peculiar spelling of 'Swann'. Are there other Swanns than Proust's character? Were the names devised by a well-read property developer or a sneaky town hall clerk?

Or perhaps Life does have a meaning, but the meaning is a happy chance like a piece of driftwood found on a beach, which is lovely for all that no artist shaped it. Perhaps Life is full of it in the same way that the random alphabet contains all the books written or capable of being written.

In the North Pole, the old man said, 'I used to know Earl Mountbatten.'

Mountbatten had been Viceroy of India. He was uncle to the Queen.

'Did you?' I said.

'Yes.'

He thought long and hard for something that would convince me.

'He was a poof,' he said.

NOTES ON "THE CLOCK"

The first autobiographical essay I wrote was a version of this one. Its themes of Time and Memory reflect the concerns that have led me to recommend people to write their autobiography, and, finally, caused me to write my own.

By the way, Shirley is pleased I've written this book. I read it to her in the bath as I go along, and she laughs. I don't say this is a strong recommendation, but it's encouraged me to go on at a faster pace than would otherwise be the case. Motivation is crucial in writing, and books remain uncompleted for lack of encouragement as much as for any other reason. If you can find someone to whom you can read your efforts, someone who is sympathetic to your objective – most likely a member of your family – you'll be helped enormously. My family has been very supportive of this exercise and you'll probably find the same.

My point is: don't be secretive. You may be surprised how much others will appreciate your efforts.

The bath is optional.

Although this essay was written first, I've deliberately placed it late in the collection because I felt it was necessary to work through material dealing with my earlier life to understand the present essay better. Also this piece is structurally and stylistically fairly complex and – to be frank – I was frightened of scaring the reader off.

This brings me to the matter of organising your essays, if and when you decide to gather them in a collection. In what order should you put them?

For a chronological narrative, the problem solves itself.

261

One starts at the beginning and continues. Under my suggested method, however, there are real choices to be made. For example, I seriously toyed with the idea of placing the present essay first, because there was a logic in setting down those concerns, insights or whatever one calls them that motivated me to take up the pen.

In the end I've decided to organise my material on a loose chronological principle that underlies even those essays that are not easy to fix in time: *My Holidays*, for example, which begins with my childhood but covers a lifetime in itself. So the rough order is:

(1) Essays dealing with my background and family: e.g. *Nellie* and *Gents and Gypsies*.
(2) Essays on broader subjects developing out of childhood: e.g. *Little Jimmy's Christmas* and *My Holidays*.
(3) Chronological narrative, beginning with *My School* and taking the reader through my education and career.
(4) Miscellaneous essays dealing with various themes using material not normally considered but tending to shed light on character: e.g. *Fabulous Freddie Teaches Poetry* and *Parlez Vous Williams*?

Other schemes would probably work as well or better. My aim is only to avoid the essays being seen as random and some form of ordering is necessary in order to edit them and avoid repetitions. Although they're designed to work when read individually, if a number were to be read in succession by someone trying to follow my life, I suspect the reader would feel disoriented unless there were a sense of underlying coherence and direction. To understand my point, consider how the book would be if *A Dream of Red Tulips* were immediately followed by *Fabulous Freddie Teaches Poetry*. I suggest you'd be left without any clear idea of the kind of book you were reading, and this wouldn't encourage you to read on.

At all events, think about this when you devise your own scheme.

You may have noticed that missing from the above is any form of 'ending'. In the conventional sense, of course, no 'ending' is necessary – or even possible. 'Endings' belong to the realm of plots: to fiction and, to a lesser degree, to history. Life on the surface is just stuff that happens, and an autobiography is always a work in progress rather than the completed thing. There would be a certain truthfulness in allowing this account of my life just to break off at the end of whatever essay happened to be last; or even part way through an essay; or a paragraph; or a sentence; or a …

… but that would hardly be fair, would it?

The best reason for including an 'ending' is that writing an autobiography is purposive. We do it in order to achieve something; and, if we come to a point at which we want to stop, it's natural to want to review the whole and decide whether the objective has been achieved.

No matter how natural seeming your writing style may be – and mine isn't particularly so – it's an illusion to suppose we're describing life 'as it is'. We are necessarily editors and shapers of our own stories, and I'm quite unapologetic about this.

Look again at Lionel's tales about his friends as he told them to me in his flat and at the Washington and the North Pole. After twenty years I completely lost track of whom I knew and whom I didn't. Stories and recollection had interpenetrated each other and become hopelessly confused.

This was brought home to me after Lionel's memorial service. It was held at the Friends Meeting House opposite Euston Station; and Bruce Kent and other luminaries from the Campaign for Nuclear Disarmament showed up. After the service the mourners (a thoroughly cheerful and disreputable lot) swiped Lionel's T-shirts and coffee mugs as souvenirs, and afterwards we gathered at a pub near Camden Town Hall, drank beer, chatted and tried to discover who'd acquired the pornographic novels Lionel had written. Nick Webb and his wife Sue were there.

Nick had recently published three of my own novels, but I knew him mainly as a friend of Lionel whom he called 'The Captain'. They used to go on holiday together. The publishing connection was new and previously we'd met only two or three times over a couple of decades and, although I thought I knew him well, it was primarily as an object in Lionel's stories.

So we talked, and I asked him – somewhat nervously since I might be expected to know the answer – 'Were we at university together?'

You see, *I no longer knew*.

Don't look to me for accuracy. I don't want simply to set down 'stuff that happened'. I'm looking for a sense of what it has all meant: what the shape of my life has been, and why. I have some thoughts about an appropriate coda to this book, but at this point they're still fluid. In fact the 'ending', even when written, will only ever be provisional.

As for the detail, well…

At a stylistic level, one of my aims has been to convey a sense of how funny I've found things: not least my own absurdity. I hope I've conveyed something of the joys I've experienced, the people I've loved, the disappointments I've encountered (which to my mind don't amount to much), and a vivid feeling of being alive. If the details have become shaded in order to accomplish this, the compromise has been in the interest of a form of truth that I, at least, consider important.

When you compose your own story – if you've enjoyed life – tell a few jokes.

Structurally the essay is made up like this (with rough dates):

(1) Encounter with the old man at the North Pole in 1987
(2) Discussion of my relations with Lionel
(3) Introduction to an evening at The Clock circa 1992
(4) Lionel's stories and what they meant.
(5) A university reunion in 1987
(6) A reunion with my classmates in 1988
(7) How I came across Proust at school (1965)
(8) Returning to Proust in1990 and again in 2001
(9) Anthony Powell and more about The Clock (1992)
(10)   Bicycling along Swann's Way (1988 to date)
(11)   The Encounter with the old man at the North Pole (1987)

It should be immediately evident that the events of this essay weave a path backwards and forwards through time. A subject is discussed briefly, dropped, then picked up again and developed further. At the point where the subjects change, you should be able to discern links such as a cross reference between the two adjoining elements or a developing theme. It's the effectiveness of these links that determines how coherent the essay is from the point of view both of easy reading and of making sense.

Essentially the underlying thinking is neither chronological nor truly logical. Rather it's associative. As I was writing and imagining each of the parts, I thought, 'That reminds me of the time when...' And in turn the memory led me the next part – and so on.

The essay form lends itself well to associative thinking because its shortness prevents the associations from sprawling out of control. And associative thinking – in my opinion at least – is a very useful approach to writing autobiography. In principle it makes the entirety of life accessible all at the same time. All events, thoughts and feelings, no matter when they happened, are laid out like pieces of a puzzle. And what makes the pieces fit is not the order in which they're produced but the pattern that we see on them.

The elements of the present essay have no real connections in time, but they all form parts of a discernible pattern.

FALLING IN LOVE AGAIN

When I was fifty-three years old I fell in love with my wife again. But first...

'Would you like to come with me to Castle Day?' I asked Shirley as we went down the stairs of the Sociology Department at Durham.

She said 'yes', and a week later we were in love.

Shirley's background is similar to mine in essential respects. She comes from Salford, less than ten miles from Oldham. Where our two families differ is that in hers the generations have become confused. Her grandparents died young, leaving Shirley's mother, Ada, to bring up her brothers and sisters almost as if they were her children. This was compounded when Shirley was born sixteen years after her oldest sister, so that, for example, Jean's son, Alan, is more like a cousin than a nephew. And so it cascades through the generations.

The effect is a large, closely integrated family in which aunts and nieces are of a similar age and in former days used to go on holiday together, as Auntie Susie did with Jean; and Shirley's Uncle Bill was like her brother. Some husbands complain about their in-laws, but mine are marvellous and I love them. They're decent, good-tempered, kindly and caring of each other – though I'm not sure I'd have bought a used car from Shirley's brother John.

But, come to think of it, my son Tom did.

We fell in love in our last term at university and went to London together: Shirley to study for social work and I to study for the Bar. That was in 1969. The following year we arranged a holiday at Slapton in Devon and, because of

267

this, in a light-hearted way we thought maybe we should get married.

Marriage in Shirley's family could be a tense affair. Ada had promised her father that she'd never see her brothers or sisters marry a Catholic. But Bill married Molly (who died of drink) and Ada paid for the affair but, on a point of principle, wouldn't attend the church.

'She was very proper,' says Auntie Susie. 'When she was given some frilly underwear for the wedding, she said, "Oo, I can't wear those!" But, in the end, we got her to put the fancy knickers on top of her passion-killers. It would have been all right except that our Ada forgot she had two pairs on, and when she went to the toilet, she only pulled one pair down. "I've weed myself!" she says to me and our Gladys. She was dead upset but we couldn't stop laughing.'

Bill and Molly's wedding reception divided into two: the prim English element in one room, and the Irish in another singing rebel songs.

Shirley's parents died in her teens. Ada was run over by a bus. When it came to our wedding, Jean volunteered to pay for a respectable ceremony. It was generous of her because she and Norman, a central heating engineer, lived fairly simply in a small terraced house. We refused because we had no religious convictions and saw no need to put on a show. Instead we decided on a registry office followed by a reception at Jean's house. Shirley bought cold chicken legs and other party food at Lewis's store in Manchester and the whole business cost about forty pounds.

Knowing our families, it was a mistake to let them gather at Jean's and start on the drink prior to the service. We couldn't get them out of the house. Shirley and I slipped away in Norman's rusty Ford Anglia and turned up at the registry office without witnesses or guests. Unable to begin the ceremony we paced up and down the bombsite outside, hoping that *somebody* would turn up and that he or she would be reasonably sober.

They did turn up – all of them – more than the registry office was designed to hold. And if not exactly sober, they were at least vertical as they jostled in the cramped space and whispered and giggled.

'Are there any bridesmaids?' asked the Registrar.

'I'm one,' said Mike Runge.

'And I'm the other,' said Mick Mills.

So we were married. And afterwards we returned to Jean's house and continued the jollity. For a bet my brother Denis ate an entire French loaf made into one enormous sandwich, and Mick Mills sang the following song:

Never let your braces dangle.
Dingle – dingle – dangle!
One old sport, his got caught
Right up in the mangle.
Over the rollers – ee by gum! –
Came out flat as linoleum!
Now he's singin' in Kingdom Come:
'Never let your braces dangle!'

Throughout it all, Nellie sat quietly drinking gin and orange with her friend Mrs Mason, and scarcely said a word until Shirley and I were about to leave, when she smiled at us both and said very pleasantly, 'If you don't mind, I won't come to the door to see you off, because I think I'm too drunk to stand.'

We spent that night in a nearby hotel. Unwisely we'd told them we were newlyweds, so they prepared for the rough stuff by putting old, darned sheets on the bed. The following day we took the train to Torquay, passing through Paignton, where I'd spent happy holidays as a child. And so on to Slapton with its pitch black country nights, my first sighting of the Milky Way, the owl haunted ruined tower of the Chantry where we stayed, and the walled garden where we made love.

I have two particular memories of our first year together. We had a flat at the home of Frank and Joan Rodriguez and midnight on New Year's Eve found us in bed in darkness, listening as boats on the Thames sounded their horns: a beautiful, melancholy chorus like whale song. And for the rest…what were we supposed to talk about? What was supposed to happen in those long evening silences that Shirley and I now spend together so companionably? We had a mistaken notion they were meant to be filled with conversation and we stared at each other in guilt and embarrassment, wondering if we'd done the wrong thing.

To celebrate our first anniversary, we bought Annie, a golden Labrador bitch with a doubtful temper. It was a mad idea for two young people living in a flat, but Frank and Joan were as indulgent as parents even when Annie peed on Frank's lawn leaving brown spots. She stayed with us for ten and a half years, dying in the first winter after we returned to the North West in 1981.

In due course we passed our respective exams. Shirley worked for a year in Lewisham as a probation officer. I worked as a clerk and receptionist at the Social Security office in Greenwich, trying to handle the clients tactfully enough so that we didn't have to batten down the hatches once a week and call the police to throw them out. All of this was to save a hundred pounds to pay for my pupilage.

One memory of our time in London has stuck with me. I was teaching visiting American students. The girls were Jewish Princesses and the boys were nervous of the Vietnam draft. As we finished term and they returned home, one of the girls said to me (sincerely I think): 'Have a nice life.' She meant we'd never meet again – nor have we – and it was brought home to me that each day we part from people, not realizing the partings are final; so that only after several years will a name come to mind and we struggle to recall where and when we last met and there's a lingering regret that something wasn't said or done that should have been. This poignancy of everyday life still affects me.

In 1972 we moved to Durham and I set about the career as a lawyer that would lead me five years later to my downfall in the matter of the Tiberius Club. Our first home at 5 Priors Close was a small, modern semi-detached house, thoroughly nondescript in retrospect but infinitely more luxurious than anything we were used to. We were enormously proud of it as we set about trying to reinvent ourselves as a middle-class couple. In our enthusiasm and naivety we must have appeared absurd at times. Even now we have a tendency to overdress, but it's become a style with us and we don't care what anyone else thinks.

Tom was born in Durham in 1974 and Alex in 1976. Hannah was a blessed accident in 1982.

In material terms our struggles weren't too great. We had no parental money behind us, but we both held professional jobs (with interludes in Shirley's case) and neither of us is extravagant – Shirley will still buy second hand clothes if she likes them, and she looks wonderful. Like other young couples we had to be careful. In our case that drew us closer together.

Was I – am I – a good husband? I think that's a question only Shirley can answer. I've always been faithful. I hope I'm generally good tempered. I cook and do other stuff around the house. I'm indulgent towards the children. I like Shirley to have other friends and I'm not in the least jealous. On the other hand I sometimes get drunk; I can be childish and pompous; and, as I've admitted elsewhere, I'm rather a silly man in my view.

'Why do you love me?' I ask her.

'Because you make me laugh,' she says.

And? And?

Mentally I'm hopping from foot to foot like a child looking for a sweet. *Please, Mummy, say something nice!*

'Because you make me laugh.'

That, it seems, is all there is. I'd hoped for more, though without particularly feeling I deserved it. The fact is that my wife laughs at me. Damn!

And why do I love her? I get tongue tied by emotion when I search for an answer. She's beautiful and affectionate and forgiving and...and...and... I think that, above all, it's because she has integrity: she has honesty without any touch of cruelty. I never feel I'm looking at someone who's opaque to me, someone whom I should fear in a corner of my heart.

We're both demonstrative people. We kiss and hold hands in public and dance in the street at the drop of a hat and generally wear our hearts on our sleeves. We've never really taken middle class restraint on board.

We sometimes leave the toilet door open. We talk about farts.

When I was fifty-three years old I got drunk at a dance, made Shirley miserable and experienced a conversion. I realized the blindingly obvious, namely that I was impossibly stupid and that for practical purposes any problems we had experienced in marriage were all my fault and that whenever we disagreed about something Shirley was almost certainly right and I was wrong and that if I ever wanted to be happy I'd better take these points on board and act accordingly.

Since that time I've done my best to follow the lesson, and it's delivered the happiness I looked for. It hasn't cured me of being an idiot, but I've abandoned the practice of idiocy, bar the occasional lapse. Or so I think – you really had better ask Shirley, who's on the receiving end of my character and can be trusted to be truthful.

I also fell in love again.

You should understand: I'd never *not* loved Shirley in

the thirty years we'd known each other. But now I fell *in* love again in the same way I had when we agreed on the Sociology Department steps to go to the Castle Day fête and we were twenty-one years old. I found my heart fluttering when I saw her and my mouth becoming dry and generally felt so overflowing with emotion that I wanted to laugh, cry and dance a jig at wholly inappropriate moments.

And – ridiculous to say – that's pretty much how things stand.

'What are you looking at?' Shirley asks when, of an evening, she catches me glancing slyly at her as she works at her papers.

'I love you,' I say.

'Silly bugger,' she says softly, and smiles.

I don't care. I wear the title of 'Silly Bugger' like a medal earned in a thirty-five year campaign to love my wife as much as she deserves. I want the words 'Silly Bugger' on my gravestone. I want them in my passport under 'Occupation'. The blue plaque put upon my house by a Grateful Nation will read: 'Jim Williams – Famous Author and Silly Bugger.'

Did I say I love my wife?

I'd hoped that my transformation was because my Great Brain had at last understood The Real Nature Of Things and that I'd arrived at Wisdom by my own merits. But apparently it isn't so.

Quite recently I read a newspaper article in which it was explained that there's a general and pronounced tendency of people to become happier in their forties and fifties. Rich or poor, fat or thin, intelligent or not – they say it doesn't matter. It seems we're conscripted to happiness with little regard for our personal qualities.

How humiliating! All that education and experience apparently wasted as far as happiness is concerned.

However to complain about the terms is to complain

about winning a million pounds in the Lottery. My happiness may not be deserved, but I don't intend to hand it back.

Still the facts of the case are that my wife laughs at me and my happiness is a matter of dumb luck.

Sigh.

How many times do we kiss each day and say, 'I love you'? A dozen? More? I don't really know. We do these things at all hours for no obvious reason. But when I go to work I kiss Shirley as if we are partners in a tragedy, because, once I go through the door, we may never meet again in this life.

And when I come home I'm overwhelmed with relief because a woman who loves me is smiling at me.

Between the lines of these essays I've tried to write them as if they're a love letter to my wife.

I try to live my life as if it's a love letter. But I fail of course. It's probably more like a bad romantic novel. Most likely one that I wrote.

A VISIT TO POUSSIN

A few years ago, Shirley and I discovered the Wallace Collection during one of the trips to London that we make now and again to shop and go to the theatre. We also used to dance in the late afternoon at the Waldorf, where a small band led by a singer in a red *tarboosh* played quicksteps and tangos while we drank a glass of champagne and ate cucumber sandwiches. Now, alas, the dances seem to have stopped.

I like the Wallace Collection. It embraces variety in a small space and, in a short visit, I can look at French paintings of *fêtes galantes* (which, if you don't know them, are paintings of French aristocrats and their mistresses getting plastered and playing music) and Italian *maiolica*, both of which appeal to me.

The Wallace collection is also the home of *A Dance to the Music of Time,* the painting by Poussin, which inspired Anthony Powell's novel and gave him his title. The picture shows figures dancing in a circle, each one representing an aspect of human life as it changes over time. It was Poussin, too, who painted shepherds standing by a tombstone inscribed *Et In Arcadia Ego*, as a reminder that Death is present even when we're most happy.

I've suggested that, in principle, any material from your life is autobiographical if it can be shaped in a way that will tell your story. Photographs, poems, word lists – it really doesn't matter. It should therefore come as no surprise to realize that the notes to my essays are as much a part of my autobiography as the essays themselves. So at this point the distinction no longer applies and you may consider the present piece as an essay or as a note because it shares something of both.

Starting with Poussin, I want to indicate some of the places he leads me to in the way of things recollected. The motto *Et In Arcadia Ego* was used by Evelyn Waugh to introduce his novel *Brideshead Revisited,* which I lightly parodied in *The Strange Death of A Romantic*. According to Henry Lincoln and the other authors of *The Holy Blood And The Holy Grail*, the setting of the painting of the shepherds is near Rennes le Château, and Dan Brown also refers to it in his novel *The Da Vinci Code*. Rennes le Château was the home of the priest Bérenger Saunier, whose mysterious fortune is the source of much speculation. It happens to be about an hour's drive from the cottage owned by our friends the Sheltons, where Shirley and I stay from time to time. About five years ago we visited Saunier's house and also the church, which he restored while incorporating symbols of Freemasonry and Rosicrucianism for reasons he never explained.

This spring [2004] we went to a wedding in Poland. It gave us the chance of seeing the beautiful city of Kraków. While we were there, we went round the Czartoryski Museum. Though not as large as the Wallace Collection, it's very similar in style and feeling, which isn't surprising since they reflect a shared aristocratic culture of the Enlightenment. The Czartoryski Museum doesn't own a Poussin but – shades of Dan Brown – it does have a Da Vinci, *The Lady with Ermine*. I'm interested in forgery and illusion and happen to know that there's a second version of this painting in the United States and it has its supporters as the 'true' Da Vinci. I used the subject of a lost Da Vinci painting in my novel *Last Judgment.*

Where does this rambling tour of my thoughts take us? You'll notice that the various elements aren't linked by chronology or cause and effect or any rule of logic. Each image or memory in turn seems to initiate a connection in my mind with something else – not dissimilar to the way dreams work, I suspect, but this is done in my waking moments. Though unsystematic, the result isn't random. The connections are understandable and the outcome has a meaning, even if it's implicit rather than expressed. One of the things the process does is to gather the experiences and impressions of a lifetime and form them into some sort of pattern. Anthony Powell speaks of 'hearing secret harmonies', and I think that patterns of this kind are what he's referring to. Together they make up the dance to the music of Time.

It was probably the meeting with Lionel at The Clock that was the mainspring causing me to write these essays. It provided me with a key to reading Powell's book and, ultimately, Proust. If you re-visit that essay – which was the first I wrote – you'll see that it's organized on a pattern of connections and can be understood as a manifesto for the entire exercise. The principle behind all the essays has been to make the entirety of my life available as the source material for any theme or subject and so to find the patterns that bind the whole together.

It isn't without significance that I begin and end with pictures: that of the red tulips which Little Jimmy drew in wax crayons at the age of five, and Poussin's great painting which Shirley and I saw at the Wallace. If Little Jimmy had been incapable of dreaming of tulips, Poussin's painting would have been meaningless to me. Those events form, if you like, the border of the tapestry I've tried to create through the essays as I weave memories, impressions and ideas together. It's for you to decide if my method has been successful and if it can do anything for you.

Tonight, after I've finished this piece and put it away, Shirley and I are going dancing to a band called Plus Four and a singer called Paul Bentley. They'll play old Sinatra numbers, and we'll probably dance, though Shirley has recently hurt her ankle and not fully recovered. I'm looking forward to Christmas, which we'll spend quietly at home with the children. On Boxing Day we'll host a large family party because Shirley has taken over from her mother, Ada, as the great female force responsible for such things.

A month ago I wasn't certain Nellie would make it this far, but she has, though she's very tired. Fabulous Fred Day, who taught me to love poetry, has just come out of hospital with a new lease on life and that makes me happy because he and Penny have young children.

In short life goes untidily along and no dramatic event brings this book to a conclusion.

Now that I'm finished I'll read this last essay to Shirley while she takes a bath. I imagine she'll laugh gently and murmur, 'Silly bugger.'

Fortunately it seems that she loves her silly bugger, even if he doesn't understand why.

It's enough.

Jim Williams
22 December 2004

POSTSCRIPT

AND WHAT HAPPENED NEXT?

I've already said that writing your autobiography is a dangerous business. During the course of composing this one, my friends Lionel Trippett and James Hale died, as did Uncle Joe, the chief 'gypsy' in my dad's family. My mother was clearly in a terminal decline when I finished the book in December 2004 and she died in March 2005, worn out by a life well lived. Fabulous Fred Day was suffering from a brain tumour, when I wrote the essay 'Fabulous Freddie Teaches Poetry'. He died in November 2005, much missed by his many friends.

Nothing is guaranteed, but I'm still okay. Shirley and the children still love me; I'm in work and my health is good. Writing the book has given me great satisfaction and caused me to reflect on my life and appreciate more keenly the love I have felt for and received from others. However I doubt it has made me any wiser, though I live in hope.

I have many dear friends and relatives whom I've not been able to mention in the book. The reason is that I've written these particular essays rather than others of equal interest and importance, in which they would have figured prominently. It has no other meaning. The omission makes me sad, but I don't know what to do about it. You will face the same problem if you choose to follow me.

I've decided to publish the book because this year (2007) I shall be sixty years old. If it interests anyone else, I am truly grateful.

If you enjoyed reading *A Message to the Children* then please share your reflections with others by posting a review online.

Connect with Jim Williams and Marble City Publishing

http://www.jimwilliamsbooks.com/

http://www.marblecitypublishing.com

Join Marble City's list for updates on new releases by Jim Williams at **http://eepurl.com/vek5L**

Follow on Twitter:

http://twitter.com/MarbleCityPub

Read on for other Marble City releases by Jim Williams

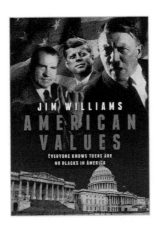

JIM WILLIAMS
AMERICAN
VALUES
EVERYONE KNOWS THERE ARE
NO BLACKS IN AMERICA

Conspiracies are not meant to be understood.

America in the Fall of 1963. The aging "Big A" has been President since he beat Roosevelt in 1932 and passed the Defense of American Values Act to establish his dictatorship.

Thirty years on, the United States is locked in a war to conquer South America. Racial minorities are persecuted, homosexuals killed, and African Americans have disappeared from public view. The country is worn-out and dilapidated, and people wait to see who will succeed the Old Man. In high places, Nixon and the Kennedys manoeuvre against each other under the watchful eye of J. Edgar Hoover.

Harry Bennet is a foreign correspondent for the Manchester Guardian, posted in Washington and treading warily in the political minefield. He is helped by his best friend, Jeb Lyman, but it is a dangerous friendship since Jeb is a high official in the feared General State Police and deeply implicated in the politics of the regime. Yet Harry has to trust him to protect the woman he loves, Maria, whose racial ancestry may not stand up to investigation.

Harry learns of a mystery patient secluded in one of Washington's hospitals. Following up the lead takes him across the decaying landscape of an oppressed America to Chicago, Las Vegas, Louisiana and Texas.

Ultimately his investigations embroil him in a murderous conspiracy to inherit the Presidency and he finally obtains an answer to the terrible secret hidden behind the public face of American Values.

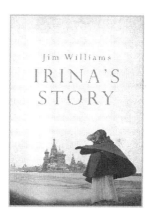

Jim Williams

IRINA'S
STORY

At the age of 90, Irina Uspenskaya is the last surviving witness
of these events. In her Moscow apartment, while her young
relative Slavochka and his friends in "the International
Syndicate" aspire to become successful drug dealers, Irina
collects the letters and diaries of her parents' generation and sets
down the tale of what happened to them all.

In turn she describes the doomed marriage of her father Nikolai
and her mother Xenia, who love but never understand each
other; her idealistic aunt Adalia, who marries the sinister
Grodsky; her disreputable uncle Alexander and his feisty wife
Tatiana. These and a host of other colourful characters populate
the story and we see their world through their eyes and
understand it through their thoughts and writings.

Our guide, Irina is wry, funny, insightful and humane. Born with
a disability, she views events through detached yet sympathetic
eyes and reflects on her own history and her unrequited love for
a boy she met as a little girl and the family and children she will
never have.

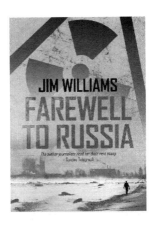

The unthinkable has happened at the Soviet nuclear plant at Sokolskoye. An accident of such terrifying proportions, of such catastrophic ecological and political consequence that a curtain of silence is drawn ominously over the incident. Major Pyotr Kirov of the KGB is appointed to extract the truth from the treacherous minefield of misinformation and intrigue and to obtain from the West the technology essential to prevent further damage. But the vital equipment is under strict trade embargo....

And in London, George Twist, head of a company which manufactures the technology, is on the verge of bankruptcy and desperate to win the illegal contract. Can he deliver on time? Will he survive a frantic smuggling operation across the frozen wastes of Finland? Can he wrong-foot the authorities ... and his own conscience? Is it possible to say farewell to Russia?

Farewell to Russia is the first of Jim Williams's astonishingly prophetic novels about the decline and fall of the Soviet Union.

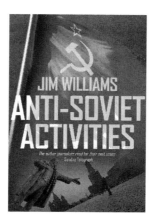

For Colonel Pyotr Andreevitch Kirov there is only one inescapable truth in modern Russia – if the old order does not change, it is impossible to bury the past.

When Kirov's routine investigation into black market antibiotics is linked to the former head of the KGB – and Kirov himself is put under investigation by his own men – the course for collision is set.

As the old and new factions in the Soviet machine grapple for power, the stock in trade is the hardest currency known to the Socialist Republic … murder. Will Mikhail Gorbachev share the same fate?

Anti-Soviet Activities is the second of Jim Williams's astonishingly prophetic novels about the decline and fall of the Soviet Union.

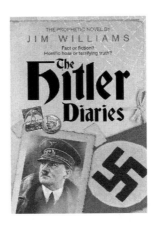

A stunning literary prophecy! The international bestseller that caused a sensation when it was published 9 months before the famous Hitler Diaries forgery scandal.

A French aristocrat and his mistress are murdered. A mysterious businessman offers the Fuehrer's diaries to a new York publishing house. Are they a hoax or a record of terrifying truth? A controversial historian and his beautiful assistant are commissioned to find out the answer following a trail that draws them into a terrifying web of conspiracy and slaughter as competing forces fight to publish or suppress Hitler's account of the War and of secret negotiations with his enemies.

But are the Diaries genuine or just a plot to destabilise contemporary politics? A shattering revision of history whose revelation must be prevented at all costs: or a fake, just a sinister manoeuvre in the Cold War?

If the Hitler Diaries are authentic, then who left the bunker alive?

A disillusioned soldier looks for love. An exiled Emperor fears assassination. Agatha Christie takes a holiday. And George Bernard Shaw learns to tango.

In the aftermath of World War I, Michael Pinfold a disillusioned ex-soldier tries to rescue his failing family wine business on the island of Madeira. In a villa in the hills the exiled Austrian Emperor lives in fear of assassination by Hungarian killers, while in Reid's Hotel, a well-known lady crime novelist is stranded on her way to South Africa and George Bernard Shaw whiles away his days corresponding with his friends, writing a one act play and learning to tango with the hotel manager's spouse.

A stranger, Robinson, is found murdered and Michael finds himself manipulated into investigating the crime by his sinister best friend, Johnny Cardozo, the local police chief, with whose wife he is pursuing an arid love affair; manipulated, too, by Father Flaherty, a priest with dubious political interests, and by his own eccentric parent, who claims to have been part of a comedy duo that once entertained the Kaiser with Jewish jokes. Will Michael find love? Will the Emperor escape his would-be killers? Will any of the characters learn the true meaning of the tango?

THE
STRANGE
DEATH
OF A
romantic

JIM WILLIAMS

The poet Shelley wasn't murdered. This book tells you whodunit.

A group of glamorous English socialites spend the summer of 1930 holidaying on the Italian Riviera where the poet Shelley died in a sailing accident in 1822. To pass the time, they tell amusing stories, much as Shelley, Byron and their friends had done a century earlier. For their theme they choose the death of Shelley and the stories progress towards a solution to the "murder mystery". Yet is that truly what the stories are about? Or, despite their witty surface, are they a code for dark and dangerous secrets hidden behind an urbane façade?

Guy Parrot, a naive young doctor, finds himself falling in love with the beautiful and enigmatic Julia, the truth of whose past flickers between the lines of the stories, tantalising both Guy and the Reader. Guy discovers that truth, and its terrible reality leads to two murders and the destruction of his happiness and sanity.

In 1945, in the aftermath of war, Guy returns to Italy with the army and is given an opportunity to re-examine the events of fifteen years before. This time will he understand what happened and finally redeem himself?

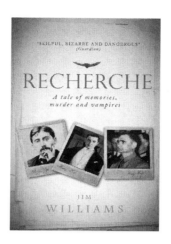

"A skilful exercise, bizarre and dangerous in a lineage that includes Fowles' *The Magus*."

Guardian

You get to be a lot of people when you are a vampire.

Meet old Harry Haze: war criminal, Jewish stand-up comedian, friend of Marcel Proust and J. Edgar Hoover. John Harper encounters him while spending the summer in the South of France with his mistress Lucy, and is entranced by Harry's stories of his fabulous past. Then Lucy disappears without explanation and both John and Harry fall under suspicion.

Yet how are we to know the truth when it is hidden in the labyrinth of Harry's bizarre memories and John's guilt at abandoning his wife? Nothing in this story is certain. Is Lucy dead? Is Harry a harmless old druggie or really a vampire? Deep inside his humorous tales is the suppressed memory of a night of sheer horror. And it is possible that one of the two men is an insane killer.

THE
ARGENTINIAN
VIRGIN
a story of love, betrayal and murder unpunished
JIM WILLIAMS

Summer 1941. France is occupied by the Germans but the United States is not at war. Four glamorous young Americans find themselves whiling away the hot days in the boredom of a small Riviera town, while in a half-abandoned mansion nearby, Teresa and Katerina Malipiero, a mother and daughter, wait for Señor Malipiero to complete his business in the Reich and take them home to Argentina.

The plight of the women attracts the sympathy of 'Lucky' Tom Rensselaer and he is seduced by the beauty of Katerina. Tom has perfect faith in their innocence, yet they cannot explain why a sinister Spaniard has been murdered in their home and why Tom must help them dispose of the body without informing the police.

Watching over events is Pat Byrne, a young Irish writer. Twenty years later, when Tom has been reduced from the most handsome, admired and talented man of his generation to a derelict alcoholic, Pat sets out to discover the facts of that fateful summer: the secrets that were hidden and the lies that were told. It is a shocking truth: a tale of murder unpunished and a good man destroyed by those who loved him most.

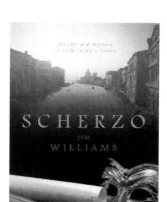

MEET two unusual detectives. Ludovico – a young man who has had his testicles cut off for the sake of opera. And Monsieur Arouet – a fraudster, or just possibly the philosopher Voltaire.

VISIT the setting. Carnival time in mid-18th century Venice, a city of winter mists, and the season of masquerade and decadence.

ENCOUNTER a Venetian underworld of pimps, harlots, gamblers, forgers and charlatans.

BEWARE of a mysterious coterie of aristocrats, Jesuits, Freemasons and magicians.

DISCOVER a murder: that of the nobleman, Sgr Alessandro Molin, found swinging from a bridge with his innards hanging out and a message in code from his killer.

Scherzo is a murder mystery of sparkling vivacity and an historical novel of stunning originality told with a wit and style highly praised by critics and nominated for the Booker Prize.

Janet Bretherton, a widow at 60, suspected of her husband's murder and involvement in the fraud which brought his company down, exiles herself to Puybrun, a small village in a picturesque corner of south-west France, where she nurses her grief and tries to rebuild her shattered world. She meets six other Englishwomen who live the expatriate life. Earthy has fled from a hippy camp in a damp corner of Wales. Carol claims to have slept with every man in the world called Dave. Belle has a husband, Charlie, who may or may not be real because no one has ever seen him. Joy is married to the appalling Arnold. And Veronica and Poppy try to discover the basis for the love they have for each other. The women form a group in which they take turns to teach each other the lessons life has taught them. At the same time, they grow more confident and gradually reveal the secrets of their pasts.

When Janet finds she has attracted the attention of Leon, thirty years younger than she is, yet seems to find her still sexually desirable as he invites her to go dancing with him, she asks herself: What are his real motives? And does she care? In the end, the process of discovery reveals a terrible secret which forces the women to decide how much they love each other: how far they can rely upon each other ... even when the question is one of murder.

In the pretty Devonshire town of Dartcross an elderly lady diarist struggles with her memory to write a history of her colourful past, her hateful cat and her murderous husband. At the same time, Janet Bretherton and her friend Belle try to discover a purpose to their retirement. Is it enough to discuss the latest novels in their readers' group, go to the theatre or attend a séance? Perhaps, instead, they should try to solve the mystery of the dead Polish man whose body is found by the river?

The Demented Lady Detectives' Club is both a whodunit and a funny yet poignant account of a group of women growing old and seeking love and meaning in both the past and the present. The unnamed lady diarist finally faces up to the horror she has buried in her memory and the love she has lost. And Janet has to deal with the tender feelings she is still capable of evoking in a man who is twenty years her junior.

Lord T'ien Huang controls the universe through poetry, telepathy and the violence of his insane Angels. His subjects consider him to be God. Emperor of a universe ruled by the Ch'ang, immortal but not invulnerable, his interest is aroused by Sebastian, a novice monk on the remote and wasted planet of Lu, who can see and speak to God. Should he destroy the boy or toy with him?

Sebastian is rescued from the Lord T'ien Huang's avenging Angels by Mapmaker, an ancient Old Before the Fall with a forgotten history of betrayal, and they journey to the snowbound north. They are accompanied by Velikka Magdasdottir, a girl belonging to the Hengstmijster tribe of warrior herdswomen who maintain a veiled harem of husbands.

In the frozen wastes they encounter the remains of the Ingitkuk who rebelled against the Ch'ang in antiquity and lost their witch princess, She Whom the Reindeer Love. Mapmaker knew her when she died half a millennium ago as Her Breath Is Of Jasmine.

Will Mapmaker lead Sebastian, the Hengstmijster and the Ingitkuk to their doom against the Ch'ang? Can Sebastian master his own powers? How will they survive against the Angel Michael, thawed and frozen more times than he can recall, with his power to destroy humanity by the billion?

Printed in Poland
by Amazon Fulfillment
Poland Sp. z o.o., Wrocław

59201791R00181